Elections @ 4-5

Throughout its history members of 4-5 Gray's Inn Square have appeared in all of the most important election law cases, including the Literal Democrat case, the Liberal Focus case, the Birmingham Postal Ballot case, the Tower Hamlets (Respect) case and the Winchester 1997 Parliamentary By-election case.

Members of chambers also regularly advise on election law in relation to all major electoral events, including the 2020 GLA Elections, the 2019 and 2017 General Elections and the 2016 EU Referendum, and in respect of all local, mayoral and PCC elections.

The barristers at 4-5 Gray's Inn Square advise local authorities in respect of all local authority functions which, according to the Encyclopaedia (and our experience), range alphabetically from abattoirs to zoos.

We have unparalleled experience in respect of the involvement of local authorities in public law matters and challenges by way of judicial review. We frequently advise on matters of public procurement and competitive tendering.

Members of chambers have acted for local authorities and (we confess) against them in most of the major planning and environmental cases in the last decade.

Please contact our Senior Clerk Emily Mottin, who will assist you with your initial queries. Emily can be contacted at clerks@4-5.co.uk

GRAY'S INN SQUARE

4-5 Gray's Inn Square
Gray's Inn, London WC1R 5AH
2nd Floor, Two Snow Hill, Birmingham B4 6GA

DX 1029 LDE
+44 (0)20 7404 5252
clerks@4-5.co.uk

www.4-5.co.uk

RUNNING ELECTIONS

9th EDITION

Roger Morris
Mark Heath

APS BOOKS
Yorkshire

APS Books,
The Stables, Field Lane
Aberford, West Yorkshire,
LS25 3AE

APS Books is a subsidiary of the APS Publications imprint

www.andrewsparke.com

Ninth edition published worldwide by APS Books

ABOUT THE AUTHORS

ROGER MORRIS

Roger Morris was Chief Executive of both the City of Durham (1981-1986) and Northampton Borough Council (1986-2004), and has been involved in running elections for some fifty years, serving as East Midlands Regional Returning Officer in 1999 and 2004 for the European Parliamentary elections. He has been President of the Association of District Secretaries (1979-1980) and of SOLACE (1995-1996), and has written widely, including *Parliament and the Public Libraries* (1977); *Solicitors and Local Authorities* (1983); *Local Government Ground Rules* (1990); with Roger Paine, *Will You Manage? The Needs of Local Authority Chief Executives* (1995); and *Local Government, Local Legislation: Municipal Initiative in Parliament from 1858-1872* (2017). He is a Solicitor and currently Chair of the Law Society's Board for the Diploma in Local Government Law and Practice. He was awarded an OBE for services to Further Education in 2014.

MARK HEATH

Mark Heath is a Solicitor who since 1990 has held various roles at Southampton, including Solicitor to the Council, Director of Corporate Services, and latterly Chief Operating Officer. He partially retired from Southampton in 2016, and is now a part-time Consultant for a firm of Solicitors (VWV) specialising in public sector work. He continues to serve, however, as Southampton's Electoral Registration and Returning Officer, to which he was first appointed in 1994 having previously been Deputy Returning Officer.

He was the South East Regional Returning Officer for the 2009, 2014 and 2019 European Parliamentary Elections, the Regional Counting Officer for the South East for the AV Referendum in 2011, and has also served as the Police Area Returning Officer for Hampshire for the Police and Crime Commissioner elections in 2012, 2016 and 2021. He is a member of several groups convened by Government or the

Electoral Commission on electoral law, policy and practice.

He has been 'hands-on' in electoral matters now for many years. His first involvement in elections was conceding an election petition in 1985, something he would like to avoid doing in the future, if possible. This experience he feels has contributed to his genuine interest in the electoral process, also linked to a belief that democracy is worth supporting, and if "done", should be "done well".

CONTENTS

INTRODUCTION

Newly appointed chief executives, who are usually not lawyers (let alone "electoral anoraks"),[1] often ask whether there is something they can read about running elections. Certainly it is not essential to be a lawyer to be a successful returning officer. It is, however, worthwhile to have a topical and current working knowledge of electoral law, and it is upon that basis that the authors have prepared this text, now in its eighth edition, which tries to describe the management tasks and challenges involved, and to help in resolving actual problems facing returning officers.

This is not a publication about election law as such. Rather it is about responsibility for the management of elections and polls, a concept now better recognised by Parliament (despite its title) since the passing of the Electoral Administration Act 2006, and continued in the current Elections Bill. It goes without saying that having properly run, free and fair elections is a cornerstone of democracy in any community. Similarly every chief executive (or indeed anyone else who may be responsible) should recognise that running elections properly and efficiently is a key aspect of job retention and success. Increasingly there are formal performance indicators seeking to measure consistent and efficient practice across the country, and the public, your employing authority, and your own staff all need to have confidence in what's happening from their own standpoints.

These pages should help that confidence. They draw input from the various SOLACE courses of recent years on running elections, and the authors welcome comments on their relevance, helpfulness, and on any omissions. In 35 concise chapters and two appendices we present a series of themes (relating to England and Wales) which you won't find – not like this anyway – in traditional textbooks or encyclopaedias like *Parker* and *Schofield*. Moreover, both experienced returning officers and electoral administrators will find the publication useful in checking reference points,

---

[1] A phrase coined by George Howarth MP in a Parliamentary debate, and quoted in *Hansard*.

particularly for specific provisions in legislation.

Running elections is a very personal, and sometimes lonely, responsibility. We hope that this book will be a companion in carrying that responsibility. Everyone who carries that responsibility needs to think about the issues we present. Our intention is simply to help you to have the confidence to make your own decisions, as you must, usually within a very unforgiving timetable. (The power to correct certain procedural errors given by s 46 of the Electoral Administration Act 2006 is welcome, but does not remove the personal accountability that everyone who manages elections has.)

There is a very high standard of electoral management and administration in this country which often makes the whole process appear on the surface almost mechanical and routine; but even the most experienced returning officer will always be wary, for dangers commonly lurk beneath dark electoral waters.

Because references to the Representation of the People Acts and Regulations occur so frequently they are abbreviated to "RPA" or "RPR" appropriately. We have tried to refer to the law as we understand it applicable on 1 February 2022. In 2021 we published a *Supplement* to the preceding edition of guidance on the changes necessitated by the Covid-19 situation. Many of those temporary provisions are now spent, but previous experience and guidance remains relevant, and we have incorporated it in chapter 35.

The changes to be introduced by the current Elections Bill are referred to in this book alongside the subsisting law. Similarly major changes have been made in Wales by the Senedd and Elections (Wales) Act 2020 and the Local Government and Elections (Wales) Act 2021, as the legal regimes of the two jurisdictions increasingly diverge. Until the change of name, and the re-enactment of electoral law and subordinate rules, have been fully assimilated the position in Wales will be especially complicated.

If you find errors, or consider that any issues are not covered which should be, please email Roger Morris at rm@rjbmorris.net. We also thank Ian MacKellar of the *Hunts Post* for his innovative contribution to chapter 18, which we have reprinted from past editions, when Roger's co-author was David Monks, then Chief Executive of Huntingdonshire District Council.

ROGER MORRIS
MARK HEATH

CHAPTER 1
THE BACKGROUND TO ELECTION LAW

As one of the oldest and longest-running democracies, elections in the UK go back hundreds of years, and there are echoes of this still on the statute book, particularly in relation to Parliament. The word "candidate" is traced by *The Oxford English Dictionary* to the early seventeenth century, and is derived from the Latin *candidatus* – meaning "clothed in white" – since it was the custom for those standing for office in ancient Rome to wear a white toga.

The present system is still essentially Victorian in construction and tone, with the secret ballot dating back to the Ballot Act 1872 and even earlier legislation. Although changes are gradually being made, fundamental reform of our voting process is well overdue to reflect the technology, the lifestyles and the expectations of the first quarter of the twenty-first century. We have a tradition of caution over the pace of electoral change: the Ballot Act itself, which received royal assent on 18 July 1872, was originally provided by s 33 to remain in force only till the end of 1880, a stipulation which the House of Lords had inserted in the Bill. Together with other related legislation, it was not made permanent until the passing of the Representation of the People Act 1918. (The general election of Saturday 14 December 1918, incidentally, was the first to be held on a single day; that of January 1910 had been the longest in British history, taking place over 26 days.) Nevertheless, we may salute a system which served well for several generations, was a model for others, and was so enduring that it survived all that time when so much else was changed – including the scope of the franchise for whom the processes were originally devised. That system's virtues, while in need of reform, at the same time deserve fresh evaluation in this era of 'fake' news, internet manipulation and allegations of hidden and uncosted influences.

The written procedures and documentation still need to be compared against that original purpose – to be honest, fair, and at once both secret for the individual voter and open to inspection for the confidence of candidates and the electorate at large. It will be much harder to safeguard and even improve the reputation for integrity than it will be to improve the physical act of voting, and remove any justification for the use of sealing wax! In fact, of course, much has anyway changed over the years. In the Public Libraries Act 1850 those voting on whether to adopt the Act had to sign their names on their votes, whereas today we still expect to vote by marking a cross, the traditional mark of the illiterate. In s 2 of the Ballot Act 1872, the returning officer was forbidden to vote, even in secret, yet if a tie resulted he had to give his casting vote, so publicly declaring his preference! (This provision has now been thankfully repealed, but returning officers can draw lots in the event of a tied result: see chapter 20.)

Another historical principle, and one still very important today as part of the safeguards of integrity, constitutional checks and balances, is contained in the appointment of returning officers. Through statutes and Parliamentary and constitutional procedures, the Crown dissolves and summons Parliaments. A writ – the term still survives here despite its abolition in everyday legal use – is issued as an instruction to officials acting locally to "return" the writ (hence "returning officer") with the name of the elected candidate on it.

That official, however, is not appointed directly by the Crown, or Parliament, or any Minister, but by the prescribed local authority for all, or a substantial part, of each constituency concerned. Though the returning officer is technically either the county High Sheriff or a district chairman or (lord) mayor – see chapter 5 – the official who does all the management and administrative work, styled the "acting returning officer", is appointed by that local authority, by virtue of being appointed electoral registration officer.

The network of rules about how to manage, run and participate in elections is detailed and, as already stated, is now in urgent need of fundamental reform, but it must meet three principal objectives. It has to be clear and fair to administer, and deal with all the likely eventualities; it has to be demonstrably and openly fair to candidates and voters, so that they can scrutinise what takes place and check compliance with the law for themselves; and it has to be secret in terms of voters' choices, yet able to be reviewed by a court if legally challenged.

The rules have also to be considered against that original social and technological background, so different from that of today. That approach may well produce a different verdict from contemporary opinion: those differences may be instructive in checking how proposals for reform would affect the requirements of principle that have been found to serve well in the past.

A problem both in reading and describing election law is its repetitive and convoluted nature. Many rules are all but identical for different sorts of elections and polls, and are set out separately for each in different regulations. There is considerable scope, reform and modernisation apart, for simply rationalising what is there. The past twenty years alone have seen four new systems of elections added – for the Welsh Assembly (subsequently called the Welsh Parliament, and now known as the Senedd); for the Greater London Authority; for referendums for directly elected mayors; and most recently for the election of police and crime commissioners. A fifth system, for the European Parliament, was remodelled, and then became obsolete when this country left the EU. (Outside the scope of this book, changes for the Scottish Parliament and the Northern Ireland Assembly have come about also.) Regulations for referendums on regional assemblies have been made, a new context given for referendums originally created under the Government of Wales Act 2006, and polls for business improvement districts and other issues introduced. Yet again, provisions were enacted in the Localism Act 2011 for local polls on council tax levels, council governance changes and neighbourhood development plans. (Indeed the passing of the Localism Act 2011 represented a major shift in English practice at least, with its broad extension of the referendum principle to wholly new areas of local democracy and public voice.) The range and scale of changes in systems and principles, as opposed to the detailed conduct of elections and polls, has been greater in that time than in the whole of the one and a quarter centuries from the Ballot Act of 1872 to the election of the Labour Government of 1997. There may still be more changes to come: the prospect of direct elections to the House of Lords has for the present receded, but will probably be canvassed again in due course. It is to the credit of the creaking Victorian structure that so much significant change has been able to be grafted onto it.

Nor have the detailed conduct issues been neglected. In the last fifteen years or so, the combination of elections has become increasingly normal rather than exceptional, with consequent complications in the inter-relation of different timetables and requirements in the same polling systems. On 25 May 2005 the then Department of Constitutional Affairs (DCA) published *Electoral Administration: A Policy Paper For Discussion*, and the subsequent Electoral Administration Act 2006 and its dependent statutory instruments made substantial changes to the actual process of voting, as well as to many ancillary matters which had already begun to be modified in the years leading up to the 2006 Act. The more recent changes have most visibly and publicly affected the postal voting process, as the Government reacted to the first significant public loss of confidence in the integrity of the voting system itself since Victorian times. Other changes too, however, have taken place, many of which have greatly added to the administrative burdens of election staff already struggling to cope with ever more intricate demands in an unforgiving, short timetable. It is an irony, no doubt, that while on the one hand electronic and text message voting have been piloted in recent years, elections staff now find themselves doing things like checking signatures and supervising handwritten copying of the unedited electoral register in a world where large-scale repetitive clerical work (and the experience of performing it accurately) is increasingly unusual. As noted above, it was back in the time of the Public Libraries Act 1850 that voters had to sign their name to vote ...

A consolidating Elections Act, simplifying the cumbersome "representation of the people" style, would be a useful step in itself. The previous authors have argued for such steps to be followed in other places, so far without success; the 1999 Report of the Home Office Working Party on Electoral Procedures (chaired by Home Office Minister Mr George Howarth MP, published on 19 October that year, and of which the former co-author David Monks was a member) did acknowledge that reform was overdue and presaged the election pilot legislation introduced in 2000, on which see now chapter 25. The Law Commission (rather than the Electoral Commission) has worked on the long overdue process of considering reforms: the Commission's consultation paper *Electoral Law in the United Kingdom* was published on 15 June 2012, and then *Electoral Law: A Joint Interim Report* (with the Northern Ireland and Scottish Law Commissions) was published on 4 February 2016.

The real problem with regulations as they change and modify existing election rules is that they are produced in a "jigsaw" style. Thus, there is never a *de novo* start from a blank sheet of paper to produce a composite set of rules for a particular election when there is substantial change (such as in the European elections of 1999 and again of 2004). The existing rules are always modified or replaced to a certain extent and the poor practitioner has to juggle with a number of weighty texts to try and see the whole picture. At last from 2 January 2007 the local elections rules for England and Wales, including parishes and communities, were consolidated for the first time since 1986, and twenty sets of regulations and amendments were almost entirely revoked. From 2022, however, the rules in England and Wales have diverged again, following the Local Government and Elections (Wales) Act 2021 and associated provisions such as the Local Elections (Communities) (Wales) Rules 2021, SI No 1460 (W. 375). Some Regulations, however, remain in force for England that still retain the words "and Wales" in their titles.

At this stage it is also worth noting that the vast majority of these regulations used to emanate from the Home Office who, traditionally in our system of government, promoted electoral legislation. This was the situation for very many years but began to change significantly some twenty-five years ago.

The predominant Government Department for all practical purposes in the elections field is now the Department for Levelling Up, Housing and Communities ('DLUHC'), which has succeeded the Cabinet Office ('CO'). It publishes regular updates outlining its work and progress with electoral legislation, etc. Within the DLUHC, the unit dealing with this work is the Elections and Democracy Division. Ministerial responsibility for the law and policy on the conduct of elections now lies with the DLUHC.

The Electoral Commission was created to oversee elections practice generally and to establish a resource of best practice; the Commission is the subject of chapter 2. The Commission's increasing range of specialist publications are now web-based, and generally published separately for England, Scotland and Wales. See also the other publications mentioned in appendix 1.

Note that *in England* (following the Local Government Act 2000) by virtue of section D of sch 1 to the Local Authorities (Functions and Responsibilities) (England) Regulations 2000 SI No 2853 (amended by reg 2(4) of SI 2007 No 2593), deciding election-related matters is not to be the responsibility of an authority's executive. They must be dealt with either by the full council; by a traditional Local Government Act 1972 committee (many authorities now have a separate elections panel); or, where appropriate, by officer delegated powers. In England the 2000 Regs were further amended in this context by SI 2007 No 2593, and also by SI 2008 No 516 which inserted regs 2(6A) and (6B) to exclude from an authority's executive the making of requests for single-member areas and changing a scheme for elections. *In Wales*, in a council operating executive arrangements, 8(4) of the Local Government and Elections (Wales) Act 2021 stipulates that power to change the local voting system cannot to be the responsibility of that executive. The position hitherto has been prescribed by SI 2007 No 399, also section D of sch 1 and in addition (relating to authorities operating alternative arrangements where election-related matters are not to be responsibility of an authority's board), section D of sch 1 to SI 2007 No 399.

The Local Government and Public Involvement in Health Act 2007 made extensive changes to the rules about executive responsibilities, whole and partial-council elections, and also – under the banner of community engagement – to the powers to review, reconfigure and group parish councils, and to create new ones, including in London. The Coalition Government introduced the Parliamentary Voting System and Constituencies Act 2011, under which the unsuccessful Alternative Vote referendum was held on 5 May 2011, and provisions were also made in that Act for redrawing constituency boundaries and reducing their number.

The detailed legal rules and regulations about all kinds of elections are to be found in standard practitioner works like *Parker* and *Schofield*. Of course this book can be no substitute for them. It seeks only to provide a general map to an ever more intricately constructed territory.

Particular care must be taken in Wales to check the implementation dates of new legislation, and the current situation for provisions referred to in this book.

CHAPTER 2
THE ELECTORAL COMMISSION

Many countries (particularly in the Commonwealth) established Electoral Commissions long before this country. The Electoral Commission in the UK came into existence on 30 November 2000. It developed partly as a result of discussions in the Howarth Committee (Home Office) following the 1997 Parliamentary election. The Howarth Committee (so called because it was chaired by the then junior Minister in the Home Office, George Howarth MP) consisted of civil servants, returning officers (including one of the former joint authors, David Monks), electoral administrators, representatives of the political parties, etc and was charged with reviewing electoral practice after the 1997 general election.

Although a Commission had been talked about before 1997, it was only in November of that year that the Government asked the Neill Committee (reviewing standards in public life) to consider the funding of political parties and to make recommendations for change. In October 1998 the Neill Committee recommended the establishment of a Commission to deal with political donations and other matters. The Government then took this forward into the Political Parties, Elections and Referendums Act 2000, establishing the UK Commission (see ss 1-21 and sch 1). The Commission's general functions are set out in ss 5-13 of the 2000 Act (as amended), and were augmented by Part 1 of the Political Parties and Elections Act 2009 (following the operation of which, however, the Commission lost its former electoral boundary functions in ss 14-20 of the 2000 Act).

The Commission is a UK-wide body, independent of Government, non-partisan and answerable directly to Parliament, via the Speaker's Committee. Its priorities have been variously expressed over its two decades, and have been successively redrawn in the light of contemporary public and political preoccupations. An interim Corporate Plan for the period 2020-21 to 2024-25 was last updated on 22 June 2020. The Commission's current vision is "to be a world-class public sector organisation – innovative, delivering great value and getting right what matters most to voters and legislators." This vision is to be achieved through a five-year work programme with four goals, last updated on 12 May 2021. The goals are about securing free and fair elections; a trusted and transparent system of regulation in political finance; being an independent and respected area of expertise; and providing value for money and best use of resources.

The way in which the Commission was established, and the means by which it is funded, were designed to emphasise distance from the Government of the day. The employees of the Commission are not Crown servants. When the Political Parties and Elections Bill was originally introduced in July 2008, the Commission initially had misgivings about the principle of nomination of four Commissioners by political parties, but that no longer applies and the current approach is considered to work well. (The Chair cannot be from a political party.)

The Commission's five-year plan and estimates must be presented to the Speaker's Committee (s 2 of the 2000 Act), consisting of both front-bench and back-bench MPs. After each financial year the Commission is required to prepare a report about the performance of its functions during that year; this is laid before Parliament.

Clauses 14 and 15 of the current Elections Bill, by inserting ss 4A-E into the 2000 Act, will allow the Secretary of State (subject to consultative and procedural requirements) to prepare and publish a "strategy and policy statement" of

"(a) strategic and policy priorities of Her Majesty's government relating to elections, referendums and other matters in respect of which the Commission have functions, and

(b) the role and responsibilities of the Commission in enabling Her Majesty's government to meet those priorities."

The statement may also include "guidance relating to particular matters in respect of which the Commission have functions" and associated matters, while the Commission must annually publish "what they have done during the period in question in consequence of the statement." Section 13ZA of the 2000 Act will empower the Speaker's Committee to examine the performance by the Commission of their duty under s. 4B(2).

The Commission's initial Chair and five Commissioners were originally appointed by Royal Warrant on 19 January 2001 on a recommendation from the House of Commons. There are now ten Commissioners. The Chair's term will run from 2021-2024 inclusive. Provisions about the selection and backgrounds of Commissioners are now contained in ss 4-7 of the 2009 Act.

The Commission's remit covers all elections (including also now those for Scottish local government, which were formerly excluded), but it is not responsible for the actual process of managing or conducting elections. This remains a function for returning and acting returning officers under existing arrangements. The Government remains responsible for electoral legislation and the underpinning policy, but has a statutory duty to consult the Commission on proposals for change in key areas, and the Commission has a statutory duty to keep electoral law under review: s 6 of the Political Parties, Elections and Referendums Act 2000. Additional provisions about election guidance and the financing of the Commission's work concerning Wales were made by s 28 and sch 2 to the Senedd and Elections (Wales) Act 2020, which inserted para 16A into sch 1 to the 2000 Act.

Most of the early work of the Commission was focused on its own establishment and tackling party registration as well as dealing with donations to the parties. The Commission is required to maintain up to date registers of political parties in Great Britain and Northern Ireland; these, of course, are very important to returning officers in the nomination periods running up to elections (see chapter 12). It also is empowered to make grants to certain political parties under the Elections (Policy Development Grants Scheme) Order 2006, SI No 602, most recently amended by SI 2022 No 26 (see s 12 of the Political Parties, Elections and Referendums Act 2000).

The work of the Commission has broadened into reviewing aspects of electoral law and practice, based on its reports on recent elections and other matters, and into developing and monitoring performance. The approach to projects varies, but has included significant consultation with the Society of Local Authority Chief Executives and Senior Managers (SOLACE) and the Association of Electoral Administrators (AEA). The Commission has produced many reports on specific electoral topics such as postal voting, electoral turnout, electoral cycles, voting age, political engagement, nomination procedures, etc. As mentioned in chapter 1, the Commission now publishes a wide range of reports, information and guidance, most of which is publicly available on its website. For the public generally there is also www.electoralcommission.org.uk. The Commission's power to publish a report into spending by a referendum campaign was upheld by the Court of Appeal in *R. (Vote Leave Ltd.) v. Electoral Commission* [2019] *The Times*, 27 December.

In April 2002 the Commission had absorbed the functions of the Local Government Commission for England, which became "The Boundary Committee for England" with responsibility for reviewing local electoral boundaries through periodic electoral reviews. That change was reversed, however, by the Local Democracy, Economic Development and Construction Act 2009, s 55 of which established the Local Government Boundary Commission for England (a similar body had existed prior to 1992), and effectively removed all the Commission's role in boundary and electoral area review matters. (On boundary reviews see chapter 27.)

Following discussions with returning officers during and after the June 2004 European Parliamentary elections, the Electoral Commission identified the need for there to be an ongoing source of strategic advice to the Commission, and to the DLUHC, on UK-wide electoral issues. The idea was to establish a partnership approach at a time of change and renewal to discuss electoral administration, modernisation and reform. Chaired by the Commission's Chair, the twelve existing regional returning officers and the DLUHC are also represented. The Forum meets quarterly, and has considered matters such as the latest legislation, performance standards and the timing of counts.

In 2006, on an experimental pilot basis, the Electoral Commission appointed four regional co-ordinators. The areas selected were the East, North West, South West and South East. Those appointed were all experienced returning officers. The concept was to provide a regional centre of support and guidance in the English regions, whilst still recognising the independence of each local returning officer. The Commission continued with regional co-ordination in 2007 (as part of its plan to strengthen its regional presence), but in a modified form. Following the regional co-ordinator pilot, the Commission now has home-based staff around the English regions to provide them with the same kind of support already available in Scotland and Wales.

Fraud prevention (see also chapter 29 on the integrity of the process) has become an important concern, particularly since around 2005 when a succession of prosecutions, mostly involving postal votes, drew attention to the relative lack of security in the absent votes procedure (and also, though to a lesser extent, to the risk of personation – claiming to be someone you aren't – because of the lack of any rigorous identity check on would-be voters presenting themselves at polling stations). The Commission has been much concerned both in advising electoral registration officers and others about the prevailing system and also in advising how it might be changed. In February 2014 the Commission published revised *Guidance on preventing and detecting electoral fraud.* The Commission also welcomed the publication on 12 August 2016 of *Securing the ballot: Report of Sir Eric Pickles' review into electoral fraud.* Since 2017 the Commission has annually published electoral fraud data on its website.

Without doubt, the establishment of the Electoral Commission was one of the most significant developments in the world of elections for many years at that time. Its impact continues to grow, and returning officers must keep abreast of its work.

CHAPTER 3
ELECTORAL REGISTRATION

A THE BACKGROUND

The registration of electors is the permanent, year-round electoral function in the UK which is carried out by an official called the Electoral Registration Officer ("ERO").

Registration is the gateway to democracy. You must be registered to vote. You can only be registered to vote if (amongst other things) you fulfil the requirements that allow you to be

able to vote. Then you are part of the relevant franchise. It has been said that:

"No area of electoral law is more important than the franchise. It governs entitlement to vote at UK elections. Along with electoral boundaries and voting systems, it is a core parameter of representative democracy and the right to free elections." (Law Commission)

Electoral registration, the compiling and keeping of the electoral register, is a separate function from running actual elections. It is inevitably and increasingly intertwined with it, however, and that in itself has brought issues. Over recent years this has become a much more complex topic (and far from the task traditionally regarded as mechanical) that is virtually sufficient to be covered in its own dedicated textbook! Registration work now has its own set of performance standards stipulated by the Electoral Commission (see chapter 26), and the situation overall has not been helped over the last twenty years or so by high profile cases and allegations of "roll-stuffing" (packing the electoral roll with fictitious voters), though not more recently. Nevertheless, together with postal voting, this has remained a controversial issue. Besides the allegations of fraudulent entries there remain considerable concerns over non-registration, to which reference is also be made later.

Registration was introduced in 1832 to record and check the property qualifications for voting by adult males. As the electoral regime evolved, the registration process remained tied to the household/property. In every household, one person was asked to tell the ERO who lived there, their age and citizenship – the key franchise requirements. The electoral register provided a snapshot of who resided and was eligible to vote in a household on a particular day within the canvass period.

B INDIVIDUAL ELECTORAL REGISTRATION

Individual Electoral Registration ('IER') replaced the household system, with individuals taking responsibility for their own registration. This significant change was brought about by the Electoral Registration and Administration Act 2013 ("the 2013 Act"). As of 10 June 2014, IER has been in effect in England and Wales, and was followed by Scotland on 19 September 2014, after the referendum on Scottish independence. Since then those wishing to register to vote have been able to apply online to register.

The law effectively created five different registers, namely:

A. the UK Parliamentary register, which includes overseas voters;

B. the local government register;

C. the register for non-national European citizens residing in the UK;

D. the register of peers who live abroad; and

E. Gibraltar's register.

In practice, the ERO must so far as possible combine the entries for the first four registers, marking the names to indicate which elections electors are entitled to vote in. Following "Brexit", given that 3 of the 5 registers existed solely for the EU Parliamentary Elections, this list is now reducing to two.

Registers are structured geographically. The law requires it to be framed in separate parts for each parliamentary polling district. Some parliamentary polling districts cross local authority boundaries. Where that occurs, the entries should be divided into separate parts for each electoral area within that polling district. Each polling district is delineated by different letters eg 'EV', which are then used in making up electoral numbers for the relevant polling district. The Parliamentary polling district is the default administrative area for all elections, and this rule is geared at making the registers divisible into polling station registers.

Names and addresses must, so far as reasonably practicable, be arranged in street order. This also helps returning officers to decide on the polling station provision and location in each polling district. Where it is not practicable to do this, names can be arranged in alphabetical order or in a combination of alphabetical and street order.

The law relating to the management of electoral registration can be found within the RPA 1983. Section 8 provides for EROs to be appointed by local councils. Section 9 requires these officers to maintain registers and sets out their core content. Section 9A governs what steps are involved in maintaining the register in Great Britain.

Wales has seized the opportunity to make use of its rights as a devolved administration to set its own policies for non-reserved polls. In this context, in Wales, a person aged 16 or over on the relevant date who meets the residency qualification and is not subject to any legal incapacity to vote is entitled to be included on the local government register. An elector must be 18, however, to be included on the UK Parliamentary register. This means that in Wales the local government register will include 16 and 17 year olds as full electors, and 16 they are entitled to vote in both Senedd elections and local government elections held on or after 5 May 2022.

Relevant provisions are amended to give effect to this. For example s 8(5A) of the RPA 1983 was inserted, in relation to Wales, by the Senedd and Elections (Wales) Act 2020, s 23.

Note that it is specifically the ERO who is to be the acting returning officer for Parliamentary election purposes under s 28(1)(a) of the 1983 Act – so the original appointments are very important. The term "registration officer" is not used, however, in defining the returning officer for local elections in s 35(1), (1A) and (3) of the RPA 1983, or therefore (since the local returning officer designation is followed) in the definition of "counting officer" for several kinds of referendum (see M, P, Q and R in chapter 5).

Questions sometime arise as to the so-called independence of the ERO and their relationship with their employing authority. Is this a similar post to that of returning officer with personal autonomy and responsibility? Certainly, when acting as ERO the post holder has a certain level of independence, as the functions in relation to the registration of electors are placed on the ERO personally, and not on the council by whom that officer is appointed. It is important, however, to note that the relevant local authority must pay any expenses properly incurred by an ERO. Generally, however, chief executives' (or proper officers') salaries are inclusive of this role, and separate fees in the style of elections are not usually paid.

Deputies to the ERO need to be approved by the council concerned under s 52(2) (as amended) of the RPA 1983. Where the ERO is unable to act or there is a vacancy, s 52(3) provides that the duties may "be done by or with respect to the proper officer of the council by whom the registration officer was appointed." The word "whom" here refers to the council, and not to the proper officer. As to possible redundancy and entitlement to a redundancy payment, see the comments about this in relation to returning officers at the end of chapter 5.

C PREPARING AND PUBLISHING THE REGISTER

The duty to "prepare and publish in each year" in s 9 of the RPA 1983 used to give the ERO considerable discretion in how to set about the task, and how far to go in obtaining the responses which local residents are by law obliged to provide. The scheme in Great Britain now also gives expression to accuracy and completeness. Section 9A of the 1983 Act qualifies the duty to take steps to maintain the register to refer specifically to the purpose of:

Securing that, as far as is reasonably practicable, persons who are entitled to be registered in a register (and no others) are registered in it. (Section 9A(1)(a))

The ERO is required by section 9A(1) of the 1983 Act to maintain the register, and "*must take all steps that are necessary for the purpose of complying*" with this duty, and for the purpose of ensuring completeness and accuracy.

Section 9A(2) provides that the steps include:

1. for the purposes of a register of parliamentary electors in Great Britain, or a register of local government electors in England, sending to any address at least one communication to be used for the canvass;

2. sending more than once to any address the form to be used for the canvass in certain circumstances;

3. making on one or more occasions house to house inquiries;

4. for the purposes of a register of parliamentary electors in Great Britain, or a register of local government electors in England, making on one or more occasions contact with persons by telephone;

5. making contact by such other means as the registration officer thinks appropriate with persons who do not have an entry in a register;

6. inspecting any records held by any person which he is permitted to inspect under or by virtue of any enactment or rule of law;

7. providing training to persons under his direction or control in connection with the carrying out of the duty.

Nevertheless, the five kinds of "necessary steps" set out now in s 9A(2) of RPA 1983 need not necessarily be slavishly followed in every case, or be taken in any particular order. It is the view of both the Commission and the present authors that s 9A allows an ERO to exercise judgement about the steps listed according to the circumstances in each case.

It should not be forgotten that s 69 of the Electoral Administration Act 2006 (which requires local electoral officers, defined to include EROs, to take such steps as they think appropriate to encourage the participation by electors in the electoral process in their area) applies to registration as well as to voting.

Before IER, the canvass under the household registration system was conducted by sending out a canvass form and, as we noted above, making house-to-house enquiries on one or more occasions. A canvass form completed and returned by a person in the household constituted an application to register for each person appearing from the form to be entitled to be registered. As a result, it was the main way in which electors became registered, although the introduction of rolling registration meant that it was possible for applications to be made outside a canvass period as well.

Under IER, the canvass is a request for information as to who resides in the household. A returned canvass form gives the ERO that information but is not an application to register any of the reported residents. Each must individually apply to register by returning an invitation to register form to the ERO.

In 2018 the Government proposed reform to the canvass, saying:

"Electoral Registration Officers from all parts of Great Britain have observed that the current annual canvass of electors is outdated and cumbersome. The one-size-fits-all approach, incorporating

numerous prescribed steps, takes little account of differences within and between registration areas. It is heavily paper based, expensive and complex to administer. It is also clear that the current process leads to confusion for the citizen. We are determined to ensure the citizen is at the heart of the process and has a positive interaction with our democratic system. It is therefore important that we modernise and streamline the process of the annual canvass to ensure that it is fit for purpose."

Arising from this, the Government brought forward the Representation of the People (Annual Canvass) (Amendment) Regulations 2019, SI No 1451. These regulations removed the previous requirement to canvass all households in the same way, that is, by sending up to three full canvass forms with pre-paid pre-addressed envelopes, with the addition of a household visit where the property has not responded. The Government's stated policy intention was that these changes would allow EROs to better focus their resources on households more likely to have experienced changes in composition, ie where additions to or deletions from the register were required. It established a mandatory national data matching service (and provided for a one-off test of that service), allowing EROs discretion over the conduct of their annual canvass of the electors on their electoral registers. It set out the new matched and unmatched property routes, one of which EROs must follow based on the results of their data match step, as well as an exemption process for certain properties. Similar provisions were made for Wales in SI 2020 No 50 (W.6).

The Electoral Commission advised at the time that the success of this canvass reform was highly dependent on new data-sharing mechanisms and careful planning and implementation activities being completed in good time ahead of the start of the 2020 annual canvass in July that year.

The Commission also noted that additional reforms could further improve the efficiency of the electoral registration process including:

"...

•enhanced digital data sharing between organisations holding public data and EROs;

•automated and automatic registration; and

•the integration of electoral registration into other public service transactions."

(Report on UK Government's draft statutory instrument to reform the annual canvass: July 2019)

It is important to remember that the online system provides an opportunity for applications to register to be made, and once that is completed it remains an application pending the

ERO's decision, something that is often lost on the public who believe that once their online application has been submitted, they are registered.

Section 10ZC (1) of the 1983 Act requires EROs in Great Britain to register a person ("P") if:

(1) an application for registration is made by someone who appears to the ERO to be P;

(2) any requirements imposed by or under the 1983 Act in relation to the application are met; and

(3) P appears to the ERO to be entitled to be registered.

D OBJECTIONS TO REGISTRATION

There is the possibility of the ERO receiving objections to registrations that they will need to process. Note generally the possibilities for hearings (regs 29-32 of RPR 2001). These regulations make provision for objections made in respect of persons already entered in the register. Such objections can now be made pursuant to s 12(4) of the 2006 Act, though registration officers may now dismiss such objections without a hearing if they believe the objection is clearly without merit. Reg 13 of the 2006 Regs now gives further power to registration officers to undertake a review of a person's entitlement to registration and objection. Provision is made for when such reviews must be heard and how they are to be heard, with due notice being given to the person whose name appears on the register.

As can therefore be seen, the ERO's role is more "active" under this regime than previously. As well as the ERO needing to consider objections to registration, they also need to undertake data matching against national databases such as that of the Department for Work and Pensions, and they have the power to ask for evidence as proof of identity.

E QUALITY OF THE REGISTER

There have been (and still are) concerns over the quality of the register in certain areas. The Electoral Commission reported the accuracy and completeness estimates for England, Scotland and Wales for both the Parliamentary and local government registers published in December 2018. In England, the local government registers were found to be 89% accurate, and the accuracy of the Parliamentary registers also stood at 89%. The local government register was 83% complete, while the Parliamentary register was slightly more complete, at 85%.

The Commission's research confirmed that age and mobility continue to be the strongest variables associated with lower levels of completeness. The Commission added:

"Earlier this year we published the findings from a series of feasibility studies exploring how electoral registration reforms could be delivered, to help inform the debate about registration reform. These studies looked at the potential for giving EROs access to data from other public service providers; integration of electoral registration into other public service transactions; and automatic or more automated forms of registration.

The options explored in the studies could help address some of the specific challenges highlighted in this research. For example:

•For people who have recently changed address, including those who move more frequently, registering to vote may not always be an

immediate priority. Regular access to reliable data from a wider range of public services about people who have recently updated their address details would allow EROs to make contact directly with them at their new address to encourage them to register to vote.

•Integrating electoral registration applications into other public service transactions could make it easier for individuals to keep their registration details up to date and accurate. This could be particularly effective for those who have moved recently and who are in the process of updating their details with other agencies and public bodies.

•Making better use of existing public data sources could also help to improve levels of completeness among some of the specific under-registered groups identified in this study. Data from the education sector – such as information held by the Education and Skills Funding Agency Learning Records Service, which collects data relating to learners in England, Wales and Northern Ireland registering for relevant post-14 qualifications, and the Scottish Qualifications Authority – could help EROs identify attainers and other young people. Also, data from the Department for Work and Pensions could potentially be used by EROs to register young people to vote automatically when they are allocated their National Insurance number ahead of their 16th birthday."

(*Addressing the challenges of accuracy and completeness*: September 2019)

While people do not register for a range of reasons – some wish to conceal their identity from authority for financial or tax reasons; others do so to seek personal anonymity from society in general; yet others fail to register for reasons connected with inertia and ignorance. Whatever the motivation, this is a highly unsatisfactory situation in a modern western democracy, and one that should be remedied with some vigour. Moreover, all those involved with the administration of the electoral process know that an accurate and comprehensive register is a key building block in running a successful election, and the Electoral Commission has made the existence of complete and accurate electoral registers one of its key objectives.

F COMBINED REGISTERS

Registers for different kinds of elections are combined so far as possible (s 9(2) RPA 1983), with various letters printed to indicate particular limitations or entitlements. These various letters are as follows for electoral registers in force from 16 February 2001:

"(1)   Paragraphs (3) to (7) [Paragraphs (3), (5) and (6)] below specify the marks to appear against a person's [entry] in the register to indicate that he is registered in one or more of the four registers (those of: parliamentary electors; local government electors; relevant citizens of the Union registered as European Parliamentary electors, and peers overseas registered as European Parliamentary overseas electors) [of the two registers (those of: Parliamentary electors and local government elections)] which are required to be combined.

(2)   Where no mark appears against a person's [entry] in the register of electors, this indicates that he is registered in the registers of Parliamentary and local government electors.

(3)   To indicate that a relevant citizen of the Union is registered only in the register of local government electors, the letter "G" shall be placed against his [entry].

(4)   To indicate that such a citizen is registered in both that register and the register of such citizens registered as European Parliamentary electors, the letter "K" shall be placed against his [entry].

(5)   To indicate that any other person is registered only in the register of local government electors, the letter "L" shall be placed against his [entry].

(6)   To indicate that an overseas elector is registered only in the register of Parliamentary electors, the letter "F" shall be placed against his [entry].

(7)   To indicate that a European Parliamentary overseas elector is

registered only in the register of such electors, the letter "E" shall be placed against his [entry]."

(Regulation 42: Representation of the People (England and Wales) Regulations 2001, SI No 348.)

In addition, reg 111(7) of the RPR 2001 SI No 341, as amended by RPR 2002, SI No 1871, requires that in any copy of the full register sold under regs 112-114, "the letter 'Z' shall be placed against the name of any person whose name is not included in the edited version of the register".

Sections 13A and 13B (added into the RPA 1983 by the RPA 2000) deal with ongoing alterations to the register, and the final date for changes effective for any given election (normally close of nominations). Section 13B is further amended by s 11 of the Electoral Administration Act 2006: if an alteration in a published version of a register is to take effect after the fifth day before polling day it will be ineffective for that election (s 13B(1)).

G. OFFENCES

Just as there are statutory penalties for failure to supply correct information for inclusion in the electoral register (reg 23 of RPR 2001), so it is not unknown for people to try and register – perhaps using a name or address of convenience – solely for the purpose of establishing credit references or separating themselves from poor credit records associated with other addresses. Giving false information to such an end is of course an offence. This was revised and strengthened by s 15 of the Electoral Administration Act 2006 which amended Section 13D RPA 1983 (provision of false information). (After a statutory hearing the registration officer at Winchester some years ago rejected as spurious an attempt to register with the same name as the then Conservative MP.)

In March 2008 a special High Court election hearing in Slough found Eshaq Khan (a Conservative councillor) guilty of corrupt and illegal practices to secure his election. He was stripped of his seat and banned from standing for five years. The Court heard that he had won his marginal seat in the Central Ward after his team registered hundreds of "ghost voters" in the month before the election and then cast votes using fraudulent postal ballots. They registered fictitious voters at derelict houses and claimed that as many as twelve voters were living at two-bedroom flats or three-bedroom houses. They managed to add some 450 names to the register in the final weeks before the poll, almost all of whom voted for Khan by post. His Labour opponents succeeded in striking 145 of these 'ghost' names from the register.

The judge, Richard Mawrey QC, made a couple of highly barbed criticisms of the then system of electoral registration:

"There is no reason to suppose that this is an isolated incident. Roll-stuffing is childishly simple to commit and very difficult to detect. To ignore the probability that it is widespread, particularly in local elections, is a policy that even an ostrich would despise.... Great Britain's system of voter registration may well have been a quaint but demand has made it lethal to the democratic process."

Stories of similar practices sadly circulated around the time of the May 2010 general election. On 1 May 2010 *The Times* reported "Bundles of fictitious names put on the roll" in Tower Hamlets, London –

"Scotland Yard has launched criminal investigations into four allegations of bogus voter registration. Bundles of fictitious names have been put on the electoral roll in the London Borough of Tower Hamlets in what looks like a blatant attempt to steal the elections. It will raise concern in an area notorious for election fraud and where a last-minute flood of applications to vote means that more than 5,000 have been accepted without any checks enough to sway Thursday's results".

On 9 May 2010 (after the 6 May general election) *The Sunday Times* reported on 27 names that were registered to a London flat above a florist's shop in Southall. Fifteen names had been added just before the deadline; the owner said that the flat had been rented out and that they had no knowledge of the voters.

The response to such corrupt and allegedly corrupt practices resulted in the introduction of IER, but there are warnings here to those responsible for electoral registration. Mass over-registration at domestic addresses (not being houses in multiple occupation) must raise suspicions, especially when accompanied by applications for postal votes; in one case in East London 200 names were registered as living in a disused factory. The Birmingham case (local elections, June 2004) clearly establishes that it is not the role of the returning officer/electoral registration officer to investigate fraud, but if genuine suspicions are aroused or allegations received that have some prima facie validity, they should be reported to the police for further investigation. Most police forces now have much increased awareness of these issues, and some have considerable experience of their investigation.

The Representation of the People (England and Wales)(Amendment) 2002 Regulations, SI No 1871, amended the provisions of the RPR 2001 SI No 341 about sales and supply of electoral registers.

H. PUBLIC INSPECTION AND COMMERCIAL USE

Under regs 6 and 9-11 of SI 2002 No 1871 there can be public inspection of the full register, but only under supervision. Consequently, many EROs now consider that such registers can now only be inspected at their offices, and not as before at public libraries and area offices etc. The Electoral Commission advised, however, in 2006 that where EROs are sufficiently confident that library and other council staff can offer an appropriate level of supervision it would be helpful if inspection facilities can be provided. It is a criminal offence to copy the register by more than handwritten notes, and what is now reg 7(3) of the RPR 2001 (inserted by reg 6 of SI 2002 No 1871) makes it an offence to use any such hand-written notes for marketing purposes. Regulation 15 of the 2002 Regulations inserts regs 92-115 into the RPR 2001, SI No 341. These prescribe in detail authorised and unauthorised use of the full register and the wider use permitted of the edited register published under reg 93. Note that restrictions on unauthorised use of the full register apply equally to the ERO and their staff: reg 94. Some EROs have required others within their authorities to give undertakings only to use the register for permitted purposes.

Where there is a duty to supply a copy of the register, that duty is to supply it "in data form" unless a written request for a printed copy has earlier been made: see reg 102 (3) and similar provisions for other free supply situations. Under regs 15-16 of the RPR 2006, SI No 752 (amending reg 97 of the RPR 2001 and adding regs 97A and 97B), the British Library and the National Libraries of Wales and Scotland now receive data copies from all electoral registration officers, and reg 8 of the RPR (Amendment) Regs 2009, SI No 725 also amends reg 99 of the RPR 2001 in relation to what is now the Statistics Board. The Security Service, GCHQ and the Secret Intelligence Service may now, upon application, receive a free copy of the full Register. Differently (and strangely!) the Environment Agency, the Financial Conduct Authority and anybody carrying out the vetting of any person for the purpose of safeguarding national security are now included in the definition of government departments under reg 113 of the RPR 2001 (as amended by reg 23 of the RPR 2006), and so they may now purchase a copy of the register using the usual pricing procedure. Elected representatives and local constituency parties' candidates have rights to the supply of free copies of the full register under regs 103, 104 and 105; all are bound by restrictions with criminal penalties if they use the copies of the relevant parts of the register for any purpose other than that for which it has been lawfully supplied or disclose any information from it not published on the edited version of the register to anyone else.

Credit reference agencies are amongst the other categories to which full copies of the register may be supplied, although reg 114 provides for sale to them, not free supply. They are similarly bound by the narrowly defined purpose for which they may use the information. Indications have suggested that a third, or even approaching a half, in some places, of electors are choosing to opt out, thereby calling into question what commercial value the edited versions of registers have.

The cost of the full register, where it can be sold, remains the same as before (reg 111(5) and (6)). Reg 110 prescribes the cost of copies of the edited register, and reg 111(6) the cost of the list of overseas electors. Note that in any sale of copies of the full register under regs 112-114, "the letter 'Z' shall be placed against the name of any person whose name is not included in the edited version of the register" (reg 111(7)).

In data form it will cost £20 plus £1.50 per 1,000 entries (or part thereof), and in printed form £10 plus £5 for each 1,000 entries (or part thereof) (so long as the registration officer has enough copies left to sell – see reg 48(4)). The former provisions about supplying data and labels are not continued, as today's technology has rendered them unnecessary when every registration officer is a "data user". Separate charges are made for the list of overseas electors. (See reg 48, RPR 2001.)

I ANONYMOUS REGISTRATION

Provisions for anonymous registration were introduced for the first time by s 10 of the Electoral Administration Act 2006, inserting ss 9B and 9C into the RPA 1983 and supplemented by the Representation of the People (England and Wales) (Amendment) (No 2) Regulations 2006, SI No 2910. In the past this has caused registration officers some problems, as members of the armed or security services, or those threatened with violence by a former partner, have been registered in various ingenious ways (if at all) – as being resident at the Town Hall for instance, or as "other voters" in a list at the end of the regular register.

Under these provisions, which came into force after the May 2007 local elections (see regs 31G-J of ROR 2001, added by reg 12 of SI 2006 No 2910), an applicant for anonymous registration must provide a written claim that their safety (or that of another person of their household) is at risk. The registration officer must be satisfied as to the evidence – eg a document from the court or an attestation made by someone such as a Chief Constable concerning the safety of the applicant. The registration officer must maintain a record of anonymous entries and take proper precautions for its safe custody. The record is only to be used for registration, elections or jury service. The record may not otherwise be disclosed, except by order of the court. The provisions about evidence in support of anonymous registration applications were augmented (in relation to court orders, injunctions and attestation) by reg 6 of RPR (Amendment) Regs 2009, SI No 725.

J SERVICE AND OVERSEAS VOTERS

The Service Voters Registration Period Order 2010, SI No 882 extended the validity period of registration as a service voter from three years (to which it had previously been extended by SI 2006 No 3406) to five.

Until 2015 the number of overseas voters registered to vote had never risen above 35,000. In the annual ONS electoral register figures of December 2016 this had risen to 264,000. This was largely because of an overseas voter registration campaign in the run up to the 2015 General Election and interest in the 2016 referendum on the UK's membership of the EU.

At the UK General Election of 2017 there were a record 285,000 registered overseas voters. The Government has estimated that this is about 20% of eligible expats under the current 15-year limit.

After the 2015 General Election the Government indicated that it would bring forward a Votes for Life Bill in the Queen's Speech of 27 May 2015. The Government indicated that its provisions would scrap the 15-year rule, would make it easier for overseas voters to cast their votes in time for them to be counted, and would allow for the secure and accessible registration of overseas voters.

During Business questions on 21 July 2016, the then Leader of the House, David Lidington MP, indicated that extending the franchise was a complex matter :

"...because we would have to not just extend the franchise but establish a new system of voter registration, which is not straightforward given that voter registers no longer exist for periods that go back earlier than 15 years. We have to find some way of allocating those individuals to constituencies and verifying a previous place of residence."

On 7 October 2016 the Government published a policy statement, "A democracy that works for everyone: British citizens overseas" which set out how the 15-year rule would be removed and how all eligible British citizens who had lived in the UK would be given a lifelong right to vote in Parliamentary elections. British citizens living abroad would have to provide either a verifiable national insurance number, or a current UK passport, or an identity attestation, in order to be registered as an overseas voter. Overseas voters would continue to be registered at a previous address in the UK and the ERO would need to be satisfied of their connection with that address. The registration would last for twelve months, and then have to be renewed. A commitment to introduce votes for life was also included in the Conservative Party manifesto for the 2017 General Election.

The Government has included this within the Elections Bill currently before Parliament (see chapter 33).

Overseas postal voters have had issues with receipt and return of their ballots, with consequential advice that proxy votes may be better. If the 15-year rule is to be abolished, other methods of voting for what may be a significantly increased number of overseas voters may need to be considered.

An unintended consequence of IER is that registration is now largely event driven. That is to say that when a poll or election is called, the online service receives many applications. Unfortunately, a lot of those are duplicates, and many of those applications are made just prior to, or on the date of, the deadline to register. This can mean a major peak of work on registrations just prior to polling day for the election staff. The consequence of this is that the capacity in the election's office, at exactly the moment when most election staff should be focussed on polling day and the count, may be on registration matters and consequential issues.

All this puts even greater strain on both the manpower and software systems in the elections office at the most critical of times. This is an aspect of registration that is inevitably and increasingly intertwined with the running of elections, and is a legitimate matter of concern to returning officers as well as to EROs.

When at times a significant proportion (33% has been quoted) of applications are duplicates, that wasted effort at that time in an election timetable is a genuine and significant concern.

CHAPTER 4
DIFFERENT KINDS OF ELECTIONS AND POLLS

A. European Elections
B. Parliamentary Elections
C. Senedd (Welsh Parliament) Elections
D. Greater London Authority Elections
E. London Borough Elections
F. County Elections
G. Metropolitan Borough, Shire District, Borough or City Elections
H. Parish or Town Council Elections
I. Welsh Unitary and Community Council Elections
J. Parish and Community Polls and Local Polls
K. National Referendums
L. Regional Referendums
M. Elected Mayor and Petition Referendums
N. Elected Mayor Elections
O. Police, Fire and Crime Commissioner Elections
P. Council Tax Referendums
Q. Governance Changes Referendums
R. Neighbourhood Planning Referendums
S. Business Improvement District (BID) Ballots and Business Rate Supplement (BRS) Ballots

In England and Wales there are several different kinds of elections: indeed several different kinds of polls.

Elections and polls are not the same thing. An election is a process for choosing a person to hold a particular office or job; a poll (as the word itself originally implied) is a procedure of counting heads or votes to ascertain winners and losers or decide questions – and sometimes to decide about lost deposits. A ballot (interestingly, the word chosen to title the original Ballot Act 1872) is similarly a process of voting, once (according to *The Oxford English Dictionary*) by depositing small balls in an urn or box, and sometimes but not always a secret process. The term hustings, originally an Old English and Old Norse word, referred before the Ballot Act 1872 to the temporary platform from which the nomination of candidates was made, and from which they addressed the electors: hence it came to refer to the whole proceedings of Parliamentary elections. (The first election under the 1872 Act, incidentally, was at Pontefract on 15 August 1872.)

If an election is called and only one candidate is validly nominated, or there is only one candidate left at the close of the candidature withdrawal time, that person will be declared elected unopposed without a poll. There is no need for a headcount of who supports whom.

Similarly a referendum is about deciding the answer to a question, not about choosing someone to hold office. There is no equivalent of being elected (or "returned") unopposed, and a poll is always necessary to obtain the totals of answers of those entitled to express their preferences by voting or polling.

We will refer to each of the various kinds of current elections in turn. On combined elections see chapter 25.

A. EUROPEAN ELECTIONS

The last European Parliament elections, prior to the UK leaving the EU on 31 January 2020, were held on 23 May 2019.

B. PARLIAMENTARY ELECTIONS

The House of Commons is elected for a maximum of five years, and MPs had traditionally been alone in not being elected for a fixed term, because the Prime Minister could ask the Queen to dissolve Parliament and so trigger a general election. Parliament had to be sitting when the Prime Minister asked the Queen for a dissolution, making Parliamentary recess dates important. Formerly only seventeen working days had to elapse between the dissolution of Parliament and polling day; that minimum was extended to twenty-five working days by s 14 of the Electoral Registration and Administration Act 2013.

The position changed after the passing of the Fixed-term Parliaments Act 2011. Subject to an exception involving certification by the Speaker that the House of Commons has resolved that there should be an early dissolution, Parliaments ordinarily are to continue for a fixed five-year term. In fact, however, general elections were held on both 8 June 2017 and 12 December 2019, the latter following the Early Parliamentary General Election Act 2019. The next general election is currently scheduled for 2 May 2024, though this date will cease to be significant if the current Fixed-term Parliaments Act 2011 (Repeal) Bill becomes law.

Parliamentary elections are conducted generally under the RPAs 1983 and 1985. Sch 1 to the RPA 1983 is known as the Parliamentary Elections Rules. Note also the Parliamentary Elections (Welsh Forms) Order 2007, SI No 1014, as amended by SI 2010 No 1078 and SI 2015 No 803.

The House of Commons currently comprises 650 constituencies, fixed every few years by the Parliamentary Boundary Commission via the procedure now set out in the Parliamentary Constituencies Act 2020. There are 533 constituencies in England, 59 in Scotland, 40 in Wales and 18 in Northern Ireland. (The 'electoral quota', the average number of electors per constituency, is currently about 73,200.) For historical reasons, the constituencies are divided into county constituencies and borough constituencies, now set out in the Parliamentary Constituencies (England) Order 2007, SI No 1681 (as amended by SI 2009 No 698), and for Wales in the Parliamentary Constituencies and Assembly Electoral Regions Order 2006, SI No 1041 (as amended by SIs 2008 No 1791 and 2011 No 2987). The distinction between borough and county makes little practical difference (though sub-agents can be appointed in county constituencies – see chapter 12), but the returning officer is different. For county constituencies, the returning officer is the high sheriff of that county; for borough constituencies, it is the appropriate district council chairman or the mayor of the borough (or mayor or lord mayor of a city, as appropriate). Constituency boundaries may well mean that borough or county areas are not exactly coterminous with local government units. Remember that a borough or city with an elected mayor (see M and N below) will as a result have a chairman and not a mayor as its civic figurehead, and it is that chairman, not the elected mayor, who will be the returning officer.

A referendum was held on 5 May 2011 under the Parliamentary Voting System and Constituencies Act 2011 on whether the first-past-the-post method of election should be changed in favour of the alternative vote ('AV') method for Parliamentary elections: this change was not endorsed, so SI 2011 No 1702 was made repealing the provisions that otherwise would have been required. Part 2 of the 2011 Act made major changes to the definition and allocation of constituencies. There are in future to be 600 constituencies, but that change from 650 has not yet been implemented. See chapter 27 on area changes. The officer who runs the actual Parliamentary election process is the acting returning officer, on which see s 28 of the 1983 Act.

A Parliamentary election begins with the receipt of a writ from the Clerk of the Crown ordering that an election be held. That writ is returned – hence "returning officer" – when the election is completed and the result declared. The candidate declared elected cannot become an MP unless the Clerk of the Crown has received back the properly completed writ. See also chapter 20 on this procedure.

The Recall of MPs Act 2015 provides for recall petitions on any one of three grounds set out in s 1: essentially imprisonment; suspension by the Commons for at least ten sitting or fourteen calendar days; or conviction of an offence under s 10 of the Parliamentary Standards Act 2009 (false or misleading allowances claims). If the petition officer – the acting returning officer for the relevant constituency – receives a notice from the Speaker, arrangements must be made for signing of the petition by the electors as set out in ss 7-11.

The procedure requires a signing period of six weeks, on each working day between 9am and 5pm (reg 15), from the 'designated date': see ss 7 and 9(2). No more than ten places are to be provided for signing. A petition is successful if at least 10% of electors sign in favour; the petition officer determines whether the petition has been successful: ss 14(2)-(3). If so, the petition officer must notify the Speaker; the seat then becomes vacant, and a by-election follows.

The associated voting processes are set out in the Recall of MPs Act 2015 (Recall Petition) Regulations 2016, SI No 295, reg 149 of which amended the wording of the petition signing sheet in s 9(4).

The first petition under the 2015 Act was triggered in North Antrim in July 2018, but did not attract the requisite 10% signatures. In 2019 the MP for Peterborough lost her seat following a petition (reputedly costing around £0.5m) in which 27.6% of voters signed; shortly afterwards the MP for Brecon and Radnorshire also lost his seat when 19% (10,005) voters signed a petition; he stood again, but was not re-elected in the by-election on 1 August 2019.

C. SENEDD (WELSH PARLIAMENT) ELECTIONS

The former National Assembly for Wales, or Welsh Assembly, was renamed the Senedd Cymru (or Welsh Parliament) under the Assembly's Senedd and Elections (Wales) Act 2020. Elections to the Senedd, which comprises sixty seats, are held every five years and next due on 7 May 2026, though the date can be varied by up to a month. They are run under the Government of Wales Act 2006 (see ss 3 and 4), originally following a referendum held on 18 September 1997 under the Referendums (Scotland and Wales) Act 1997. (The Scottish equivalent was held on 11 September 1997.) The first former Welsh Assembly elections took place on 6 May 1999 (likewise for the Scottish Parliament). What follows below now refers primarily to the Senedd, although the titles of provisions and statutory instruments which have not yet been replaced of course retain their former titles and terms.

The Government of Wales Act 1998 created five Assembly electoral regions (as they then were), corresponding with the five Welsh European constituencies as they were before the European Parliamentary Elections Act 1999 (see sch 1 to the 1998 Act). The five regions are now as defined by s 2(3) of the Government of Wales Act 2006, and alterations are provided for by sch 1 to that Act. Each region returns four Senedd seats; there is also one member for each of the forty Senedd constituencies (which correspond with the Parliamentary constituencies). On the relevant boundaries, see the references to SIs 2006 No 1041 and 2008 No

1791, comprised in s 2(1) of the 2006 Act, substituted by s 13(1) of the Parliamentary Voting System and Constituencies Act 2011. (SI 2011 No 2987 has since further amended these provisions.) Where a Senedd electoral area comprises parts of more than one local authority, the relevant electoral registration officer is designated by the Representation of the People (National Assembly for Wales) (Relevant Registration Officer) Order 2007, SI No 1372.

As to the election process itself, see the National Assembly for Wales (Representation of the People) Order 2007, SI No 236, as amended by SIs 2010 No 2931 and 2016 Nos 272 and 292. A person may not be an Senedd constituency candidate for more than one Senedd constituency: Government of Wales Act 2006, s 7(1). Nor may a Senedd member also be a Westminster MP: s 16 of the 2006 Act. Schedule 1A, setting out further disqualifications for candidature or election to the Senedd, was added to the 2006 by s 29 of, and sch 3 to, the Senedd and Elections (Wales) Act 2020. See also the Senedd Cymru (Disqualification) Order 2020, No 1255.

Each Welsh voter has two votes: one vote for a Senedd constituency candidate under the simple majority system ('first past the post'), and one usually for a regional registered political party list with the election held under the additional member system of proportional representation (though it is possible for an individual to stand in an election for the regional seats). Section 9 of the Government of Wales 2006 provides for the allocation of seats to electoral region members.

The National Assembly for Wales (Elections: Nomination Papers) (Welsh Form) Order 2001, SI No 2914 validates "Annibynnol" as the Welsh equivalent description to "Independent". See also the Local Elections (Declaration of Acceptance of Office) (Wales) Order 2004 SI No 1508 for F, G and I below. Amendments were made to the rules on access to election documents by the Representation of the People (National Assembly for Wales)(Access to Election Documents) Regulations 2007, SI No 1368. Amendments to forms prescribed for combined elections were made by art 2 of SI 2016 No. 292. The Candidate Election Expenses (Senedd Elections) Code of Practice (Appointed Day) Order is SI

2021 No 264 (W. 70).

Section 78 of the Government of Wales Act 2006 contains a wide-ranging duty for the Welsh Ministers to promote and facilitate the use of the Welsh language going well beyond the scope of the Welsh Language Act 1993. As to the referendum held in Wales on 3 March 2011 about whether additional powers should be devolved to what is now the Senedd, see K below.

D. GREATER LONDON AUTHORITY ELECTIONS

Following a London referendum held on 7 May 1998, the Greater London Authority was established by the Greater London Authority Act 1999. The first elections were held on 4 May 2000, and the next elections will be on 2 May 2024. This three-year term – instead of the usual four – from 2021 is the result of the continuation for five years of the 2016 term caused by the Covid 19 pandemic. (As to the counting officer arrangements for the referendum involving each London Borough and the City of London, see s 3 of the Greater London Authority (Referendum) Act 1998.)

The Greater London Authority consists of the Mayor of London, also directly elected for the first time in May 2000, and twenty-five members together comprising the London Assembly. Of these twenty-five, fourteen are members for Assembly constituencies and eleven are members at large for the whole of Greater London. They are known respectively as "constituency members" and "London members": see s 2 of the 1999 Act. The term of office of the Mayor and all Assembly members is four years.

The Mayor is returned under the simple majority system ('first past the post') unless there are more than three candidates, when a supplementary vote system of first and second preferences applies. But each elector has three votes: one for the Mayor (with two preferences); one for their Assembly constituency on a simple majority "first past the post" basis; and one for a list of registered political party candidates (or for an individual candidate) for Greater London as a whole. The rules for counting those votes are set out in Part II of sch 2 to the 1999 Act, sch 3 to which amends the RPA 1983 in relation to these kinds of election. No one may be a candidate in more than one assembly constituency: s 4(9). Nor can someone already elected as Mayor or as a constituency member be also elected as a London member of the assembly: see para 8(4) of Part II of sch 2 to the 1999 Act.

The Assembly constituencies are prescribed under s 2(4) of the 1999 Act by the Greater London Authority (Assembly Constituencies and Returning Officers) Order 1999, SI No 3380. The detailed rules for these elections are set out in the Greater London Authority Elections Rules 2007, SI No 3541 (as amended by SIs 2012 No 198, 2016 No 24 and 2019 No 1426), a series of statutory instruments which illustrate both the intricate complexity of the election process today and the benefits of systematic consolidation. The first eight of the schedules to SI 2007 No 3541 comprise the Constituency Members Election Rules; the London Members Election Rules; the Mayoral Election Rules; and the Manual Count Rules; and then again the Constituency Members Election Rules; the London Members Election Rules; the Mayoral Election Rules; and the Combined Manual Count Rules. The two sets of four Rules regulate dedicated and combined elections and/or polls respectively, following rr 3 and 5 of the instrument. (See also chapter 26 on combined elections.) See also the Greater London Authority (Declaration of Acceptance of Office) Order 2002, SI No 1044, and the Greater London Authority Elections (Election Addresses) Order 2003, SI No 1907 (as amended by SI 2008 No 507).

E. LONDON BOROUGH COUNCIL ELECTIONS

London borough council elections for the 32 London boroughs established by the London Government Act 1963 are run under rules essentially similar to those for county and district councils elsewhere, on which see sections F and G following. They are whole-council elections held every four years and are next due on 5 May 2022. The London Councillors Order 1976, SI No 213 was made under s 8(2) of the Local Government Act 1972. "Relevant election years" for London boroughs – in 2014 and every fourth year afterwards – are defined for the purposes of Part 1A of the Local Government Act 2000 by s 9R(2), inserted by Part 1 of sch 2 to the Localism Act 2011.

The City of London has some special provisions of its own but is largely brought into the scope of the same provisions as other municipal elections by s 191 of the RPA 1983. The City's timetable under which members of the Common Council were elected annually in December has now changed; from March 2005 elections have been held every four years, but those due in March 2021 were postponed to March 2022 as a result of the Covid 19 pandemic. City aldermen are elected for six-year terms. See also the City of London (Ward Elections) Act 2002 (a local Act), and the Representation of the People (Variation of Limits of Candidates' Election Expenses) (City of London) Order 2005, SI No 153.

F. COUNTY ELECTIONS

County council elections, ie elections to county councils comprising a tier of two-tier local government, are held every four years. County council elections are run under the RPA 1983 and the Local Elections (Principal Areas) (England and Wales) Rules 2006, SI No 3304, s amended by SI 2011 No 563. In 2001, because of the foot and mouth disease outbreak, the elections were delayed by the Elections Act 2001 and run alongside the Parliamentary general election on 7 June. In 2005 they were also run on the same day as the Parliamentary general election on 5 May. They are next due on 1 May 2025, although the elections due in 2021 for Cumbria, North Yorkshire and Somerset County Councils were postponed to 2022 because of pending local government reorganisation there.

"Relevant election years" for county councils, however – 2021 and every fourth year afterwards – are defined for the purposes of Part 1A of the Local Government Act 2000 by s 9R(2), inserted by Part 1 of sch 2 to the Localism Act 2011.

Counties are divided into electoral divisions, not wards, prescribed for each county by a statutory instrument made following a review by the Boundary Committee for England, a separate part of the Electoral Commission. (There are no two-tier counties outside England.) These electoral divisions are the equivalent of wards for district or borough (city) elections, and may indeed have the same names or areas in some cases. Section 89 of the Local Government

Act 2000 amended ss 14 and 17 of the Local Government Act 1992 to enable county electoral divisions to have more than one councillor (and see also G below on ss 84-7 of the 2000 Act); this was a new feature in the county council elections of 2005. The Government in its White Paper *Local Leadership, Local Choice* (Cm. 4298, 24 March 1999) suggested that a way of enhancing local democracy was to increase the number of elections – indeed, to allow the electorate to vote annually in some form of local election, hence the aforementioned powers.

The returning officer for the county is that authority's proper officer (see chapter 5). In practice the returning officer is likely to delegate much, if not all, of the task of actually managing the procedures to counterparts in the constituent county districts.

Polling hours at all local elections (except parish and community polls) were extended from 7am to 10pm by the Local Elections (Principal Areas and Parishes and Communities) (Amendment)(England and Wales) Rules 2006, SI No 390, now consolidated into r 1 of the local elections conduct Rules SI 2006 No 3304. These have since been variously amended by SIs 2011 No 563, 2014 No 494, 2015 No 103 and 2018 No 1308.

G. METROPOLITAN BOROUGH, SHIRE DISTRICT, BOROUGH OR CITY ELECTIONS

This heading refers to metropolitan boroughs outside Greater London and to shire district councils in the English two-tier system. Possession of borough or city status makes no practical difference for this purpose.

Metropolitan borough elections have traditionally been held by thirds, and are next due on 5 May 2022. Shire district council elections are held, according to the choice made by the council or prescribed by order, either every four years (the next generally due on 4 May 2023) for the whole council, or every year other than the county election year for a third of the council, or every two years if by halves. Metropolitan borough and shire district elections are run under the same legislation and rules as county elections, on which see F above.

"Relevant election years" for both metropolitan and non-metropolitan districts, however – 2014 for the former and 2011 for the latter, and every fourth year afterwards – are defined for the purposes of Part 1A of the Local Government Act 2000 by s 9R(2), inserted by Part 1 of sch 2 to the Localism Act 2011.

Sections 84-86 of the Local Government Act 2000 had allowed the existing patterns of whole council elections or elections by thirds to be varied, and for the Secretary of State to alter election years by order under s 87. Part 2, ss 31-54 as amended, of the Local Government and Public Involvement in Health Act 2007 enables districts (both metropolitan and shire) currently subject to elections by thirds or by halves to resolve to change to whole-council (or so-called 'all out') elections. Consultation, a specially called council meeting, and a two-thirds majority are all required, but the "permitted resolution periods" of s 33(3), (6) and (7) were deleted by s 24(2) of the Localism Act 2011. A district council in England may now resolve to change its election scheme at any time. Once a council has passed a resolution to change its scheme, it may not change it again for five years, beginning with the day on which the first resolution was passed: s 31A of the 2007 Act (inserted by s 24(6) of the 2011 Act). If a council resolves to move to a scheme of whole-council elections, it must also specify in its resolution the first year in which a whole-council election will be held. The only restriction is that district councils in two-tier areas are prevented from specifying the year of their county council ordinary elections. Once the council has held its first, it will then hold whole-council elections in every fourth year thereafter.

A council formerly on thirds, but now whole-council, may resolve to revert: s 39(1); there are detailed supplementary provisions about the terms of those elected, how the various patterns are to operate, and the role of the Electoral Commission (which, if a resolution seeking elections by thirds or halves is passed, must consider under s 43 whether an electoral review is necessary). A principal council with whole-council elections may also request single-member electoral areas under the procedure of s 57 of the Democracy, Economic Development and Construction Act 2009 Act. (Section 55 of the 2007 Act, which had inserted s 14A into the Local

Government Act 1992 for a similar purpose, was repealed by the 2009 Act.)

Metropolitan boroughs and shire districts are divided into wards, likewise prescribed for each authority by a statutory instrument following a review by the Boundary Committee for England, a separate part of the Electoral Commission.

The returning officer for district elections is that authority's proper officer (see chapter 5). Polling hours were extended from 7am to 10pm by SI 2006 No 390 referred to in F above.

H. PARISH OR TOWN COUNCIL ELECTIONS

Parish councils have whole-council elections every four years, usually on the same day as district councils (see s 16 (as amended) of the Local Government Act 1972), though where districts are elected by thirds parish councils may be organised similarly in a geographic rotation; see also chapter 26 on combined elections. Town councils are effectively parish councils with town council status, which does not affect their election arrangements at all. Parish council elections have on occasion been delayed if a general or European election is to be held on what would otherwise be a parish (and district) election day – as in 1979 and in 2009. Postponement because of the Covid 19 pandemic also occurred in 2020. The provision in s 16 of RPA 1985 for automatic postponement for three weeks of parish and community council elections, however, where they would otherwise have fallen on the same day as both Parliamentary (or European) elections and also ordinary local elections was repealed by s 15 of the Electoral Registration and Administration Act 2013.

Under s 53 of the Local Government and Public Involvement in Health Act 2007 there is power for districts to alter the years of ordinary elections of parish councillors; this is not to move away from whole-council parish elections, but to ensure that the parish elections "are to be held in years in which ordinary elections of district councillors for a ward in which any part of the parish is situated are held."

Larger parishes are sometimes divided into wards, which will either have been prescribed by the statutory instrument establishing the parish arrangement or by the district council in whose area the parish is situated. (Parishes have to be wholly contained within one district council area, and can be comprised within metropolitan borough or unitary authority areas as well. Since the passing of the Local Government and Public Involvement in Health Act 2007, which placed the whole status and structure of parishes on a new footing, they may also be created within London boroughs, which formerly was not possible. See also D in chapter 27.)

The returning officer for parish elections is the proper officer appointed for the purpose of the district, borough or unitary council within which the parish is situated. Where parishes (or groups of parishes) do not have councils, but only parish (or 2007 Act alternative style community, neighbourhood or village) meetings (in which all the local government electors can meet together), they do not have elections. See also J below on parish and community polls.

Parish councils are the only councils which can co-opt members. This can occur if either insufficient candidates stand at the main elections, or when a vacancy occurs. The first case is prescribed by s 21 of the RPA 1985; secondly, in the case of a casual vacancy, the parish clerk must publish a notice giving the parish electors fourteen days (ie days valid for election timetable purposes - see r 2 of Part I of sch 2 to the Local Elections (Parishes and Communities)(England and Wales) Rules 2006, SI No 3305 – during which to requisition an election. If ten electors sign a requisition, a by-election will be held; if not, the parish council can co-opt a local elector, ie someone who would have been entitled to stand as a candidate in an actual election, to become a parish councillor. See r 5 of the 2006 Rules, which prescribe the running of parish and community elections which are not combined with any other elections. They were also variously amended by SIs 2011 No 562, 2014 No 492, 2015 No 104 and 2018 No 1309.

Section 76 of the Local Government and Public Involvement in Health Act 2007, by inserting s 16A into the Local Government Act 1972, gave parish councils in England a new power to appoint councillors, as opposed to co-opting them. Regulations may be made accordingly under s 16A(2) (there are none so far), and under s 16A(3) parishes must also have regard to any guidance they are given. Under ss 1 and 8(2) of the Localism Act 2011 parish councils may be eligible to benefit from the power of general competence if they meet the prescribed conditions in SI 2012 No 965.

Polling hours were extended from 7am to 10pm by SI 2006 No 390 referred to in F above.

I. WELSH UNITARY AND COMMUNITY COUNCIL ELECTIONS

The arrangements for the 22 Welsh principal councils – counties and county boroughs (some with city status) as styled under s 1 of the Local Government (Wales) Act 1994 – have hitherto been essentially similar to those for principal councils in England as described in section G above. Major changes have now been made, however, by the Local Government and Elections (Wales) Act 2021. The next elections for unitary, town and community councils in Wales are on 5 May 2022, with many changes in boundaries, wards and numbers of representatives following the completions of long-running reviews. Sections 14 and 15 of the 2021 Act change the electoral cycles for principal councils and community councils from four to five years.

The principal authority areas are apportioned into electoral divisions, and s 53 of the Local Government Act 1972 originally established a Local Government Boundary Commission for Wales equivalent (at the time) in terms of boundary reviews etc. to that for England. What is now termed the Local Democracy and Boundary Commission may now conduct reviews of electoral arrangements under ss 11 and 138 of, and sch 1 to, the Local Government and Elections (Wales) Act 2021.

The eleven counties and eleven county boroughs in Wales are now comprised in a revised Part 1 of sch 1 to the 1994 Act referred to above. See also the Local Elections (Principal Areas)(Welsh Forms) Order 2007, SI No 1015, as amended by SIs 2014 No 918 and 2017 No 145.

Under ss1-3 of the Local Government (Wales) Measure 2011, local authorities must now after each ordinary election conduct a survey of councillors and unsuccessful candidates for election, and provide the results to the Welsh Ministers. The Local Elections Survey (Wales) Regulations 2012, SI No 685 (W.93), as amended by SI 2016 No 1220 (W.291) set out the questions, and the form in which they are to be asked.

Community councils are the Welsh equivalent of English parish councils. The election rules and circumstances are essentially the same for both save in respect of Welsh language usage, on which see the Local Elections (Communities) (Welsh Forms) Order 2007, SI No 1013, as amended by SIs 2014 No 919 and 2017 No 146. The main regulations are now the Local Elections (Communities) (Wales) Rules 2021, SI No 1460 (W. 375). The explanatory note terms schedules 1 and 2 to these the Conduct Rules, though that does not appear in the text itself. See also s 35 of the Local Government Act 1972 (as amended) on community councillors.

Polling hours were extended from 7am to 10pm by SI 2006 No 390 referred to in F above.

J. PARISH AND COMMUNITY POLLS AND LOCAL POLLS

Parish polls are a kind of referendum, though their results are not binding in the strict legal sense. They are held under para 18 (2) of Part III of sch 12 to the Local Government Act 1972 and only apply to parish meetings. Polls consequent on the Welsh equivalent community meetings were abolished by s 162 of, and sch 13 to, the Local Government and Elections (Wales) Act 2021. A parish with a council may still require a poll if that decision is taken by the whole parish acting under sch 12 as a parish meeting. In England a poll can be held where under para 18(4) at least ten or a third (whichever is the less) of the local government electors present so demand.

In England a notice must be given to the district council proper officer to conduct a poll on the submitted question under the Parish and Community Meetings (Polls) Rules 1987, SI No 1, as amended by SI 1987 No 262. The parish meeting requiring the poll has to pay for it; the district council will fix a scale of charges, including returning officer fees.

Rule 1 of the schedule to SI 1987 No 1 prescribes the hours for polling as 4pm to 9pm. This remains the case for parish polls despite material published alongside the Local Elections (Principal Areas and Parishes and Communities)(Amendment)(England and Wales) Rules 2006, SI No 390 to the effect that, following the lengthening of local elections polling days to run from 7am to 10pm by r 2(2), all polling hours have now been synchronised. The temporary Coronavirus amendment provisions brought in by SI 2020 No 1355 have expired.

There have been occurrences in certain parishes of requiring polls on national or general topics that are not specific to that parish in the immediate sense. Robust opinion from leading counsel has it that the parish poll procedure was not intended for this purpose, but mainly as a way of validating or authorising the collective view of electors of a parish. Section 9(1) of the Local Government Act 1972 specifically states that "...there shall be a parish meeting for the purpose of discussing parish affairs..." The argument then proceeds on the basis that, for example, the national currency of the United Kingdom is not an affair of the parish, it is an affair of the nation.

It has to be said, however, that this view is not undisputed. Indeed, the National Association of Local Councils do not support it and there are difficult issues around; for instance, GM crops being grown in certain fields within the parish – surely usage of that field is a local, not a national matter? These problems were considered in 2000 when some parish polls were apparently conducted on national issues (e.g. UK currency) but other districts refused. The issue did not proceed into the courts and remains unresolved. Parish polls, however, continue to take place. David Monks, the previous joint author, conducted polls about skateboards and wind turbines in Huntingdonshire.

Some examples of parish polls held on wider topics are quoted in *Parish Government 1894-1994* by KP Poole and Bryan Keith-Lucas (National Association of Local Councils, 1994), pp 247-8. On the

Parish and Community Meetings (Polls) Rules 1987 see Home Office Circular RPA 308 issued on 17 February 1987.

Under s 116(1) of the Local Government Act 2003 a local authority may conduct a poll about any service, or the expenditure on such service, within its functions to provide. It is for the authority to decide who is to be polled and how to poll them, though regard must be had to any appropriate guidance: ss 116(2) and (3). Such polls need not include, therefore, the whole of the usual electorate, and their results are not formally binding. An interesting example took place in May 2011: the two neighbouring Suffolk Councils Babergh and Mid Suffolk held a referendum on merging (overall the proposal was rejected).

K. NATIONAL REFERENDUMS

The UK's first national referendum – on whether the UK should join the European Economic Community (then commonly referred to as the Common Market) – was held on 5 June 1975. Outside London, where the Greater London Council still existed and was the organisational unit, it was run on a district council basis: see s 2(1)(a) of the Referendum Act 1975. The count was organised nationally by the Chief Counting Officer, who under s 2(4) and (5) appointed counting officers for counties. Accordingly the legal process chosen fully utilised the then new local government two-tier systems of April 1974 and May 1975 in both England and Wales and Scotland.

Two referendums each have subsequently been held on devolution for Scotland and Wales. The Scotland Act 1978 provided via s 85 and sch 17 for a referendum on Scottish devolution, held on 1 March 1979 and organised via the then Scottish local government units of regional and islands councils under a Chief Counting Officer. Section 80 and sch 12 of the Wales Act 1978 provided similarly with counting officers for each Welsh county reporting to a Chief Counting Officer. The Welsh referendum was also held on 1 March 1979.

The Referendums (Scotland and Wales) Act 1997 similarly covered both. Section 1 of this Act provided for a Scottish referendum on 11

September 1997, the Chief Counting Officer appointing a counting officer for each Scottish local government area. Arrangements for Wales were similar under s 2 for the Welsh poll on 18 September 1997, a counting officer being appointed for each Welsh county or county borough area by which the polling was organised and the constituent part of the national total counted.

General enabling powers for national and regional referendums were provided by Part VII, ss 101-129, of the Political Parties, Elections and Referendums Act 2000. The Chief Counting Officer will be either the Chairman of the Electoral Commission or someone he or she appoints under s 128(2), and a counting officer for each "relevant area" under s 128(3) will organise the local polling. Relevant areas are English metropolitan boroughs and shire districts, Welsh unitary councils, London Boroughs and the City of London. Orders under s 129 will provide for the detailed conduct of any referendum. The 5 May 2011 alternative vote ('AV') referendum was held under Part 1 of the Parliamentary Voting System and Constituencies Act 2011: nearly 68% of the 19.2m voting – a turnout of some 42.2% – voted against adoption of the proposal. As the change to the alternative vote system was not approved in the 5 May 2011 referendum, SI 2011 No 1702 was made repealing the provisions that otherwise would have been required. The 23 June 2016 referendum on EU membership was held under the European Referendum Act 2015. The turnout was 72.2%, with an outcome of 51.9% to 48.1% in favour of leaving.

As to the concept of "permitted participants" in any referendum, see s 105; as to the designation of those for whom assistance may be available see ss 108-110; and as to actual or notional referendum expenses and their restriction see ss 111-118. Section 120 provides for returns on referendum expenses.

In all or any part of Wales, the Welsh Ministers may conduct a poll under s 64 of the Government of Wales Act 2006 "to ascertain the views of those polled about whether or how any of the functions of the Welsh Ministers (other than those under section 62) should be exercised." Such a poll will be run as if it were a local election in the area(s) in question. Sections 103-106 of, and sch 6 to, the 2006 Act also provide for a referendum commanded by Her Majesty by Order in Council "to be held throughout Wales about whether the Assembly Act provisions should come into force." No general regulations for conducting Welsh national referendums have yet been made (and none had been made under the now repealed s 36(4) of the Government of Wales Act 1998, the former equivalent of s 64). The rules for conducting the 3 March 2011 referendum, however, about increased law-making powers for the what was then called the National Assembly for Wales were contained in the National Assembly for Wales Referendum (Assembly Act Provisions) (Referendum Question, Date of Referendum Etc.) Order 2010, SI No 2837. It was run on local authority boundaries.

The 2011 referendum question (art 4(1)) was "Do you want the Welsh Assembly now to be able to make laws on all matters in the 20 subject areas it has powers for?" accompanied by the Welsh equivalent (also with one word printed in bold). A statement by a lengthy dual-language statement seeking to explain what powers and limitations the Assembly currently had preceded it. The procedure and timetable provisions, and all the associated rules, were similar to those for other referendums, and indeed for the 2004 North East regional referendum referred to in L below. About 63.5% voted 'yes' on an overall turnout of 35.2%, with only Monmouthshire of the 22 Welsh unitary authority areas narrowly voting against. As to Welsh local authority referendums, see L below.

L. REGIONAL REFERENDUMS

The Government announced plans in 2002 for regional referendums to be held, once certain conditions were satisfied, on whether regional assemblies should be established, and subsequently Parliament passed the Regional Assemblies (Preparations) Act 2003.

Although it was expected that the North East, North West, and Yorkshire and the Humber regions would all have referendums, in the event only that for the North East proceeded in an all-postal referendum closing on 4 November 2004 (under SI 2004 No 1963).

The Electoral Commission assisted the Government on preparatory work. The regulations were based on the units of organisation being district or unitary councils under a Chief Counting Officer - again see s 128 of the Political Parties, Elections and Referendums Act 2000, K above, and the Regional Assembly and Local Government Referendums Order 2004, SI No 1962. Section 128(2) makes the Chief Counting Officer the Chairman of the Electoral Commission, or someone appointed thereby. Under para 9(1)(a), for local government referendums the Chief Counting Officer is whoever is "the Chief Counting Officer for the Regional Assembly referendum in the region", and the duties are contained in para 10. Schedule 1 to SI 2004 No 1962 comprises the Regional Assembly and Local Government Referendum Rules for the conducting of these polls. (The Chief Counting Officer delegated his functions in the North East regional assembly referendum to the regional returning officer.) Voting in referendums is all-postal: see para 5 of SI 2004 No 1962. The Coalition Government expressed the view that the powers to conduct these regional referendums should be abolished, though the powers remain in force.

For the conduct of local government referendums in Wales, see the Local Authorities (Conduct of Referendums) (Wales) Regulations 2008 SI No 1848. Schedule 3 to the Regulations provides the Local Government Act Referendums Rules, and sch 4 the necessary modifications of other enactments.

The North East rejected proposals for an assembly in 2004, but if any future referendum vote were to held with the result in favour, then of course further provisions would be required for the election of the assemblies themselves.

The expense limits for permitted participants (see K above) were prescribed by the Regional Assembly and Local Government Referendums (Express Limits for Permitted Participants) Order 2004, SI No 1961.

As to Greater London's referendum on 7 May 1998 about whether there should be a Mayor of London etc, see D above. See K above for polls under s 64 of the Government of Wales Act 2006 and referendums about whether Assembly Act provisions should come into force under s 103 of that Act.

M. ELECTED MAYOR AND PETITION REFERENDUMS

The Local Government Act 2000 introduced the possibility of referendums on whether councils should in principle have elected mayors. The principal provisions are ss 34-36 and 45 of the 2000 Act. (As to so-called 'metro mayors' see N below.)

A referendum is a necessary step before a council can adopt the elected mayor approach for its executive arrangements. The Secretary of State at DCLG can direct that a referendum be held (s 35), or require it by order (s 36). A referendum must also be held if an authority receives a valid petition or combination of petitions (s 34), but none of these provisions apply to an authority whose population at the end of June 1999 was under 85,000. The first referendum was held at Berwick-upon-Tweed on 7 June 2001 alongside that day's general election, and the first 'yes' vote was given after Watford's referendum on 12 July 2001. By the time the House of Commons Transport, Local Government and the Regions Committee took evidence for their September 2002 report *How the Local Government Act 2000 Is Working*, 23 authorities had held referendums on the mayor and cabinet model, with eight areas voting in favour (para 48). (See Annex 1 to the DETR evidence ref LGA 22, quoted as at the end of February 2002.) A referendum at Bury on 3 July 2008 was only the third held anywhere since 2005 (all rejecting the proposal), while at another referendum at Stoke-on-Trent on 23 October 2008 voters decided to end their six-year elected mayor period. (A new choice had to be made there because the type of executive arrangements adopted by Stoke-on-Trent, the elected mayor and city manager system, had been abolished by the 2007 Act. In 2012 Hartlepool voted to abolish the role of elected mayor, as did Torbay in 2016. The elected mayoralty has, however, been retained despite moves against it in Doncaster, Middlesbrough and Lewisham. The only elected mayor referendum held under former rules in Wales was by conventional polling at Ceredigion on 20 May 2004 (the proposal was not approved).

Petitions are governed by the Local Authorities (Referendums) (Petitions) (England) Regulations 2011, SI No 2914. The proper officer must publish at the outset and each year thereafter the verification number. That number, five per cent of the local government electorate, is the number of signatures required for a valid petition. Separately the fact of publishing the notices must itself be publicised in at least one local newspaper – see regs 4 and 5 of the 2011 Regulations. Regulations 11 and 13 in particular deal with the procedure for the proper officer on receiving a petition, and publicity for that receipt.

The rules for running referendums are set out in the Local Authorities (Conduct of Referendums) (England) Regulations 2012, SI No 323, where the responsible manager of the poll process is called the counting officer, not the returning officer, although in fact reg 9 designates as counting officer the RPA 1983, s 35(1) or (3) returning officer for local elections (see chapter 5). These 2012 Regulations have been amended by SI 2014 No 924.

As to combined elections, see regs 10-13 (and chapter 26). Basically if the referendum timetable would yield a poll date within 28 days either side of a European, Parliamentary or ordinary local election, the polls must be combined (reg 10(1)). For the DLUHC (formerly ODPM, DETR and CLG) guidance on referendums, see the (substituted) chapter 13 of the *New Council Constitutions: Guidance Pack* Volume 1 – *Local Leadership, Local Choice* originally issued in October 2000. The hours of polling were extended from 7am to 10pm by reg 26 of the RPR 2006, SI No 752, amending reg 12 of SI 2001 No 1298.

Parliament determined under the Localism Act 2011 (sch 2 to which inserted the requisite provisions into the Local Government 2000 as s 9N) that referendums on whether to introduce elected mayors would be held on 3 May 2012 in Birmingham, Bradford, Bristol, Coventry, Leeds, Manchester, Newcastle upon Tyne, Nottingham, Sheffield and Wakefield. (Leicester had already voted to adopt the system and elected a mayor in 2011, while Liverpool anticipated Parliament's decision by proceeding directly to an actual mayoral election on the same day as these other referendums. Salford elected a mayor then also, having chosen to do so on 26 January 2012. Of the ten cities actually holding referendums under the Parliamentary Orders, only Bristol voted in favour.

N. ELECTED MAYOR ELECTIONS

Once it has been determined following a successful referendum under M above that an elected mayor is to be elected, that election will be conducted (ordinarily for a four-year term) under ss 39-44 of the Local Government Act 2000. With necessary adaptations, the election is conducted like other local elections under E, F and G above. The first such mayoral elections were held on 2 May 2002. The relevant regulations are the Local Authorities (Elected Mayors) (Elections, Terms of Office and Casual Vacancies) (England) Regulations 2012, SI No 336 (as amended by SI 2014 No 2172), and for the process itself, the Local Authorities (Mayoral Elections) (England and Wales) Regulations 2007 SI No 1024, as variously amended by SIs 2012 No 2059, 2014 No 370, 2018 No 20 and 2019 No 351.

Para 2(1) of the 2001 SI No 2544 Regulations provides for an election to be held on either the first Thursday in May or in October first occurring after three months have elapsed after the relevant mayoral referendum date. Para 3 prescribes when the second ordinary election is to be held according to the type of authority concerned (the ordinary term of four years is prescribed by s 39(6) of the 2000 Act, but is subject to these regulations). As to casual vacancies, see para 7. See also the Local Authorities (Elected Mayor and Mayor's Assistant) (England) Regulations 2002, SI No 975, and the Local Authorities (Elected Mayors) (England) Regulations 2004, SI No 1815, and SIs 2005 No 2121 and 2008 No 3112. The first Bristol mayoral election following the successful 3 May 2012 referendum was held on 15 November 2012 in combination with the first police and crime commissioner elections.

There are some further noteworthy procedural differences between ordinary council elections and those for elected mayors. They include:

i) the returning officer must prepare and distribute a booklet containing all the candidates' election addresses, recharging them the cost of printing, but not delivery;

ii) a new voting system, set out in sch 2 to the Local Government

Act 2000, and under which supplementary vote system will be used if there are three or more candidates;

iii)nomination requirements include a proposer, a seconder and 28 other sponsors, together with £500 deposit.

Additional provisions about the timing and process etc of elections for elected mayors, and extensive powers to make relevant Regulations, were inserted as Part 1A (ss 9H-9HE) of the Local Government Act 2000 by Part 1 of sch 2 to the Localism Act 2011. In s 9HE(1)(b) the Secretary of State is given power about "the questioning of elections for the return of elected mayors and the consequences of irregularities." There must be prior consultation with the Electoral Commission, but such Regulations may modify or except provisions either of, or made under, the Representation of the People Acts – so allowing statute in principle to be amended or disregarded by statutory instrument.

So-called 'metro mayors' for the eight combined authorities were introduced by the Cities and Local Government Devolution Act 2016, inserting s 107A into the Local Democracy, Economic Development and Construction Act 2009. They have been created and elected for four-year terms for Cambridgeshire & Peterborough, Greater Manchester, Liverpool City Region, North of Tyne, Sheffield City, Tees Valley, the West of England and the West Midlands. Schedule 1 to the 2016 Act inserts sch 5B accordingly into the 2009 Act.

These elections are run under the Combined Authorities (Mayoral Elections) Order 2017, SI No 67, as amended by Nos 2018 No 19 and 2019 No 350.

O. POLICE, FIRE AND CRIME COMMISSIONER ELECTIONS

The reforms introduced by the Police Reform and Social Responsibility Act 2011 led to the first elections of police and crime commissioners on 15 November 2012 in 41 police authority areas outside London (where the Mayor of London already has an equivalent role). (The overall national turnout that day, including spoiled ballot papers, was some 15.1%, varying between 11.6% in Staffordshire and 19.5% in Northamptonshire. In 2016 it was 27.2% overall, and in 2021 – delayed by the Covid pandemic from 2020 – it was 33.2% overall across the 34 areas, with turnouts generally much higher in Wales than in England.) Commissioners normally have a four-year term, but the delay from 2020 has resulted in a three-year term for those elected in 2021, so that the next elections will be held on 2 May 2024.

The Policing and Crime Act 2017 introduced measures enabling PCCs to submit a proposal to the Home Secretary to take on governance of a Fire and Rescue Authority where a local case was made. Where this happens, the PCC is re-titled a Police, Fire and Crime Commissioner ('PFCC'). In this book we generally refer just to PCCs.

These PCC elections are conducted under the Police and Crime Commissioner Elections Order 2012, SI No 1917, as amended by SIs 2015 No 665 and 2016 No 300, using first and second preference voting for a single commissioner in each area. Since police authorities cover more than one local authority, the Secretary of State is required under s 75 to designate a local authority, whose head of paid service is designated the "appropriate officer" and is currently set out in SI 2020 No 134, as amended by SI 2021 No 258. See also for Wales in particular SI 2016 No 300. The detailed rules for polls are otherwise very similar to other elections, the form of declaration of acceptance of office being provided by SI 2012 No 2553 and Welsh forms by SI 2012 No 2768 (though a Welsh nomination paper is provided by SI 2016 No 300). As to combining these with other polls, see sch 4 to the 2012 Order, SI No 1917, as amended by para 12 of SI 2006 No 300.

See also chapter 29 on these elections.

P. COUNCIL TAX REFERENDUMS

Section 72 of, and schs 5 and 6 to, the Localism Act 2011 introduced the requirement for referendums to be held by billing authorities in England on proposed council tax increases defined as excessive. These replaced the former regime of Government 'capping.' The rules are contained in what became Chapter 4ZA inserted into the Local Government Finance Act 1992. (Note that numerous amendments of Chapters 4ZA and 6 of the Local Government Finance Act 1992 were further made by reg 11 of, and sch 2 to, the Local Government (Structural Changes) (Finance) (Amendment) Regulations 2012, SI No 20, "to ensure" as the Explanatory Note says "that Chapter 4ZA of part 1 of the 1992 Act operates appropriately whether an authority sets its council tax under Part 4 of the 2008 Regulations, or Chapter 3 of Part 1 of the 1992 Act.")

Following determination of an excessive increase under ss 52ZC (as amended) and 52ZD of the 1992 Act, arrangements must be made under s 52ZG(3) by the billing authority for a referendum to be held either not later that the first Thursday in May in the financial year for which the increase is proposed to be applicable or on alternative date specified by Order by the Secretary of State. Those entitled to vote are those entitled to vote on the referendum date for an electoral area (ward or electoral division) of the billing authority who are also registered at an address within the billing authority's area: s 52ZG(5). Under s 52ZH (as amended) the outcome of the referendum is binding for the purposes of the relevant council tax calculations, and if the referendum is not held as required s 52ZI stipulates that "the authority has no power to transfer any amount from its collection fund to its general fund." Similar provisions and referendum duties arise in relation to precepting authorities in England as to billing authorities under ss 52ZN-52ZP (as amended), although it is the duty of the billing authority, and not the precepting authority, to organise the referendum itself. Section 52ZO(2)(b) and (4)(b) envisage the possibility that there may be one than referendum in respect of a precepting authority's basic amount of council tax. The cost of a council tax referendum is borne by whichever billing or precepting authority has necessitated it.

Regulations about council tax referendums are made under s 52ZQ: see SIs 2012 No 444, 2013 No 409 and 2014 Nos 231 and 925. Section 52ZR (as amended) gives the Secretary of State power to direct in certain circumstances that the referendum provisions are not to apply. Schedule 6 of the Localism Act 2011 sets out extensive further minor amendments in relation to these referendums. Schedules 5 and 6 have no application to Wales.

Q. GOVERNANCE CHANGES REFERENDUMS

Chapter 4 of Part 1A of the Local Government Act 2000, inserted by s 21 of, and sch 2 to, the Localism Act 2011, provides for a change by a local authority in England from one form of governance to another: ss 9K-9KB. In some cases such a change requires approval in a local referendum. These cases are first, where *either* there is proposed a s 9K change from one form of governance to another, *or* a s 9KA change to a different form of executive, *and* "the implementation of the local authority's existing form of governance or existing form of executive was approved in a referendum under this Chapter": s 9M(2). "The second case" (s 9M(3)) "is where the local authority resolves that a proposed change in governance arrangements is to be subject to approval in a referendum."

Sections 9MA and 9MB provide for the process of proposals leading to the holding and giving effect to the necessary referendum. A third situation is set out in s 9MC, where a local authority receives a qualifying petition for change which, under Regulations yet to be made, is to be put to a referendum. Fourthly, the Secretary of State has power to make a direction for a referendum under s 9MD, and fifthly there is power by order under s 9ME(1) to provide similarly about the holding of a referendum by authorities "on whether they should have a relevant type of governance arrangements." Each of these situations is prescribed in detail in the Act, and requires elaboration in Regulations yet to be made. Once a referendum (styled "A") has been held under these provisions, an authority cannot hold, or be required to hold, a further referendum (styled "B") for ten years – unless A was held under a s 9N order, or A rejected a change to a mayor and cabinet executive, or unless B is required to be held by a s 9N order. It was under s 9N orders that the elected mayor referendums referred to in M above were held on 3 May 2012 were held. For an example of the form of one of these, see SI 2012 No 327, which refers to Coventry.

While Part 1A of the Local Government Act 2000 does not apply to

Wales, note (as set out in M above) that the Local Government (Wales) Measure 2011 also sets out circumstances in which proposed governance changes or council amalgamations will also necessitate referendums. Paragraph 6 of SI 2013 No 3005 (W.297) makes amendments to the Local Authorities (Referendums) (Petitions and Directions)(Wales) 2001, SI No 2292 (previously amended by SI 2003 No 398 (W.55)).

R. NEIGHBOURHOOD PLANNING REFERENDUMS

Section 116 of, and schs 9 and 10 to, the Localism Act 2011, by inserting extensive new provisions into the Town and Country Planning Act 1990, introduced the concept of neighbourhood development plans and orders. We need merely notice here that in two additional sets of circumstances referendums may be required as part of that initiative.

If the pre-conditions of para 12(4) of the additional sch 4B to the 1990 Act are met, a referendum must be held on the making by the authority of a neighbourhood development order. The area involved must, as a minimum, be the area that the order will cover, but the authority may decide to extend it: para 12(7)-(9). Paragraph 14 prescribes the referendum arrangements; voters must both be on the electoral register for local elections of councillors and have an address within the referendum area as their qualifying address for such local elections.

If "the draft order relates to a neighbourhood area that has been designated as a business area under section 61H" para 15 requires that an additional referendum must also be held. The complexities of this are the subject of the Neighbourhood Planning (Referendums) Regulations 2012, SI No 2031 made under para 16; unusually they may "make provision for excluding a person's entitlement to vote in the additional referendum" under para 15(5). Business referendums are the subject of para 17, inserted in 2013; the 2012 Regulations have been variously amended by SIs 2013 No 798, 2014 No 333 and 2016 No 934.

Matters such as the dates of polling, the questions to be asked, the publicity, conduct of events and counting are all required to be prescribed; the Act is silent on whether the two referendums may or must be held on the same day where both are required to be held. Voters in the second referendum will be non-domestic ratepayers in the referendum area who also meet such other conditions as may be prescribed: para 15(3). Regulation 16 of SI 2012 No 2031 deals with any situation where the relevant council for a referendum is not the local planning authority for that area (since the proper officer of a local planning authorities has responsibility for publishing the initial notice at least 28 days ahead that a referendum is to be held under reg 4). The Neighbourhood Planning Referendums Rules comprise sch 3 to SI 2012 No 2031, and the Combination of Polls Rules comprise sch 5. (Note that the relevant counting officer *also* has to publish a notice about the referendum, stating the date of the poll, under r 5 of the Neighbourhood Planning Referendums Rules.)

These Rules, however, apply only to para 14 referendums, as r 2(1) defines a voter as someone "entitled to vote on their own behalf." The date by which a referendum must be held is prescribed by para 2A, added in 2016. The timetable is prescribed in r 3. The Neighbourhood Planning Business Referendums Rules comprise sch 7 to the 2012 Regulations, added by sch 2 to SI 2013 No 798, and amended by para 20 of SI 2014 No 333. These business referendums should be contrasted with BID ballots referred to in S below.

The Neighbourhood Planning (Prescribed Dates) Regulations 2012, SI No 2030 stipulate that the prescribed date for paras 14(4) and (6) of sch 4B to the 1990 Act (ie for qualification to vote) is the date when the referendum is held, and that the date of any additional referendum is similarly the prescribed date for para 15(3).

S. BUSINESS IMPROVEMENT DISTRICT (BID) BALLOTS AND BUSINESS RATE SUPPLEMENT (BRS) BALLOTS

Business improvement district (BID) ballots, applicable to both England and Wales, were introduced by Part 4, ss 41-59, of the Local Government Act 2003. The Business Improvement Districts (England) Regulations 2004 are SI No 2443, and those for Wales SI 2005 No 1312 (W.94). In England the 2004 Regulations have been amended by SIs 2013 No 2265 and 2014 No 3199; see also the Community Right to Challenge (Business Improvement Districts) Regulations 2015, SI No 582.

Such ballots, where required to be held by the relevant local (business rate billing) authority under reg 5, are all-postal and conducted under the very simple rules set out in sch 2, the approach of which may be contrasted with the requirements for postal voting and conventional elections. (These references to reg 5 and sch 2 are the same in both the English and Welsh Regulations.) A successful vote to establish a BID must meet two tests. More than half the votes cast must be in favour, and the positive votes must represent more than half of the business rateable value of the votes cast. Those entitled to vote are the business ratepayers in the proposed BID area: the usual electoral register is not used in these ballots.

The first ballot took place in 2004 to establish a BID in Kingston upon Thames LBC. Subsequently there was a 71% vote in support of a BID for the Leicester Square/Piccadilly area of central London. Other parts of London (such as Camden, Holborn and Paddington) have since established BIDs, and in 2006 there were positive ballots in the centres of Brighton, Ipswich and Swansea. Not all early ballots were successful, however: those in Maidstone and Southport in 2005, and in Malton in 2006, all failed to reach the required level of support. Since then there have been many subsequent BID ballots across the UK. The effect of establishing such an area is to impose an extra levy on business premises on top of business rates (or "NNDR") to pay for improvements to the surroundings in addition to those planned by the Council.

The Business Rate Supplements Act 2009 made provision for ballots to be taken before a supplement can become payable. A simple majority of those voting is required for approval. See in particular ss 7-9 (s7 as now partly repealed by the Localism Act 2011) on the ballot provisions; several SIs have been made under the Act's various provisions, including under s 9 the Business Improvement Districts (Property Owners) (England) Regulations 2014, SI No 3204.

BID ballots may be contrasted with neighbourhood planning business referendums under R above.

CHAPTER 5
RETURNING OFFICERS AND DEPUTIES

This follows chapter 4 in providing a short summarising key as to who is which returning officer for the different kinds of elections, polls and ballots described there. The different capacities in which you may act for different elections is often confusing to those new to election management.

The same list of nineteen different kinds of elections or polls in England and Wales therefore applies:

A. European Elections
B. Parliamentary Elections
C. Senedd (Welsh Parliament) Elections
D. Greater London Authority Elections
E. London Borough Elections
F. County Elections
G. Metropolitan Borough, Shire District, Borough or City Elections
H. Parish or Town Council Elections
I. Welsh Unitary and Community Council Elections
J. Parish and Community Polls and Local Polls
K. National Referendums
L. Regional Referendums
M. Elected Mayor and Petition Referendums
N. Elected Mayor Elections
O. Police, Fire and Crime Commissioner Elections
P. Council Tax Referendums
Q. Governance Changes Referendums
R. Neighbourhood Planning Referendums
S. Business Improvement District (BID) Ballots and Business Rate Supplement (BRS) Ballots

A. EUROPEAN ELECTIONS

For each European election region the Secretary of State for Constitutional Affairs prescribed under s 6(2) of the European Parliamentary Elections Act 2002 a Parliamentary constituency acting returning officer who was to be the regional returning officer. The last designations were under the European Parliamentary Elections (Returning Officers) Order 2013 SI No 2064.

B. PARLIAMENTARY ELECTIONS

The returning officer for county constituencies (see chapter 2) is the high sheriff of that county, and for borough constituencies is the relevant district chairman or the (lord) mayor of that borough or city – see s 24 (as amended) of the RPA 1983. But this is a ceremonial role, confined to the optional duties of receiving and returning the writ and declaring the result: see s 27.

It is important to remember that returning officers so designated have no authority over the electoral process.

The relevant regulations for designating returning officers are the Returning Officers (Parliamentary Constituencies)(England) Order 2007, SI No 2878, and the equivalent in Wales, SI 2007 No 171.

The substantive duties are carried out by an acting returning officer, who is the appropriate (electoral) registration officer – see s 28. Under s 28(3) the returning officer must give the acting returning officer a notice of duties under r 50 of the Parliamentary Elections Rules (sch 1 to the RPA 1983) not later than the day after the writ is received. Rule 50 is simply about declaring the result and returning the writ.

The 'petition officer' for the purposes of the Recall of MPs Act 2015 is the acting returning officer for the relevant constituency: see s 6 of the 2015 Act.

Registration officers are appointed under s 8 of the RPA 1983 by London Boroughs, districts or boroughs/cities and unitary and metropolitan councils in England (plus the City of London), and counties and county boroughs in Wales.

Before general elections the Electoral Commission publishes a manual of *Guidance for (Acting) Returning Officers*.

C. SENEDD (WELSH PARLIAMENT) ELECTIONS

See C in chapter 4 above regarding the change of name to the Senedd (Welsh Parliament). Para 18(1) of the National Assembly for Wales (Representation of the People) Order 2007, SI No 236 (as amended by SI 2010 No 2931) prescribes a constituency returning officer for each Senedd constituency, who is either the relevant county or county borough (or city) returning officer or in a cross-boundary case the one designated by the Senedd.

Para 18(1)(b) also prescribes a regional returning officer for each Senedd electoral region, who is the appropriate county or county borough returning officer designated by the Senedd. See paras 19-24 for ancillary returning officer provisions.

The Senedd Cymru (Returning Officers' Charges) Order is SI 2021 No 315 (W. 80).

D. GREATER LONDON AUTHORITY ELECTIONS

The Greater London returning officer for elections for the Mayor of London and London members of the London Assembly is the proper officer of the Greater London Authority: see s 35(C) of the RPA 1983, inserted by para 3(2) of sch 3 to the Greater London Authority Act 1999. However, special arrangements were put in place for the election of the first Mayor in 2000 as the GLA officers were not yet appointed. The Greater London Authority Elections Rules define in r 2 both of whom they term the "GLRO" and the "CROs."

For constituency members (see chapter 4), the returning officer ("CRO") is designated (personally or by description) by the Secretary of State by statutory instrument. That person may be expected to be from the appropriate London borough, but this is not how the provision is drafted: see s 35(2B) of the 1983 Act as similarly inserted, and the Greater London Authority (Assembly Constituencies and Returning Officers) Order 1999, SI No 3380. CROs and the GLRO have a duty to co-operate with each other under r 10(1) of the Greater London Authority Elections Rules 2007, SI No 3541, and r 11 (as amended by rule 3 of SI 2016 No 24) gives the GLRO a power of direction over CLROS in relation to the matters there set out.

E. LONDON BOROUGH ELECTIONS

For London borough elections, the returning officer is appointed by the council under s 35(3) of the RPA 1983 as the proper officer for that purpose. The "proper officer" is a person defined by s 270(3) and (4) of the Local Government Act 1972.

F. COUNTY ELECTIONS

For county councils, the returning officer is appointed by the council under s 35(1) of the RPA 1983. That person will usually appoint deputies to run each constituent district group election for the relevant county electoral divisions. Such deputies will ordinarily be the equivalent returning officer in those constituent authorities.

Generally, it is the chief executive or county secretary and solicitor (or holder of the equivalently named post) who is the county returning officer. It is custom and practice to appoint district returning officers to undertake the election in their individual areas. However, it must be fairly said, this is not universally followed throughout the country. It is not unknown for service level agreements or memoranda of understanding to exist between the county returning officer and the district deputy defining the specific roles and responsibilities, mainly at district level.

G. METROPOLITAN BOROUGH, SHIRE DISTRICT, BOROUGH OR CITY ELECTIONS

As for county councils, the returning officer is appointed by the council under s 35(1) of the RPA 1983. The civic status has no significant impact on election procedures.

H. PARISH OR TOWN COUNCIL ELECTIONS

The returning officer for parish or town council elections is appointed under s 35(1) of the RPA 1983 by the district, borough or city council for the area within which the parish or town council is situated. The wording implies that the same person shall be appointed for all parish or town councils within such an area.

I. WELSH UNITARY AND COMMUNITY COUNCILS

The returning officer for Welsh county and county borough (all unitary) council elections is appointed by the council under s 35(1) of the RPA 1983. The fact that some also have city status is not significant in this context.

The returning officer for community council elections in Wales is appointed by the county or county borough council within which the community is situated: see s 35(1A) of the RPA 1983. As for H above the wording implies that the same person shall be appointed for all community councils within such an area.

J. PARISH AND COMMUNITY POLLS AND LOCAL POLLS

A returning officer is appointed under r 4(1) of the Parish and Community Meetings (Polls) Rules 1987, SI No 1 by the district, borough (or city) (England) within whose area the parish in question is situated. The district or borough, etc council must in turn "appoint an officer for the purpose of the poll" (r 4(3)).

The wording implies that a separate appointment should technically be made for each time a poll is lawfully demanded but, usually, when someone is appointed chief executive they receive a generic appointment to become returning officer for elections and parish polls generally. The contract of appointment should be checked, but it is not common to have separate and new appointments.

There is no statutory counting officer as such for local polls conducted under s 116 of the Local Government Act 2003. Such polls, while authorised by statute, are not of the same formality as other elections and polls with which we are concerned, and may not include the full potential electorate – though it is no doubt be desirable for them to be conducted in a manner not inconsistent with regular electoral practice to ensure the reliability and credibility of the results.

K. NATIONAL REFERENDUMS

Legislation will provide for a person (who will probably be the Chief Counting Officer) to be responsible for declaring the overall result. Regulations will also provide for counting officers for each constituent organising area for the referendum, and they will have responsibility for the conduct of the polls.

As referred to in K of chapter 4, the Chair of the Electoral Commission or their appointee will be the Chief Counting Officer. By virtue of s 128(2) of the Political Parties, Elections and Referendums Act 2000 this is also the case for Assembly Act referendums in Wales under s 103 of and sch 6 to the Government of Wales Act 2006. Section 101(3) of the 2000 Act had excluded a poll under s 36 of the Government of Wales Act 1998 from the definition of referendums in Part VII, ss 101-129, of the 2000 Act. That exclusion is not repeated or updated in relation to s 64 of the Government of Wales Act 2006, but as such polls are to be run based on local government boundaries and electoral registers it is presumably open to the Welsh Ministers in the s 64(3) order to prescribe that local returning officers are to act as counting officers. There is, however, some overlap between the potential extent of a s 64 poll, if it included the whole of Wales, and the national or regional definition of a referendum area as defined in s 101(1) of the 2000 Act. A minor amendments order could be made if necessary under s 160(2) of the 2006 Act.

For the 3 March 2011 referendum on whether to grant additional powers to the then National Assembly for Wales (which was approved), the Chief Counting Officer was responsible for declaring the overall result. As to deputies etc, see arts 10 and 11 of SI 2010 No 2837.

L. REGIONAL REFERENDUMS

The situation is similar to that for national referendums in K. In the 2004 North East regional referendum held under SI 2004 No 1963, the Chief Counting Officer (the then Chair of the Electoral Commission) designated his functions to the regional returning officer (ie in this case the person so appointed for the European elections by SI 2004 No 1056).

M. ELECTED MAYOR AND PETITION REFERENDUMS

The person managing a referendum for an elected mayor is styled the counting officer (under the Referendum Act 1975 the person in overall charge for each (generally county) area was called the chief counting officer). The person who is the counting officer is the person who is ordinarily the RPA 1983 s 35(1) or (3) returning officer for local elections: see E above and reg 9 of the Local Authorities (Conduct of Referendums) (England) Regulations 2012, SI No 323.

For Wales equivalent provisions apply: see the Local Authorities (Conduct of Referendums) (Wales) Regulations 2008, SI No 1848 (W.177), reg 9.

N. ELECTED MAYOR ELECTIONS

The returning officer for the election of an elected mayor is the person who is the returning officer under E, F or G above for that council's ordinary local government elections. See reg 2 of the Local Authorities (Mayoral Elections) (England and Wales) Regulations 2007, SI No 1024, principally amended by SI 2012 No 2059.

For combined authorities under the Cities and Local Government Devolution Act 2016, the combined authority returning officer is prescribed by para 6 of the Combined Authorities (Mayoral Elections) Order 2017, SI No 67, with references to relevant council returning officers defined by para 5.

O. POLICE, FIRE AND CRIME COMMISSIONER ELECTIONS

Section 54 of the Police Reform and Social Responsibility Act 2011 designates as the police area returning officer the Parliamentary acting returning officer designated by the Secretary of State. As with European Parliamentary elections, the local returning officers are the returning officers for local council elections in those authorities included within the police authority area. Designations of police area returning officers were most recently made under SI 2015 No 2031.

The functions of police area and local returning officers, including the powers to appoint deputies and staff, and in the case of the former both to give directions and to correct procedural errors, were set out in the Police and Crime Commissioner Elections (Functions of Returning Officers) Regulations 2012, SI No 1918. The current returning officers' charges Order is SI 2021 No 390.

See also chapter 29 on these elections.

P. COUNCIL TAX REFERENDUMS

No Regulations have yet been made under the powers of s 52ZQ of the Local Government Finance Act 1992 (inserted by sch 5 to the Localism Act 2011). The counting officer is likely to be designated by reference to the person locally appointed under s 35 of the RPA 1983, as for BID and BRS ballots in S below.

Q. GOVERNANCE CHANGES REFERENDUMS

The person running a governance change referendum is styled the counting officer. The person who is the counting officer is the person who is ordinarily the RPA 1983 s 35(1) or (3) returning officer for local elections: see E above and reg 9 of the Local Authorities (Conduct of Referendums) (England) Regulations 2012, SI No 323.

R. NEIGHBOURHOOD PLANNING REFERENDUMS

Regulations have been made under the powers of para 16 of the Town and Country Planning Act 1990 (inserted by sch 10 to the Localism Act 2011): SI 2012 No 2031. These 2012 Regulations have been variously amended by SIs 2013 No 798, 2014 No 333 and 2016 No 934. The counting officer is designated by reference to the person locally appointed under s 35 of the RPA 1983, as for BID and BRS ballots in S below: reg 9. There is also provision made under para 16(2)(a) of sch 4B to the 1990 Act to deal with who shall be designated "where there are two or more relevant councils any of whose areas fall within the referendum area." This is reg 10(4), whereby the Council with the larger number of local government electors registered in the referendum area, or in the alternative whichever council they agree between them, must appoint a Chief Counting Officer. That person may give directions to the other counting officer(s).

S. BUSINESS IMPROVEMENT DISTRICT (BID) BALLOTS AND BUSINESS RATE SUPPLEMENT (BRS) BALLOTS

The "ballot holder" for a business improvement district ballot is prescribed by reg 6(1) of the Business Improvement Districts (England) Regulations 2004, SI No 2443 as "the person the relevant billing authority has appointed under section 35 of the RPA 1983 as the returning officer for elections to that authority." Under reg 6(2) the ballot holder may appoint someone to discharge "all or any" of the functions. The Business Improvement Districts (Wales) Regulations 2005, SI No 1312 use the same numbering and wording for this purpose (but with the addition of "whom" after "person"). (See S in chapter 4 above for the various amendments to these Regulations.)

No specific provision is made for any fee, but it is implied that the employing authority has power to pay employees if such duties are not already within the scope of their contracts of employment and such pay would be pensionable pay in the ordinary way. The anticipated arrangements for the conduct of ballots under the Business Rate Supplements Act 2009 are similar: see SI 2014 No 3204 made under s 9 of that Act.

It is important to check carefully that you have the various proper officer or other appointments required for an election, registration and related duties - there are different provisions for different aspects of the various appointments, and though they may in practice usually be held by the same person, this does not always have to be the case. Dealing with the process for a mayoral election petition, for instance, is not really an election function in itself, while election and electoral registration duties are traditionally both viewed and budgeted separately. (There is a list of most proper officer provisions in the appendix to the *ALACE Employment Guidance Notes* available to members on the ALACE website.)

All functions relating to elections (including returning officer and electoral registration officer appointments) are declared not to be the responsibility of an authority's executive by virtue of reg 2(1) of, and D in sch 1 to, the Local Authorities (Functions and Responsibilities) (England) Regulations 2000, SI no 2853. The list of functions in D in sch 1 has been added to and amended by SIs 2007 No 2593 and 2008 No 516. There are equivalent provisions for Wales in D in sch 1 in each case to SIs 2007 No 399 and (relating to alternative arrangements, and an authority's board) No 399. See also art 2 of the Government of Wales 2006 (Amendment) Order 2019, SI No 1506.

In London returning officer appointments are defined by direct reference to the proper officer function: see E and N in this chapter, and s 35(3) of the RPA 1983, and para 2 of SI 2007 No 1024 noted there. Elsewhere s 35 requires the relevant council to appoint an officer "to be the returning officer ..." etc. This makes little or no practical difference in the outcome but it is important to express the appointment correctly in the official record.

For mayoral election petitions, the proper officer publishes the verification number under SI 2011 No 2914 – see M in chapter 4. For any such ensuing referendum, the counting officer in the local elections returning officer under reg 9 of SI 2012 No 323 (in England) or para 11(1) of SI 2004 No 870 (in Wales) – see M in this chapter. Then for an actual mayoral election itself, the returning officer is again the returning officer for local elections under SI 2007 No 1024 as amended – see N in this chapter. In each case the authorising provisions are slightly differently drafted.

A returning officer (or acting returning officer) should always appoint at least one deputy. This is a personal, not council, appointment, and should be specific to each election (you never know when you may be ill, incapacitated, or just out of the office).

Deputies are appointed under the appropriate statutory authorities – eg s 28(5) of the RPA 1983 for Parliamentary elections, s 35(4) of the 1983 Act for local elections, and reg 5 of SI 2012 No 1918 for police and crime commissioner elections. It is good practice to appoint a deputy for all purposes; it may also be useful to appoint one or more additional deputies for limited purposes such as receiving and adjudicating on nomination papers, or conducting the count (necessary if more than one venue is to be used). Returning officers often talk about giving their deputies full or limited powers delegations. Some software systems will provide forms for this purpose. (Technically a deputy cannot appoint further deputies, so a district chief executive who is a deputy returning officer for a county election should ask that county's returning officer to do this.)

Distinguish *deputy returning officers* from *deputies to registration officers*, who need to be approved by the council concerned under s 53(2) (as amended) of the RPA 1983. Where a registration officer is unable to act or there is a vacancy, s 52(3) provides that the duties may "be done by or with respect to the proper officer of the council by whom the registration officer was appointed." The word "whom" here refers to the council, and not to the proper officer.

Your status as returning officer or deputy etc is important for other reasons. Service as a deputy returning officer is not pensionable, but service as a returning (or acting) returning officer is pensionable, as is also a regional and/or local returning officer role in European elections. Why the difference?

That difference is contained in reg 3 of the Local Government Pension Scheme Regulations 2013, SI No 2356. To be eligible to pay pension contributions and receive benefits, you have to be employed by a "Scheme employer", ie basically a body (including ordinary local authorities) defined in sch 2 to the 2013 Regulations. As a deputy returning officer is a personal appointment made not by the council but by an individual returning officer who is not a Scheme employer as defined, such service is not reckonable service as an "active member" of a pension scheme.

If returning officer service is pensionable, always pay the appropriate contributions, and check that your employing council also pays the relevant employer contribution in each case (recovering their costs wherever possible from the DLUHC for Parliamentary elections and similarly for the Senedd). On retirement, a pension entitlement from election work is treated separately as though involving a different employer separate from a main local government job. The calculation has different rules from conventional salary calculations. On these rules see the current edition of the Association of Local Authority Chief Executives (ALACE) advice document *ALACE Employment Guidance Notes* (available on the ALACE website), especially section 9. With the employing council's consent, a retiring returning officer may choose to have entitlements relating to pre-2014 service reckoned on a whole-number consecutive period of any three consecutive years ending on 31 March within the period of ten years ending with the last day of active membership. For post-2014 pension benefits, the CARE ('career average revalued earnings') basis makes the calculation simpler, and it is based on the member's actual pay for the year, i.e. the same basis as used to calculate benefits for the principal employment (with a $1/49^{th}$ pension build up rate revalued annually in line with inflation). See also chapter 22 on the pensionability of election fees, and staff payments generally.

A frequent practice nowadays is to consolidate election payments within the overall salary package, prior to retirement, as this enhances available years, thus increasing the value of the pension. This practice has been accepted by pension authorities (not without difficulties in some areas), but it is important to consider it well in advance of retirement. Note, however, that consolidation is only possible where the employing authority also pays the relevant election fees; ie you cannot consolidate Parliamentary fees, which come from the government, with your local authority salary.

Deputy returning officers whose fees are accordingly not local government pensionable may, if not subject to any overall pensions lifetime allowance limit, invest them in a stakeholder or other form of pension.

The most frequently occurring situation is for an English district chief executive to be a local returning officer for the police and crime commissioner elections, acting returning officer for a Parliamentary, deputy returning officer for a county, and the (actual) returning officer for district and parish elections. This apparent confusion will soon become second nature!

Occasionally the question of significant sickness or suspension arises. What happens if the chief executive or other postholder also designated as the (acting) returning officer is on more than temporary sick leave, or suspended? Since the election designation is technically a separate post, as discussed above, it is possible to be suspended from one post and not from the other. This, however, seems relatively unlikely. If the returning officer in question has already duly appointed a fully empowered deputy, that deputy can act throughout and no technical problem arises. Similarly suspension is in principle a neutral act, and if by general agreement the suspended officer appoints one or more deputies who together are fully empowered, again there will be no problem. (Such appointments have been made after suspension or, more alarmingly, from sick beds.)

In a situation where this is neither achievable nor appropriate for some reason the authority is entitled to use its normal statutory powers to appoint someone else to act (whether or not on a temporary basis) just as may happen if the returning officer has suddenly died or become permanently incapacitated. Rapidly called (though with proper notice) full council meetings to make these appointments in the run-up to an election are not unknown. The new appointee may then in turn appoint deputies in the normal way (and will also be well advised to check that the insurance cover is transferable and still appropriate – see chapter 9).

What about the fees payable? If a sick or suspended returning officer does not actually carry out any of the election management task, it is only reasonable that the whole of the fee is to be received by agreement by those who have deputised. Such receipts will not be pensionable anyway in their hands if they do not hold appointment in their own right (see above in this chapter). If possible, an explicit relinquishment from the original returning officer is desirable but, in any event, the report to the employing council should make the position clear.

If the council makes a separate stand-in appointment, even temporarily, that appointee has the right to receive the fees, and pay pension contributions as appropriate. In the case of elections for which the original returning officer's payment is aggregated into salary and not separately identified, a special arrangement for paying the stand-in appointee would be necessary.

Can a returning officer be made redundant, and if so is a redundancy payment due? There remains some uncertainty over this. Counsel's opinion has been given to the effect that making a payment at least is barred because the terms of the Redundancy Payments Office Holders Regulations 1965, SI No. 2007 (now to be read as if made under the Employment Rights Act 1996) do not allow this "office" to be deemed to be an employment. The present authors, however, note that (the now revoked) reg 11(5) of the Local Government Pension Scheme (Administration) Regulations 2008, SI No 239 clearly referred to this role as employment, which would have implied that a payment was due. (Calculation would presumably involve a notional average weekly pay, perhaps using the same basis as is used to calculate annual pension entitlement and dividing by 52.) Similar issues arise about electoral registration officers. There may be surprise that 150 years after the passing of the Ballot Act 1872 these points of principle remain undecided!

CHAPTER 6
POLLING DISTRICTS AND POLLING PLACES

Under the original s 18 of the RPA 1983, Parliamentary constituencies had to be divided into *polling districts* and *polling places*. This section was replaced and expanded by s 16 of the Electoral Administration Act 2006, and now ss 18A-18E and sch A1 of the RPA 1983 set out requirements as to how the division of the area into polling districts must be made so that voters have, so far as practicable, similarly convenient facilities or distances for going to vote according to the topography and local circumstances, or what the Act calls "such reasonable facilities for voting as are practicable in the circumstances." (In addition, each parish in England and each community in Wales must be a separate polling district under the rules of s 18A(3)). The polling districts also serve for compiling the electoral register and for running all kinds of elections. There is a useful Ordnance Survey website www.election-maps.co.uk.

Although it is not a strict rule requirement under s 18A(3) of the 1983 Act, in practice polling districts will usually be wholly contained within local government district wards or county electoral divisions, so that if those ward and division boundaries are not contiguous the pattern of polling districts will have to be compatible with both sets of boundaries. It is the council which determines the divisions of the polling districts, again usually by order. If an alteration is made, the registration officer must adapt the register accordingly and "the alteration is effective on the date on which the registration officer publishes a notice stating that the adaptations have been made by him" under s 18A(5)(b). The former rule – that changes to polling districts could only come into effect on the coming into force of the first register prepared from electors lists published after the boundary alterations had been made – has been dropped, giving the process of such alterations a much more flexible timetable.

The council similarly designates polling places, again usually by order, under the RPA 1983 s 18B(1). Polling places could formerly anyway be altered at any time, and that remains the case. Whereas the polling district is a convenient sub-division of the Parliamentary constituency, the polling place is a designated location or area within which the actual polling, at the polling station, must take place. Save in exceptional local circumstances there must be a polling place designated for each polling district.

The rules for the designation of polling places are set out in s 18B(4) of the RPA 1983. A polling place may be either quite tightly defined or be a wider area: indeed in the past polling places have been designated as comprising the whole of a polling district. Although the drafting of s 18B(4) (d) and (e) does not explicitly rule this out (and on a failure to designate s 18B(5) makes the polling place to be the whole of the polling district), it is implied that a polling place will normally comprise an area smaller than a polling district, and one whose identity is such as to make obvious to voters how to reach the polling station. The most important considerations are providing reasonable voting facilities according to local circumstances, and accessibility for the disabled. While accessibility to "potential polling stations" and disabled persons is the subject of rule (c), it will be noted that rule (b) refers to every polling place so far as reasonable and practicable being accessible to electors who are disabled. Councils will need to consider the import of these rules when designating, and decide the extent to which the differing wording has material significance in the local circumstances. If necessary a polling place can be wholly or partly outside the polling district: rule (d).

On the foregoing depends where an actual polling station itself is located: a polling station will usually be a single room or building: if the polling place is a single building or location that means that the polling station must be there too. If the polling place is a wider area, or the whole of the polling district, it leaves more scope for placing (or moving) the actual polling station within the scope of the polling place definition. More than one polling station may be used within one polling place: typically in a busy area two or more stations may, for instance, be set up within a single large room.

Whereas the council fixes the polling districts and places, under r 23(1) of the Local Elections (Principal Areas) (England and Wales)

Rules 2006, SI No 3304 it is for the returning officer (or, in the case of Parliamentary elections, the acting returning officer) to fix the location of polling stations (see chapter 7). That is simply an administrative act, requiring no particular powers or timetable in itself: nevertheless it is certainly good practice to invite comments before acting. Rule 23(1) of SI 2006 No 3305 applies similarly for parishes and communities.

It has always been good advice that the council should advertise any proposals to make a new order for polling districts or polling places, and should consult whichever political parties are active locally. That reduces the likelihood of arguments or difficulties later once the final decisions have been made. Sections 18C-18E introduced new procedures for the actual process of reviewing both polling districts and places: councils must under ss 18A(2)(b) and 18B(3)(b) keep both under general review at all times.

As well as the duty of general review, Parliament decided that every "relevant authority" must complete reviews of all polling districts and polling places within the timetable set by s 17 of the Electoral Registration and Administration Act 2013. This substitutes s 18C(1)-(5) of the RPA 1983. Future reviews must take place during the "compulsory review periods" comprising first the sixteen months from 1 October 2013, and then the period of sixteen months beginning 1 October of every fifth year afterwards, ie now next beginning in 2023: s 18C(2). Section 18D sets out the involvement and intervention powers of the Electoral Commission, while sch 1A to the 1983 Act, inserted by s 16(2) of the 2006 Act, prescribes in detail the review procedure.

As part of that procedure, and the duty to publish notice of any review, the authority must consult the returning officer, and that person must respond with information about polling station locations and any other prescribed information. The authority must also seek representations from people who have particular interest in disability access, give them an opportunity to comment on the returning officer's representations, receive proposals for alternative polling place designations, and give reasons for their eventual decisions. The manner of publication, and the information to be published on the completion of a review, required by paras 3(3) and 7 of sch 1A is prescribed by the Review of Polling Districts and Polling Places (Parliamentary Elections) Regulations 2006, SI No 2965.

It is likely that returning officers will want to arrange more polling stations, where they have the flexibility to do so, for elections where a high turnout is expected. (This may become particularly important if the prospective need under the Electoral Administration Act 2006 to obtain signatures for the issue of ballot papers, the implementation of which has not yet been introduced, is found to slow down the voting process significantly at busy times.) Often this will amount to doubling up two stations in the same premises, which as stated above is quite permissible and needs no prior notice or formality. The experiences at the 6 May 2010 general election in some areas where significant queues built up should prompt returning officers to re-consider whether they have adequate numbers both of polling stations and of polling station staff. This is a point also made by the Electoral Commission in its important Circular EC19(2010) dated 30 July 2010 on the *Review of polling districts, polling places and polling stations*. The 2010 occurrences led to s. 19 of the Electoral Registration and Administration Act 2013 whereby those queuing in or outside a polling station at the close of poll can now be given a ballot paper and can vote.

It is important for newly appointed proper officers/returning officers to check for themselves the status, circumstances and mapping, of their polling districts, places and stations. Regardless of the requirement for four-yearly reviews referred to above, to leave this until an election is called is to risk problems that probably cannot then be corrected. A "non-compliance" with ss 18A-18D, or "any informality relative to polling districts or polling places" will not call an election into question (s 18E(2)), but this is a procedural safeguard only: a fundamental failure to make proper provision for what is required is a very serious matter, and could render the whole proceedings void.

CHAPTER 7
POLLING STATIONS

The previous chapter has dealt with polling *districts* and polling *places*; this is concerned with polling *stations*. To repeat the definitions:

(i) a polling district is a geographical part of a Parliamentary constituency defined by an order or decision sub-dividing that constituency for the convenience and essentially similar treatment of voters;

(ii) a polling place is an area or location for, but not necessarily within, a polling district defined by an order or decision within which polling station(s) must be contained; and

(iii) a polling station is the actual room or similar space within which actual voting or polling takes place.

Rule 23(1) of the Local Elections (Principal Areas) (England and Wales) Regulations 2006 SI No 3304, provides that "The returning officer must provide a sufficient number of polling stations and … must allot the electors to the polling stations in such manner as he thinks most convenient." The equivalent provision for community council polls in Wales is r 29 of sch 1 to SI 2021 No 1460 (W. 375).

Local practice will inevitably vary as to the choice and arrangement of polling stations. Beyond the general principles that govern the creation of polling places set out in s 18B(4) of the RPA 1983, there are few rules about their logistics (as opposed to rules about opening hours, what notices to display, etc). The number of stations must be adequate: one station might be quite adequate for, say, 1250 electors if you expect a 30% turnout over fifteen hours at a local election, but need doubling up for an anticipated 70% turnout over that period at a Parliamentary election (2,500 is the guide figure from the Electoral Commission). Similarly, the first station might have a presiding officer (compulsory) and one polling clerk: two poll clerks, however, might be necessary in the second case to allow the staff both to keep proper control without too much queuing, and also to take proper breaks during a long day. The returning officer can preside at a station in person (see r 24(2) of the 2006 Regulations), but this would be very exceptional: such responsibilities may restrict the possibility of necessary responses to whatever else arises. As already noted in chapter 6, the experiences at the 6 May 2010 general election in some areas where significant queues built up prompted returning officers to re-consider whether they had adequate numbers both of polling stations and of polling station staff.

Polling stations need to be reasonably suitable for their purpose, and have access for the disabled: note s 18B(4)(b) and (c) of the RPA 1983 referred to in chapter 6. That also includes people who are so-called "semi-ambulant" – an elderly person, for instance, may find a long walk in from the pavement just as much of a deterrent as are steps to a wheelchair user or to a parent with a pushchair. The polling station staffs need mobile or other telephones to summon help urgently if needed – a non-public line should be provided to the election office so that staff can more readily get through in case of need. There should be clear demarcation if the polling stations are in the same room, with the ballot boxes positioned to lessen the chance of crossover voting. Each station needs three or four booths at least – one of which should be lower to facilitate use by someone in a wheelchair. The Electoral Commission has published good practice guidance *Equal Access to Electoral Procedures* containing comprehensive advice about identifying, setting up and using polling stations.

As well as physical access, other disability or disadvantage issues need to be considered. Newer regulations contain more explicit powers and requirements for posting of material in minority languages, for instance, and for the availability of tactile voting devices to help those with poor or no sight. Signing is increasingly recognised as an alternative to aural language for the deaf.

It is good practice to invite regularly participating local political parties to express any views about the location of polling stations. In any event, the more active local party workers (very often elected members of your authority) will no doubt put forward their own views without specific invitation. Those views should not determine, but can sometimes reasonably influence, the outcome. Similarly polling stations need to be checked for anything that might give rise to any perception of prejudice – voters must have a calm and unpressured place in which to vote.

Usually the polling station will only be the actual room or hall etc where the actual voting takes place. There may well be a connecting corridor to a hallway, or to the open air, and these will be outside what is legally the polling station itself. The presiding officer should nevertheless take care to ensure that such accesses are kept properly marked, clear of obstructions and not unduly invaded by noise or unofficial party scrutineers (see chapter 19) – even if it is raining!

Under r 22 (as variously amended) of the Parliamentary Elections Rules (RPA 1983, sch 1) returning officers have the right to requisition certain schools and public rooms funded from the public purse to use as polling stations. The public rooms are those "the expense of maintaining which is payable out of any rate". The simplicity of the schools definition has blurred in recent years as some colleges and academies (like the former grant-maintained schools) have left the traditional local education authority (LEA) control. Nevertheless, it will still include large numbers of LEA schools, though the word "education" was dropped from the LEA phrase by para 33(2) of part 2 of sch 2 to SI 2010 No 1158. It covers "a school maintained or assisted by a local authority. . . or a school in respect of which grants are made out of monies provided by Parliament." Importantly, therefore, academies will still be included within the ambit of the regime, and available like LEA schools. There are similar provisions applicable for other sorts of elections and polls.

Use of these, especially in May as summer examinations loom, is increasingly and understandably resisted by schools, but often their use is hard to avoid because of their situation at the heart of local housing estates and communities. Often returning officers are under pressure to use a particular mobile classroom, for instance, and thereby to allow the rest of the school to operate as normal. This is becoming increasingly commonplace but can lead to problems, in particular at the beginning and end of the school day when school buses, parents' cars and cars bringing electors all compete for the same parking spaces, occasionally with some apparent disregard for the safety of pupils and others.

Where schools are used, both the school itself, and the presiding officer, may experience security problems. Check that all the usual routes are open: if a school back gate is padlocked at the start of polling, all the locals who expect to use that access may be effectively denied entry, or have to go a very long way round. That will inevitably lead to problems and accusations.

Finding suitable polling station premises in rural areas regularly causes returning officers difficulties. Some villages (even larger settlements) have little choice and can only offer some venerable facility with poor access for the disabled, no car parking and even only intermittent electricity and water. The poll must go ahead, and so such alternatives as caravans and portakabins should be considered, although on grounds of health, safety and general convenience the 'least worst' choice is often highly unsatisfactory. Recriminations are vividly reported in the local media (let alone complaints from polling station staff), who are not always sympathetic to the returning officer's problems – but such is the nature of this work.

Note that the law prescribes who may lawfully be in a polling station, and that changes were made by s 29 of and para 84 of Part 5 of sch 1 to the Electoral Administration Act 2006. Those now permitted are:

i) candidates;
ii) election agents;
iii)polling agents;
iv)police officers on duty, including community support officers following s 21 of the Electoral Registration and Administration Act 2013;
v) the returning/acting returning officer and his or her staff;
vi)anyone accompanying a voter with disabilities to help them vote;
vii)   voters for the purpose of voting; and (presumably now)

viii) someone who brings a postal vote to the polling station;

ix) representatives of the Electoral Commission (staff and Commissioners);

x) observers accredited by the Electoral Commission; and

xi) people under 18 who accompany voters to the polling station.

It is legally the presiding officer, *and not the returning officer*, in whose control the station is. This should be borne in mind when visiting the station or dealing with public order and other similar issues. It is also a relevant consideration for insurance purposes. (It is the presiding officer's duty to keep order at a polling station – see r 33 of the Parliamentary Elections Rules (ie sch 1 to the RPR 1983), and elsewhere, such as SIs 2006 No 3304 r 31 for county, metropolitan borough and shire districts; 2006 No 3305, r 31 for parishes and community councils; and 2007 No 236, r 42 of sch 5 for the Senedd).

Most returning officers at briefing/training sessions prior to polling day, however, usually indicate that if presiding officers encounter specific problems at their stations that may require exercise of their personal powers, prior consultation wherever possible with the returning officer before using those powers is very important. For Parliamentary elections, the Electoral Commission publishes a *Handbook for polling station staff*, and there are equivalent publications, regularly updated, for other kinds of elections. There are also many other handbooks and publications supporting the running of various kinds of elections and polling, available via the Commission's website.

CHAPTER 8
THINGS TO DO FIRST FOR ELECTIONS; AND CASUAL VACANCIES

This chapter provides a short checklist of things to do at the outset of, or immediately before, an election or polling process. The activities themselves are discussed in the other chapters.

In practice the activities will, indeed must, often proceed simultaneously rather than sequentially: time is short, so responses have to be prompt. That time element predicates the first requirement: to check the election timetable, which will effectively map out the processes of the ensuing few weeks. Returning officers and electoral administrators will prepare a detailed project plan, including risk analysis. This has been recommended and expected good practice supported by the Electoral Commission for some years. The Commission produce templates for the project plan and risk register. There cannot of course logically be sixteen or more things to do *first* – but this chapter gives an indication of your early and most urgent priorities (which should all feature in your project plan) as an election date approaches.

Obviously it is easier to prepare for fixed date elections such as fixed-term Parliamentary elections, or local polls. At its shortest – before the timetable was extended by s 14 of the Electoral Registration and Administration Act 2013 – a Parliamentary election could previously be called in just over three weeks, whereas the timetable for ordinary local government elections was nearly twice as long at over five weeks, usually counting down to the first Thursday in May. For main elections a timetable will probably be supplied from elsewhere, and be almost the same for everyone, but of course for local by-elections you have to calculate it for yourself. We say "almost the same" because there is some limited room for local discretion over sending and opening absent votes etc, but all the key dates – close of nominations, polling etc – will be the same.

Only weekdays are valid days to count in the election timetable, and in addition certain Bank Holidays have to be left out of account (traditionally described as *dies non*). Clearly almost all elections running up to the first Thursday in May will see a number of such days discounted. As to election days and timetable, see r 2 of the Parliamentary Elections Rules (ie sch 1 to the RPA 1983), and similarly elsewhere (eg rules 1 and 2 of SIs 2006 Nos 3304 and 3305 for principal local elections and for parish and community elections respectively). Appendix 2 sets out the timetable for the local elections due on 5 May 2022. (Maundy Thursday, the day before Good Friday, formerly had to be discounted in election timetables but this was ended by s 20 of, and paras 49-54 of Part 4 of sch 1 to, the Electoral Administration Act 2006.)

The second initial step must be to check or arrange adequate insurances, as advised in chapter 9. Once these preliminaries are in place, other immediate requirements include:

(i) publishing the notice of election;

(ii)   appointing one or more deputies to assist or take over from you;

(iii)   finding out, if it is a Parliamentary election and you are the acting returning officer, if the statutory returning officer wishes to reserve the right under r 50 of the Parliamentary Elections Rules (sch 1 to the RPA 1983) to declare the result and return the writ (see in chapter 5), and if so prompting service on you of the necessary notice under s 28(3) of that Act;

(iv)   considering the requirements of the so-called (but incorrectly named) *purdah period*, which is better described as the time between the notice of election being published and polling day. Section 2 of the Local Government Act 1986 (as amended by s 27 of the Local Government Act 1988) at all times prohibits local authority publicity or activities "designed to affect support for a political party" or part of such a campaign, and the obligation to avoid doing anything which may be perceived as favouring a candidate or campaign is heightened in the run-up to an election. At the same time, the business of the council must be carried on, and those elected to office are still completing their terms and entitled to the facilities they have properly been given. This period may well present difficult dilemmas and judgements accordingly. On 31 March 2011, the then Department for Communities and Local

Government (CLG) issued a revised *Code of Recommended Practice on Publicity* (replacing an earlier *Code* originally issued in 1988) and *Explanatory Notes* with Circular 01/2011. As to election periods, see paras 7-9 and 33-35; these set out three specific bans on publishing proscribed material contained in s 125 of the Political Parties, Elections and Referendums Act 2000, reg 5 of SI 2007 No 2089 and reg 15 of SI 2000 No 2852. For a previous example of a judicial review of an allegedly biased and pre-determined decision made during a purdah period, see *R (On the Application of Kevin Paul Lewis) v Persimmon Homes Teesside Ltd* (also *v Redcar and Cleveland Borough Council*) [2008] EWCA Civ 746; [2009] 1 WLR 83. The law on pre-determination (at all times) has, however, been changed by s 25 of the Localism Act 2011, so that – in general terms – prior indications of a view on a given matter are not to amount to pre-determination. Nor is an authority necessarily precluded from taking politically sensitive decisions during an election period. See also chapter 31 on this.

(v) arranging to appoint election staff;

(vi) liaising with the election agents known at that stage. Hold a meeting with those of whom you are aware at the outset, with an agenda of useful issues to be covered, about nomination arrangements, copies of the electoral register, rules about tellers, plans for the count and how the permitted numbers of polling and counting agents will be decided etc;

(vii) booking rooms etc to be used as polling stations, and considering whether you may need to use your powers to requisition certain premises for this purpose. The powers are contained in r 22 (as amended) of the Parliamentary Elections Rules (comprising sch 1 to the RPA 1983), and refer to either (i) a room in a local authority school or one which is paid for out of monies provided by Parliament, or (ii) a room the expense of maintaining which is payable out of local taxation. ("Local education authority" has become "local authority": see para 33(2) of Part 2 of sch 2 to SI 2010 No 1158.) There are similar provisions about the returning officer's use of schools and public rooms for other kinds of elections, including local elections and parishes and communities (r 20 in Part 3 of sch 2 to both SIs 2006 Nos 3304 and 3305, and r 26 of sch 1 to SI 2021 No 1460 (W. 375) in Wales);

(viii) booking somewhere suitable to hold the count;

(ix) checking that all the required polling equipment and stationery is available and ordered;

(x)checking where you can get quotes for printing ballot papers, a highly responsible task in itself. The Representation of the People (Ballot Paper) Regulations 2015, SI No 656 substituted a new form into the Appendix to the Parliamentary Elections Rules in sch 1 to the RPA 1983. Printing ballot papers takes time, and with the exception of some pilot experiments they have traditionally been produced in "cheque book" format with counterfoils, with specialist equipment needed for both sets of sequential numbering together with perforations. Counterfoils have no longer been required since the Electoral Administration Act 2006 (though operation of the provisions about signatures remains postponed, with the requirement for signatures currently deleted from the provisions about the corresponding numbers list), but ballot paper printing remains a demanding and very responsible task. It is the authors' experience that this is not usually undertaken by in-house print units, though they often tackle other tasks such as notices of poll, nominations, etc;

(xi) decide what security measures you will use on ballot papers – under paras 86-88 of Part 5 of sch 1 to the Electoral Administration Act 2006 each ballot paper must have a unique security mark, but other means than the traditional stamping instrument are now permitted, and different marks can be used for different purposes at the same election;

(xii) considering what language translations, Braille and other notice display requirements there will be, following ss 199B and 200 of the RPA 1983 (the former inserted by s 36 of the Electoral Administration Act 2006);

(xiii) assessing the general public information/public relations/press and media requirements;

(xiv) arranging to supply free copies of electoral registers as required – see the RPR 2001, SI No 341 para 47 (as amended);

(xv) considering security considerations generally, and any special threats or risks. The Electoral Commission publishes bulletins and guidance on election security issues generally;

(xvi) considering any issues that may be expected to arise from the candidates' (conditional) rights to use certain rooms free of charge for election purposes under ss 95 and 96 of the RPA 1983, and the equivalent right for other kinds of elections, such as those for the Senedd (art 69 of SI 2007 No 236).

Although there will be much else to do (and some things, like booking a room for the count, may have been done months earlier), sorting out the items on the list will get a grip on the election process from the outset. This helps to ensure that in the busy and often stressful time ahead no vital step is forgotten or runs late with potentially disastrous consequences.

By-elections for, Parliamentary or Senedd elections are triggered at the relevant national level. For local government elections, see ss 84-89 of the Local Government Act 1972, noting where, through its proper officer, the authority has to declare a vacancy. Ordinarily a notice from two electors for the area is needed to trigger an election: see s 89(1)(b). "Area" here means "principal area" as defined in s 270(1) of the 1972 Act, ie that whole council area not just the relevant ward or county electoral division where the casual vacancy occurred. See also the second part of Home Office Circular RPA 321 (published on 2 February 1988) on a notice from two electors received before a notice of casual vacancy has been published (considered to be a valid requirement for an election to be held).

Note that if a local, parish or community election vacancy occurs within six months of the end of the fixed term of office, no by-election will be held: see eg s 89(3) of the Local Government Act 1972. This is a common type of provision for fixed term elections.

On filling Senedd casual vacancies, see s 10 of the Government of Wales Act 2006 for Senedd constituency seats, and s 11 of that Act for Senedd electoral region seats.

On filling casual vacancies in the office of Mayor of London see s 16 of the Greater London Authority Act 1999; and on casual vacancies of seats in the Assembly constituencies generally or of London Assembly members, see ss 10 and 11 of the 1999 Act.

Casual vacancies for other elected mayoral offices are the subject of para 7 of the Local Authorities (Elected Mayors) (Elections, Terms of Office and Casual Vacancies) (England) Regulations 2001, SI No 2544. There are no equivalent regulations for Wales.

CHAPTER 9
INSURANCE

It is a cardinal rule of running elections that you must have proper and adequate insurance before you start. This should always be checked well before any election process formally begins. The rubric is "do not even *dream* of running elections without proper insurance." High Court litigation costs can be very substantial. (Six- and even seven-figure sums are not unknown.) In this increasingly litigious age, protecting yourself against the possibility of expensive legal action does not need underlining. What may bear repetition, however, is the personal and separate nature of the role of the returning officer. That means that any action taken to question the validity of the returning officer's decision, or the proper conduct of the election process, will be taken against the returning officer personally. Fully adequate insurance is accordingly essential.

For elections paid for from the Consolidated Fund (like Parliamentary and PCC polls etc) the Government provides an indemnity, although this not meant to replace the need for individual insurance for returning officers but to act as a back-stop to that. It is important to always have regard to the wording of the indemnity.

The Government would probably pay, however, for the re-run of an election and offer an indemnity so that no-one would be seriously out of pocket. Returning officers are paid again on the same fee scale for re-run elections. Insurance for the May 2011 AV referendum was arranged centrally through the Electoral Commission, while the Government provided a 'Covid-19 Indemnity' for the May 2021 elections (as set out in two Cabinet Office papers of March 2021).

Authorities can, however, quite properly arrange to pay for such insurance for whoever they appoint their proper officer for Parliamentary and local elections, and should do so for all other elections; fairly commonplace is an extension of the council's general officials' indemnity policy and other policies too, such as public liability, defamation, etc. However it is done, returning officers should check policy terms for themselves.

While local policies appear to be continuing satisfactorily, there is little doubt that insurance has become progressively harder and more expensive to obtain, and well publicised anxieties over fraud allegations, votes going astray and other polling problems have contributed to this. It underlines, however, the extent of the risks involved – and the foolhardiness of proceeding without adequate and reliable cover. Different policies at varying levels will of course be needed to cover all elections. It is important, however, that any excess is checked and, ideally, eliminated. The authors have heard of election policies carrying an excess of £100,000 (at several London boroughs and other large metropolitan authorities), and in those cases they are quite worthless as protection for any returning officer. The best excess is nil, and in many cases, reducing the excess to nil is a simple matter of a telephone call and no cost.

It has sometimes been questioned whether a local authority has power to pay insurance premium costs for returning officers. The robust view is that this is simply incidental to the general power in s 112 of the Local Government Act 1972 to employ staff and the statutory duty to appoint returning officers in particular. It seems that paras 4 and 5 of the Local Authorities (Indemnities for Members and Officers) Order 2004, SI No 3082, now put the validity of such common-sense provision beyond doubt. As a guide, the level of liability cover should be no less than £1million, this being the limit quoted in one of the authors' officials' indemnity policy.

So far we have referred to the returning officer's personal liability in the context of challenged decisions or judicial review, election petitions and so on. Another important aspect, however, is the returning officer's potential employer's liability in respect of all the other employees and situations which may arise. Imagine that an employee working at a polling station is assaulted by a voter, or otherwise injured while on duty; or that a voter trips over rough paving at the door of the polling station premises; or that at the count someone claims they have wrongly been excluded by the security staff when they had a right or a ticket to be admitted. In each case the returning officer may have a claim to defend, and will require insurance accordingly. Even if these occurrences happen to council employees or on council premises, they are unlikely to come within the scope of ordinary council corporate insurances because of the distinct separate nature of the election process as an activity. Remember that election staff are employed in the personal name of the returning officer, not in the name of that returning officer's employing council (see chapter 10), and that the duty to carry employer's liability cover is statutory. Sometimes there are some tricky problems over car insurance as to whether or not individual policies cover elections staff whilst driving to the polling station (generally, such policies do not do so and staff must rely on their own insurance cover), but extensive discussion of such matters is well beyond our scope here. Nevertheless, there are a few authorities who insist on checking their polling staff's car insurance, and wisely point out to many retired staff whom they employ that they may not have adequate business cover on their policies. Again, there may be staff who damage either their person or their clothing on, for example, polling station furniture. These matters often result in small claims and regrettable arguments over excess limits on various insurance policies. Local situations vary, and it is worthwhile being aware of policy applications. As an approximate guide, the amount of cover required for such purposes should not be less than quoted above.

Returning officers should always check the extent of applicable local insurance prior to each and every election. Changes to the council's cover, such as in the level of excess, may be inconsequential for the council, and implemented without significant discussion or 'noise' within it, but will be very significant for the returning officer. The authors' experience is that councils sometimes may change their excess, which may then apply to the totality of their insurance cover including that for returning officers. As a result, returning officers will want to ensure that the returning officer-specific part of their council's cover has zero excess. This can be addressed in discussions with the insurers and does not always bring with it additional costs - but even if it does, it is certainly worth doing and the position must be checked!

Note that the Electoral Commission produces advice on risk management, an increasingly significant issue in the public sector. They have a risk log identifying the key "show stopping" moments in the electoral process. Some awareness of this is well worthwhile, and many authorities now have access to specialist risk management advice. Dealing with insurance companies and their loss adjusters, claims handlers, etc (not to mention their lawyers) can be a testing experience, especially at the end of a tiring election process.

CHAPTER 10
APPOINTING ELECTION STAFF

Elections officers will normally keep lists of people who are willing and suitable for elections work – particularly for election day appointments as polling station presiding officers, poll clerks and for conducting the count afterwards. This is essential: a Parliamentary election, for example, can easily require in excess of three hundred people on the day for just one constituency, and without a starting point it would be extremely difficult to make that many appointments in the statutory time available.

Appointments are personal to the returning officer (or deputy or local returning officer in the case of county or regionally based elections for instance), so again it is worthwhile underlining the points (see chapter 9) about having both them and yourself adequately insured. The appointments are made under r 26 of the Parliamentary Elections Rules (sch 1 to the RPA 1983) and equivalent provisions for other elections.

Local practice and expectation will no doubt play a considerable part in who is appointed. Obviously people should not be excluded from appointment on inappropriate grounds: so long as they have the right experience or aptitude, and can physically do whatever has to be done – perhaps with the assistance of one or more other polling station staff – then there should be no problem.

Many returning officers try to avoid appointing someone as a presiding officer if they have not served as a poll clerk once or twice before, but this will not always be possible, especially for last-minute appointments. There is usually general provision for training polling station staff (and particularly presiding officers), and a greater likelihood of fees or pay being made available to get people together for the training time involved. Many local authorities also provide regular in-house training.

Election staff should not be generally associated with a particular political party or viewpoint, though of course formal political restriction under s 2 of the Local Government, Planning and Housing Act 1989 is not required (though that probably would be appropriate for the permanent elections office employees). Needless to say, on polling day itself they must be scrupulously impartial, and may need to be reminded about working dressed in particular colours or styles, or behaving in any other way, which could give rise to allegations of bias. It is an offence for "officials" (as the side-note to s 99(1) of the RPA 1983 terms them) to act as a candidate's agent at any election.

Commonly local government officers comprise the elections staff, together with recently retired employees and a variety of others known to, or connected with, the elections office in some way. Avoid any sense of special relationships or patronage – though often this can be countered by recognition that overall the requisite staff are in short supply. Sometimes the assumption is made that people can readily be found from the unemployed register: indeed they may, but it will not always be easy to find people with the necessary attributes and sense of impartiality. Nor are many people willing to de-register and re-register to legitimise working for just one day for a not particularly high fee, though this latter factor is clearly an issue for them rather than for you the employing returning officer.

Returning officers can issue *certificates of employment* for polling station staff, to enable them (if working within the same constituency or electoral area where they are registered to vote) to vote instead at that polling station. The certificate should provide the registration number so that this can be entered on the corresponding numbers list, and is to be returned in a separate envelope to the count centre at the close of the poll. It is of course equally possible (and may be easier) for polling station staff to apply for postal or proxy votes, but the certificate alternative can be useful if, for instance, a late staff appointment has to be made or changed after the closing date for absent vote applications. Equivalent forms are provided elsewhere, eg for local elections in Parts 7 of both schs 2 and 3 of the Local Elections (Principal Areas) (England and Wales) Rules 2006, SI No 3304, at the same places in the Parishes and Communities equivalent Rules SI 2006 No 3305 and at r 37(5) in, and Appendix 8 to, SI 2021 No 1460 (W. 375) in Wales.

It is worthwhile referring here to a couple of issues that regularly trouble returning officers over staff appointments. Should council employees (of whatever grading) be allowed a day off at the grace of the employing authority or should they be required to take leave? The latter school of thought maintains they should not be paid twice (ie their usual salary and election fee), and puts forward the competitive requirements of many council (tendered) contracts such as leisure and refuse. The former theory is built around the basis that it is difficult to recruit staff for election duties; election fees after tax are not very generous, and you need to be able to rely on regular core staff knowledgeable in electoral matters. Practice varies locally, but the 'free day off' situation still generally prevails, albeit with varying degrees of co-operation from colleague chief officers or directors who have targets to meet and understandable service delivery pressures upon them.

Again, it is important to have some monitoring over the age of staff recruited for these duties. This is not to be politically incorrectly or unlawfully "ageist" but simply to be cognisant of the fact that insurance policies regularly exclude those over certain ages. Exclusions above ages 65, 70 and 75 are not uncommon, and some policies require specific consent to be obtained. It is prudent to have such matters checked. Some returning officers encourage younger staff, particularly at the count, and make approaches to local colleges – national insurance numbers will be required, however, and thinking about safe travel arrangements is sensible.

Many returning officers believe it is better to avoid using the same people to count at night as have been out in polling stations during the day, particularly for today's long polling hours of 7am to 10pm. Even if they are not infringing the Working Time Directive, they will be tired, unable to get to the count immediately because of their polling station closedown responsibilities, and particularly at risk of diminishing concentration if the count or recount is protracted. Some returning officers, however, take the contrary view – that presiding officers have to bring their boxes in anyway and that at some devolved rural counts (some districts may run eight to ten scattered counts separately on one night) it is often easier to ask presiding officers to stay on there to count. If there are problems over a ballot paper account there are advantages in having the presiding officer present for further enquiries to be made. It is a classic – and typical – example of the returning officer having to decide upon the most workable solution for the local circumstances.

Bank employees and others with manual dexterity used to be popular appointees for counts for obvious reasons, but such skills are rarer in these days of automatic teller machines. Be that as it may, the question of impartiality still applies, even if rather less rigidly for counting assistants than, say, for supervisors or those helping to arrange the overall process.

In many areas it is increasingly difficult to persuade people to agree to work at counts, especially in inner cities, because of the times and personal security issues involved set beside relatively low fees. Nevertheless, there is often considerable pressure from local precedent and candidate expectation influencing the returning officer to count at night directly after polls close wherever possible. While this is not a legal requirement for most elections, s 48 of the Constitutional Reform and Governance Act 2010 prescribed that in Parliamentary elections reasonable steps should be taken for counting to begin within four hours of the closing of the polls, and that the Electoral Commission should issue advice accordingly. This was done by making changes to the Parliamentary Elections Rules (sch 1 to RPA 1983), and inserting r 53ZA to the effect that if counting does not begin within the time limit the returning officer must publish (and send to the Electoral Commission) a statement of what time it did start, and what were the reasonable steps taken to comply with the statutory time limit. The Commission must refer to the receipt of any such statement in any report on that election that it publishes: r 53ZA(3). In May 2010, 45 constituencies were outside this time limit, 23 of which had counts planned for the Friday morning.

In Scotland the Secretary of State declared that the 2007 Scottish Parliamentary elections would be counted overnight, and would be declared before the Scottish local government results, a view with which the Electoral Commission disagreed (*The Register*, issue 9, September 2006, p 17), their concerns relating "primarily to the pressure overnight counting places on Returning Officers and their core staff, and to the complexities involved in administering two different proportional representation systems."

It is good practice, and recommended, that returning officers hold a briefing meeting at least for all presiding officers before polling day, usually when they attend the council offices to collect their ballot boxes. Again, local practice can vary, but it is often worthwhile having poll clerks in attendance too. Such meetings are commonly held a day or two before polling day. It is better to get the boxes out before polling day, as this gives presiding officers time to check the contents and the elections office time to address any issues which that check might throw up. In terms of the presence of the returning officer at the briefings, it is a positive sign to election staff that you as returning officer are interested in their work, intend to lead them forward through the polling process, and can at least listen to their queries – even if unable fully to answer all their questions.

CHAPTER 11
WORKING WITH ELECTION AGENTS

Candidates generally have to appoint election agents (RPA 1983, s 67), though they will actually be, or be deemed to be, their own agent in some cases: see s 70(1) of the 1983 Act. In a county (but not borough) Parliamentary constituency one sub-agent may be appointed: ss 68-69. See also paras 37-40 of SI 2007 No 236 for the Senedd, and paras 11-15 of Part 1 of sch 1 to the Greater London Authority Act 1999 for those elections.

"Permitted participants" in regional and local referendums may each appoint a "referendum agent" under the Regional Assembly and Local Government Referendums Order 2004, SI No 1962. Under para 11 of sch 1 to the Parliamentary Voting System and Constituencies Act 2011 similar appointments could be made for the AV referendum on 5 May 2011.

It will not always be clear at the outset of an election process or campaign which parties or individuals will be standing. This need not inhibit dealing and meeting with those who are already known, provided that so far as practicable similar facilities or opportunities are offered to others who are identified later.

Elections are busy and tense times for the agents too, and it will help greatly if a proper professional relationship (and hopefully some mutual trust and confidence) can be established from the outset. It will also help in the election management process generally to clarify issues at the start, and avoid needless time-taking repetition. This will help you to get on with running the election, and will help them to get on with working to try and get their candidate(s) elected, with a minimum of distraction.

It is good practice to get the known agents together at the start of an election process – particularly those acting for candidates with a significant local or national profile. You can give those agents the forms, electoral register copies, and other information they will need, such as where and when the issuing and opening of absent/postal votes will be; where and when the count will be; how to get count tickets (see chapter 17) from you; what the press and media arrangement will be; and so on. They can all ask questions, all hear the answers, and so reduce the scope for misunderstanding or later allegations that you treated one or other agent more or less helpfully. For some elections two such meetings may be appropriate – one concentrating on the imminent nomination process, and a later one based around the campaign, polling day itself and the count.

It is the tradition (and considered established good practice) that the returning officer and electoral administration staff communicate with agents, and not directly with candidates. Again, agents do not usually or necessarily bring their candidates to any meetings you arrange as returning officer.

There are fewer full time professional agents now than in earlier years, but most make some form of contact with the returning officer before nominations close, so it is normally possible to have a reasonable meeting. Many part-time agents, and secondees to the post, find the task complex and difficult to understand – it really is a role learnt through experience.

Agents will appreciate knowing how to contact you and your election office quickly – perhaps using a telephone number different from the busier public ones. They will no doubt be quick to take up with you any issues of concern as their campaign continues, and an investment of time and courtesy at the outset should pay dividends later.

That is, after all, only good customer service. It is also worthwhile providing them with links to, or copies of, the Electoral Commission's *Guidance: Candidate or Agent*. This is simple yet authoritative, and covers all the key matters with which agents need to deal.

But what are agents for? Essentially they manage the candidate's campaign for election, so freeing the candidate to undertake the actual campaigning. They will ordinarily direct events on the candidate's behalf, make contracts, publish election literature, submit the nomination and other required papers, and keep the financial records and control which will allow election accounts to be submitted to the returning officer both within the statutory period and within the prescribed expenditure limits (see chapter 24).

Achieving all that is of course their responsibility, not yours. Nevertheless, as already stated above, good and constructive co-operation (so long as you try to give it equally to all agents) will foster a mutually confident and professional relationship. Most agents are invariably grateful for all your help and understanding of their problems; after all, it is probable that you will work with them on more than one election!

CHAPTER 12
HANDLING THE NOMINATION PROCESS

Validly submitting the nomination papers is a key event of the electoral process – and a great relief – for agents and candidates. It is also important for the returning officer: the problems and ambiguities of nominations can generate a surprising degree of controversy, ill feeling and litigation. An early meting for putative candidates and agents may resolve many queries, and ease the process both for them and for the returning officer.

A returning officer will no doubt have appointed one or more deputies (see chapter 5) for all or for certain purposes: no one can guarantee to be immediately available to receive nomination papers throughout all the possible office hours. The importance of being aware of nomination submissions cannot be over-stated: a wrong decision is going to lead to particularly difficult and expensive problems and challenges. The returning officer must either decide each case personally or have full confidence in someone else validly appointed to do so – but if you have given that delegation you remain personally answerable for whatever has happened or been decided. As to when a person is legally defined as becoming a candidate, see s 118A of the RPA 1983 added in by s 135 of the Political Parties, Elections and Referendums Act 2000. Part 3 of sch 1 to the Electoral Administration Act 2006 made a number of amendments to the qualification rules for candidates to, Greater London Authority, local government and Senedd elections.

The basic rules about nominations are set out in rr 6-17 of the Parliamentary Elections Rules (sch 1 to RPA 1983, as amended), and similarly elsewhere: e.g. rr 4-13 of SI 2006 No 3304 for principal local elections and the same rules of SI 2006 No 3305 for parishes and communities. As a general approach, you should be principled but not pedantic, and accurate but not academic or arcane. The aim is to accept nominations as valid if possible, but to respect the rules as process driven. The requirements are directive, not discretionary. Always remember, however, that your purpose as returning officer is to administer the process so that the electorate can make a choice between candidates, and that you are an enabler in this, not a preliminary selector. Thus, it is helpful – and a performance indicator from the Electoral Commission – to encourage the candidates/agents to arrive in good time during the nomination period to enable fresh papers to be submitted in the event of errors (most are well aware of this and try to avoid rushing into your office five minutes before the deadline).

A lot of cases have considered questions about signatures, capital letters, commonly used names like "Jack" for "John", and so on. Section 21 of the Electoral Administration Act 2006 sought to reduce these by amending r 6 of the Parliamentary Elections Rules to allow a commonly used alternative forename or surname to appear on a nomination paper and statement of persons nominated, but in such a case (unless the returning officer considers it misleading or offensive) "the commonly used name (instead of any other name) will appear on the ballot paper" under r 6(5) inserting para 2A into the appendix of forms.

The Local Elections (Principal Areas) (England and Wales) Rules 2006, SI No 3304 and the Local Elections (Parishes and Communities) (England and Wales) Rules 2006, SI No 3305 each contain in r 10 of sch 2 a provision allowing the correction of minor errors in a nomination paper up to the point of publication of the statement of persons nominated. A similar rule for Welsh community elections is contained in r 16 of sch 1 to SI 2021 No 1460 (W. 375). "Minor errors" are not defined, but do include wrong electoral numbers and "obvious errors of spelling in relation to the details of a candidate." In the Welsh Rules errors relating to a home address form are also included. Returning officers (r 10(4)) "must have regard to any guidance issued by the Electoral Commission for the purposes of this rule." There is also a power to correct minor errors in para 12 of Part 1 of sch 3 to the Police and Crime Commissioner Elections Order 2012, SI No 1917.

The Lord Chancellor's guidance to magistrates (revised in 2005) warned about use of the suffix "JP" and says in its para 3 "There is particular sensitivity around usage in an electoral context. In this context, magistrates may refer to their status, as a matter of record and as evidence of their commitment to the local community and volunteering generally. However, they must ensure that this is not done in a way which could reasonably be thought to cast doubt on their political impartiality on the bench – the importance of maintaining a politically neutral judiciary is paramount." Nomination papers need to be signed, as do consents to nomination. The former need to be holograph i.e. actually personally signed, on the paper presented. Fax or e-mail will not do: they would in any event arguably not have been "delivered" in the way the statutory rules mean. It will be valid to accept an e-mailed or faxed consent to nomination if you are satisfied that the original has indeed been signed by the candidate, and you will normally be satisfied if there is no evidence to the contrary – even if you do not recognise the candidate's signature.

Section 22 of the 2006 Act adds r 8(1)(c) to the Parliamentary Elections Rules so as to preclude anyone from being a candidate in more than one constituency on the same polling day. Section 7 of the Government of Wales Act 2006 similarly provides that a candidate may stand in a Senedd general election for only one Senedd constituency. Neither may anyone be on more than one Senedd regional list at the same time: s 7(5). As to when someone technically becomes a candidate, see s 118A of the RPA 1983. Under the amendments made by s 17 of the Electoral Administration Act 2006 the minimum age for candidature is reduced from twenty-one to eighteen: a person must under s 17(1) be eighteen on the day of their nomination, not the day when the notice of election is published or when actual polling takes place.

Section 24 of the Political Parties and Elections Act 2009 allows a Parliamentary election candidate to withhold their home address from publication. The Parliamentary Elections Rules (r 6(4)) require a home address form to accompany a nomination paper (whether or nor the candidate wishes to withhold their home address from publication); other consequential amendments were made to protect confidentiality, and unless an election petition is under way, r 53A requires the returning officer to destroy the home address forms on the first working day after the twenty-first calendar day "after the officer has returned the name of the member elected." Home addresses cannot be withheld by election agents, or in other elections.

A deposit is required for Parliamentary elections (£500 – see r 9). A deposit of £500 is also required from candidates in mayoral elections - see r 10(1) of the Mayoral Elections Rules comprising sch 1 to the Local Authorities (Mayoral Elections) (England and Wales) Regulations 2007, SI No 1024. The figure increases to £10,000 for the Mayor of London election and, generally, there are different amounts for London elections.

A nomination is not complete without receipt of the deposit money. If that money does not arrive in cash, it must be in a form like a banker's draft which the returning officer can be sure will be honoured as good credit, and not drawn as a cheque (which could anyway be stopped) on a candidate, agent or political party. Credit and even debit cards were formerly not acceptable, but s 19 of the Electoral Administration Act 2006 changed that, and the rules now provide for their use. Where the returning officer has discretion, consider the practicalities of allowing deposits to be paid in this way before agreeing to it – especially in case a nomination arrives at the last minute allowed. The notice of election must now state the arrangements which apply for the payment of the deposit required to be made by electronic transfer of funds: see s 19(3) of the 2006 Act inserting r 5(1A) into the Parliamentary Elections Rules. The deposit may be made by legal tender, a banker's draft, or with the returning officer's consent, in any other manner (including by means of a debit or credit card or the electronic transfer of funds). Note that a returning officer may refuse to accept a deposit sought to be made by means of a banker's draft if they do not know that the drawer carries on business as a banker in the UK.

Nominations close at a fixed time, which cannot be extended. If a Parliamentary nomination, for instance, is not complete by 4pm on the closure day – for example because although a nomination paper has been properly completed and submitted a required deposit or candidate's consent has not been received – it cannot be completed later, and the nomination must be rejected. Failure to meet the deadline, even by a small margin, is not a "minor error."

It is a good idea to be on the lookout just before closing time, and also just before the deadline within which any nominations validly submitted can be withdrawn. That will help to avoid allegations that someone was wrongly ruled out of time.

A sensible view must be taken of such borderlines. An agent or candidate need not be in the actual room where you check the submitted paper at withdrawal time (which for Parliamentary elections is the same time as closure of nominations) – it will be acceptable for them to have arrived in the reception area, and so be present (so to speak) on your terms rather than theirs. But to be crossing the car park, or in the wrong building, or somewhere not within the scope of the address given for submission on the notice of election, is not acceptable and must be ruled out of time. Nomination papers are open to limited objections: see r 15 of the Parliamentary Elections Rules. After the time for withdrawals has elapsed, a statement of persons nominated must be published: see r 14.

The various Rules provide in some cases specific rights to attend nomination proceedings, and thereby both to inspect and to object to the validity of, any nomination paper or (as the case may be) list of candidates. These proceedings are not public as such. See also for Parliamentary elections r 11 of the Parliamentary Elections Rules. For local elections the approach is different; there are no specific rights to attend the nomination process, but there is a general public right to inspect and copy nomination papers; see variously rr 11 of schs 2 and 3 to both SIs 2006 Nos 3304 and 3305, and for Welsh community elections r 17 of sch 1 to SI 2021 No 1460 (W. 375).

Note that in Welsh community elections the home address forms required as part of the nomination process by rr 5(6) and 9 of the 2021 Rules may only be inspected by other candidates and agents in the same area, and – unlike in relation to nomination papers themselves in r 17(3) – it is expressly forbidden under r 18 to take copies or extracts.

A requirement in most elections is for candidates claiming political party membership to be able to stand as certified candidates for a political party registered under the Registration of Political Parties Act 1998, now replaced by the Political Parties, Elections and Referendums Act 2000.

Finally, take note of the drafting of two rules in particular. First, the requirement in r 7(4)(b) of the Parliamentary Elections Rules that on request a returning officer "shall prepare a nomination paper for signature." This simply means supplying a draft nomination paper with the election details filled in, so that the agent or candidate can fill in the personal details required and obtain the other subscriber(s) or assentor(s) counter-signatures as required.

Secondly, be clear about the reasons for rejection of nomination papers under the rules: they are set out in r 12(2) of the Parliamentary Elections Rules, plus r 12(3A) (inserted by para 3(3) of sch 2 to the Registration of Political Parties Act 1998) in relation to political parties. The returning officer cannot bring in other considerations outside the scope of the procedural requirements involved, or look behind the papers and details present if, having checked the electoral register details given, etc., there is no reason to do so. You are not expected to be a detective when checking papers, but a returning officer. Unless there is an obvious error blatant on the face of the papers it is not your role to be the inquisitor of candidates and agents. The principal commentaries record details of some of the problem cases, eg the man who, wishing to stand as a candidate in a Parliamentary election, maintained that his name was Margaret Hilda Thatcher and that his address was 10 Downing Street, though in Peckham not Westminster. Another candidate claimed his name to be Mickey Mouse domiciled in Disneyland. This is a difficult topic with no clear answers, though in the last decade or so the political parties registration procedure has brought some further formality to the process, and this is discussed below.

If at the end of the nomination period, or after the time limit for withdrawals, only one candidate stands duly nominated, then that person will be declared elected and of course there will be no poll. If no candidates stand nominated, the vacancy remains and the process has to begin again with a new notice of election. Theoretically in the case of a Parliamentary election the writ would have to be "returned" blank. See para 17(2) of the Parliamentary Elections Rules comprising sch 1 to the RPA 1983.

It is sensible for a returning officer to give an indication on the validity of a nomination paper or process as quickly as possible, even though the statutory deadline of closure of nominations may be some time away. The Electoral Administration Act 2006, s 19 has extended the deadline for adjudicating upon nomination papers by twenty-four hours – in other words, the returning officer now has a day to consider any final decision after the closure deadline. Agents may submit more than one nomination paper for a candidate, particularly at Parliamentary elections – partly to be on the safe side and partly to encourage more subscribers who are perhaps key to their campaign effort. There is no harm in this: in the official record, the nomination paper first accepted and declared will stand.

The Registration of Political Parties Act 1998 introduced the concept of political parties as such into elections for the first time. The register of parties had previously been kept by the Registrar of Companies under the then Companies Act 1985, but under s 23 of the Political Parties, Elections and Referendums Act 2000 it was transferred to the Electoral Commission. The new r 14 (5) of the Parliamentary Elections Rules, inserted by para 6 (9) of sch 21 to the Political Parties, Elections and Referendums Act 2000, requires the returning officer to send to the Electoral Commission a copy of the statement of persons nominated and, where candidates stand in the name of a registered party, also to send a copy of the r 6A certificate, on which see the next paragraph below and also para 41 of Home Office Circular RPA 436 dated 6 February 2001. As to this Act generally, see Home Office Circular 5/2001 dated 7 February 2001.

The register will not only contain the registered name of a given party (and up to twelve other "descriptors"), but also up to three emblems to be included on ballot papers. Most importantly for our purposes here, a candidate cannot use a description "which is likely to lead voters to associate the candidate with a registered political party" unless that description is authorised by a certificate from or on behalf of the party's registered nominating officer. (See r 6A of the Parliamentary Elections Rules, inserted by para 2 of sch 2 to the 1998 Act.) As to the use of one emblem where a Parliamentary candidate is the subject of an authorisation by two or more parties under r 6A(1B), see r 19(2AA), added by s 20 of the Electoral Registration and Administration Act 201.

The Registration of Political Parties (Prohibited Words and Expressions) Order 2001 SI No 82 (as amended by art 5(2)(c) of SI 2004 No 366, by SI 2005 No 147 and by SI 2006 No 3252) prevents political parties from registering using certain styles of naming or description. The register is public and is maintained by the Electoral Commission. The register itself is split between Great Britain and Northern Ireland and is available to be consulted on the Electoral Commission's website, by returning officers; in the event of difficulty they should contact the Commission to confirm that a party is registered on the latest date for the publication of the notice of election.

By virtue of s 22 of the Political Parties, Elections and Referendums Act 2000 nominations (except at parish and community council elections) must be accompanied by a certificate from a registered political party unless the description is "Independent", "the Speaker seeking re-election" or no description is given. There is also a new category of "minor party" for those involved solely in parish and community council elections. (The Elections (Welsh Forms) Order 2001 SI No 1204 has been made to validate the Welsh equivalent of "Independent", which is "Annibynnol", and "The Speaker seeking re-election", which is "Y Llefarydd yn ailymgeisio". (See also SI 2001 No 2914 for Senedd elections.) Annex B to Home Office Circular RPA 436, published on 6 February 2001, reprinted rr 6 and 6A of the Parliamentary Elections Rules as amended by the 2000 Act. Annex C following provided a useful question-and-answer briefing on candidates' descriptions.)

Related changes were made for local elections. See now r 5 of the Local Elections (Principal Areas)(England and Wales) Rules 2006 (SI No 3304) in relation to registered parties, and r 4(4) (a) applies in relation to a valid description of a nominated candidate other than "Independent". Rule 6 of the 2006 Rules allows a person to subscribe a nomination paper provided that they will be eligible to vote on polling day and that they do not have an anonymous electoral register entry. Similar provisions apply for parishes and communities in rr 5 and 6 of the Local Elections (Parishes and Communities)(England and Wales) Rules 2006, SI No 3305, although r 4 there refers differently to descriptions as simply not being allowed to exceed six words in length. (These and other changes were referred to in the context of the amending SIs by which they were originally made in Home Office Circular RPA 437, dated 20 February 2001.)

In *R v Balabanoff, Ex parte De Beer* (2002) QBD 10 April (Lawtel Document No C9500809 dated 11 April 2002) the returning officer was held not to have acted unlawfully or unreasonably in rejecting a certificate which used the term "Liberal Democrat" when the nomination papers used the term "Liberal Democrat Focus Team". In this interesting case the London Borough of Harrow's returning officer disallowed sixty nominations applying what was then r 4A(1) of the Local Elections (Principal Areas) Rules 1986, SI No 2214 (now r 5 of SI 2006 No 3304). The nominations were received close to the deadline, the Liberal Democrats' local nominations officer having apparently acted outside his authority from the party's national officer. The court emphasised that this was decided strictly on its own facts, but the case underlines the judgement a returning officer must make, and that courts may be reluctant to interfere with that judgement.

An important case on nominations arose out of the 2006 local elections in London: *Begum v Tower Hamlets* (Lawtel document no. AC9400651, Court of Appeal decision). This arose from nominations presented by the Respect Party – they were submitted in good time but were misfiled at the Town Hall and not discovered until after the close of nominations. Prior to the nominations being submitted, the returning officer (via a deputy) had indicated that she would assist with checking the papers. When, eventually, the papers were checked, it was discovered they were invalid (having used electoral numbers from an old register) and, therefore, the nominations were rejected as invalid. The candidates succeeded, at first instance, in obtaining a judicial review to countermand the election. The Court of Appeal, however (Sir Anthony Clarke, MR), held that it was wrong for candidates to have a legitimate expectation that their papers would be checked for errors. There was no legal responsibility on the returning officer to check; she had just offered to help in an informal way. It was the duty of the nominee (the agent) to present valid papers in time, and also to ensure that they contained the correct information. This responsibility could not be transferred to the returning officer. Nevertheless, the returning officer had breached what was then r 7 of the 1986 Principal Areas Rules, SI No 2214 (now r 8 of SI 2006 No 3304); she had failed to examine the nomination papers as soon as was reasonably practicable, as the papers had been misfiled, and that failure had been causative of the fact that their candidatures could not proceed. The RPA 1983, however, provided a statutory scheme that governed conduct in national and local elections. There was no provision within that statutory scheme for the High Court to grant judicial review during the course of an election. The Court should be slow to intervene where Parliament had conferred duties on the returning officers and that was so whether there was a breach of the 1986 (now 2006) Rules or an interference with a legitimate expectation. It would be a very rare case indeed in which there were sufficient grounds to justify countermanding the election (though it would be possible to challenge by way of petition after the result).

Formerly if a Parliamentary election candidate died before the result was declared, the poll was always abandoned under the previous r 60 of the Parliamentary Elections Rules. Section 24 of the Electoral Administration Act 2006 has changed that, and what happens now depends on the description of the deceased candidate (making s 24 an unusual example of the law not treating all candidates in the same way in the same circumstances). If the deceased candidate was standing for a registered party, the notice of poll must still be countermanded or polling abandoned as before: r 63. The election process must be re-run as prescribed there. The position is similar if the deceased candidate was the Speaker of the House of Commons seeking re-election: r 64.

Under the substituted r 60, however, the election continues regardless of the death of an independent candidate, and if there were only two nominated candidates either the notice of poll is to be countermanded or proceeding polling is to be abandoned, and the other candidate is to be declared elected as if unopposed. Where a poll is abandoned under any of rr 60(4)(b), 63(2)(b) or 64(2)(b), r 65 prescribes what happens to the ballot papers and documents arising from that poll. Rule 65 was substituted for combined elections by r 27C of the Representation of the People (Combination of Polls) (England and Wales) Regulations 2004, SI No 294 inserted by reg 4(11) of the similarly titled Amendment Regulations 2006, SI No 3278. The 2006 Regs 4(10) and (11) also clarify, by inserting further amendments, that abandonment of one poll because of a candidate's death will not affect continuation of another poll or referendum taking place at the same time under the Combination Regulations.

Rule 61 deals with the situation where there are three or more candidates, and an independent candidate who has died before the result is announced is found to have received the majority of votes. The returning officer must publish the voting figures but declare that, as the deceased candidate had the most votes, nobody can be returned as elected and the poll must be re-run under the procedure set out. If the deceased candidate had tied for first place they must be ignored under r 62 and the other tieing candidate returned (or lots cast between the tieing survivors if more than one).

In Wales, death of either a party list candidate or an individual candidate for a regional Senedd election (see C in chapter 4) will not result in the countermanding of the election if it still remains contested, but would do if it thereby became uncontested (see rr 65 (6) and (5) respectively of sch 5 to the National Assembly for Wales (Representation of the People) Order 2003, SI No 284. Death of a Senedd constituency candidate countermands that election under r 65(1), while at a Welsh combined election, the substitution made by r 42(1) of sch 4 to SI 2007 No 236 makes clear that death of a local government candidate does not in itself affect a continuing Senedd election.

In local government elections generally, the death of a candidate before the close of polling will require abandonment of the poll – see SIs 2006 Nos 3304 (principal areas) and 3305 (parishes and communities) respectively. The rule in each case is r 55, in both cases in sch 2, but also in each case r 55 in sch 3, which refers to combined polls. Note that, regardless of when the death occurred, proof given to the returning officer will either require countermand of the notice of poll, or if later will require the abandonment of the actual polling. Death between actual nomination and what would otherwise be publication of the notice of poll similarly is included in the requirement to countermand.

A small point, but one that may not uncommonly arise at local elections in particular, is where two candidates have the same surname, or even the same other names. Paragraph 4 of the *Directions as to Printing the Ballot Paper* under r 16(2) of SIs 2006 Nos 3304 and 3305 requires the other names (or if they too are the same, usually also the home address and description) to be printed in small capitals as well as the large capitals required for surnames. For local elections in Wales see also r 22 and the associated Appendix 2 of SI 2021 No 1460 (W. 375).

CHAPTER 13
THE RETURNING OFFICER'S ROLE DURING THE CAMPAIGN

Returning officers and their staffs will be very busy during election periods. Is there anything else to be said about their roles at these times other than to speak of following through the statutory procedure? We think there are several key areas about the returning officer's need for deliberate or positive impartiality, which are insufficiently described merely by referring to the statutory situation of being the holder of a politically restricted post.

First, it is quite likely that protagonists in an election campaign will seek to draw the returning officer into a kind of refereeing role, turning there for support in their eagerness or urgency to have someone else's conduct constrained or even declared unlawful. Candidates – and their agents – sometimes have difficulty in drawing the distinction between your role as returning officer and as, say, chief executive of the council. (See also the comments on the incorrectly titled so-called *purdah period* in (iv) of chapter 8 and chapter 30.)

You are *not* the referee in the election. Strictly speaking, you have no more power nor duty as returning officer than the various statutes and regulations give you. Nevertheless, it is often difficult to regard that as the last word, as the *Balabanoff* case referred to in the preceding chapter illustrates.

Wrongdoing in elections can sometimes invalidate the process, depending on whether the breached requirements are mandatory or procedural: note that under s 23(3) of the RPA 1983 relating to Parliamentary elections (and there are similar rules for other kinds of elections) procedural irregularities will not usually make an election invalid if the rules have substantially been met and the result has not been affected.[2] But wrongdoing can also amount to a criminal

---

[2] See also *Morgan v Simpson* [1975] Q.B. 151, Lord Denning's judgement.

offence, and will certainly do so if there is a deliberate attempt to corrupt the fairness of the process or do something declared impermissible or unlawful. The wide variety of election offences are divided into corrupt practices and illegal practices, the broad distinction between which is about seriousness and degree of wilful intent (not unlike the classic criminal law distinction between felonies and misdemeanours, which subsisted until the passing of the Criminal Justice Act 1967).

Of course, you have the same duty as any other citizen to act upon and report criminal offences, but there will be a greater expectation on you to do so as returning officer.

If not you, protagonists often argue, "Who else will see fair play? And anyway, X is publishing scurrilous leaflets without saying who is printing and publishing them (s 110 of the RPA 1983, and see also s 143 of the Political Parties, Elections and Referendums Act 2000); Y is using a loud hailer close to the open doors of the polling station; and Z is spending more than allowed but laundering the bills."

This is where tact and robust common sense come in. These allegations are technically not your concern, but some response is seemingly required; often you may "have a quiet word", try to give constructive advice, or simply suggest that formal action might have to follow if present circumstances continue. Nevertheless, in the light of s 106 of the RPA 1983 and the very public outcome of *Watkins v Woolas* [2010] EWHC 2702 involving the May 2010 general election in the Oldham East and Saddleworth constituency (see also chapter 23), it seems likely that in future there will be more allegations and counter-allegations about the truth or otherwise of election literature and debate, and that returning officers will inevitably have to guard against being drawn inappropriately into the arguments involved.

Sometimes candidates claim that their voters are being deterred by the most fanciful influences: it may be tempting to say airily "Do you think that could be true of *your* supporters? I thought you believed that they comprised the more sophisticated sector of the electorate?" Take care, however, not to underestimate the strains and tensions of being up for election (and particularly re-election): many things will probably be said of which no more will be heard after polling day. So try to stay concerned but independent, ready to give friendly advice and warnings (so long as ready to do so similarly to all candidates), yet ready to report to the police serious wrongdoing if you do come across convincing evidence of it.

Unfortunately, the media attention given to alleged (and in some cases actual) postal vote fraud over recent years has prompted a substantial increase in bringing such evidence to the attention of returning officers and electoral administrators. Evidence, as ever in criminal law, varies in its clarity and strength, but the returning officer should apply straightforward factual tests. A very clear example occurred in Burnley at the 2004 local elections. A candidate (assisted by a party worker) submitted proxy voting forms implying that hundreds of voters in a small part of one ward were unable to vote in person because they were all simultaneously taking lengthy foreign holidays. As *The Times* reported on 20 October 2006 (following a successful prosecution), "the returning officer smelt a rat and called in the police".

The second issue is about your continuing role in your substantive post – probably as chief executive, head of law and administration or similar. That continues and, although it is obviously politically restricted, it is (in a party politically controlled council) presumably work done predominately on behalf of the majority party or controlling administration.

This will not necessarily pose any problems, but in a vigorously contested election may produce some dilemmas. Suppose that the majority party uses its position to vote through resolutions and instructions which you (and perhaps other parties in particular) perceive as deliberately calculated to affect the election campaign and outcome?

Again, tact and caution will come in useful here, but there are three points in particular which it may be helpful to bear in mind.

The first is that you cannot validly or lawfully be asked to do anything which compromises your duty to the whole council, or your statutory duty to act in a politically restricted way as s 2 of the Local Government and Housing Act 1989 requires. We do not have to assume corruption or a criminal act by someone else in order to envisage something compromising arising for you. You must be polite but firm about any such situation, which could potentially involve professional misconduct.

The second point is about capacity. You are wearing two hats, one as (deputy) returning officer, and one as whatever your main post is. They are statutorily separate and, up to a point, you can act separately and distinctly. There is, of course, still some danger from the perception of others, or the possibility that your stance and conduct in one position is such as to cast a shadow across the other and jeopardise the reality of being seen to act fairly and without bias (say, for example, if you were publishing a district council viewpoint about a matter currently the subject of a parish poll you were required to conduct). Nevertheless, with a judicious approach you should hopefully be able to fulfil a regular role as an advocate of, and champion for, your council's – and hence probably its majority or effectively controlling group's – interests without jeopardising the proper conduct of your role in the election process.

The third point is about expenses. No one should forget the rules about spending money to try to procure the election of a given candidate, and bringing that into account. A reminder might be timely to anyone seeking by surrogate means effectively to deploy resources which would take a given campaign's expenditure beyond the lawful limits.

You may also be approached about campaigning facilities. Sections 95 and 96 of the RPA 1983 provide for Parliamentary and local election candidates to have free access to certain schools and meeting rooms for election meetings - in effect the same kind of definition as referred to in chapter 6 as able to be requisitioned by returning officers for polling stations. "Free" means free of any booking or hiring fee – the costs of heating, lighting and cleaning etc. still have to be paid: ss 95(4) and 96(4). There is now also a third area, added by s 67 of the Electoral Administration Act 2006, which is the issue of performance management. That is the subject of chapter 26 below.

See also chapters 30 and 31 about the difficulties of reconciling the 'day job' with the election period, and how crucial is your evident neutrality and your demeanour towards all concerned during this often very demanding time.

CHAPTER 14
POLL CARDS

Poll cards are simply the written communications sent to individual electors to tell them where and when they can vote at a particular election. They are required for most elections: the rules are prescribed in r 28 of the Parliamentary Elections Rules (sch 1 to RPA 1983, as amended), and r 25 of the Local Elections (Principal Areas) (England and Wales) Rules 2006 SI No 3304. For the Senedd see r 36 of sch 5 to the National Assembly for Wales (Representation of the People) Order 2007, SI No 236, and for local elections in Wales see r 31 of sch 1 to SI 2021 N0 1460 (W.375).

Poll cards do not include details of the candidates standing, but they must contain the information required by r 28(3) of the Parliamentary Elections Rules (as augmented by para 70 of Part 5 of sch 1 to the Electoral Administration Act 2006). They can include maps of polling stations, but even with today's technology mapping may still be quite costly compared with basic cards. There is a useful Ordnance Survey website www.election-maps.co.uk. It is also likely that, to provide identifiable maps which most electors can use, such poll cards may need to be larger, at perhaps A5 sizes, than the usual postcard size customarily used. Use of maps on cards may incur Ordnance Survey fees. Some authorities now produce poll cards which also "double up" as applications for postal votes, once signed and returned to the returning officer; clearly a rapid delivery system is required if this is to be successful.

Regulation 9 of the RPR 2001, SI No 341 formerly prescribed the form of poll cards for Parliamentary elections (form A in sch 3, not to be confused with the Form A for pre-2001 electoral register canvassing which was delivered to every household). This appeared not to extend to local elections but the style would have been very similar. For combined elections (see chapter 25) it is possible to send out separate cards, but it is much more usual to have a combined version to take advantage of the resultant cost savings. Regulation 9 was replaced by regs 46 and 47 of the Representation of the People (England and Wales) (Amendment) (No 2)

Regulations 2006, SI No 2910 which prescribed new forms and amended sch 3 to the 2001 Regulations accordingly.

It is usual to send out poll cards as quickly as possible after the statement of persons nominated has been published. Inevitably that means that some people who apply for absent voters, particularly under the late applications procedure, will still receive poll cards although no longer able to vote in their local polling station. Poll cards need not be sent to people who have applied for absent votes (see chapter 15).

It is a common misconception that intending voters need to bring their poll cards to identify themselves at the polling stations, but this is not so. Voters are identified by the statutory questions, which the polling staff put to them. Poll cards are required for all main elections, but they are not statutorily required for parish or community council elections, although those councils can ask for poll cards to be issued if they pay the cost; see r 25 of the Local Elections (Parishes and Communities) (England and Wales) Rules 2006, SI No 3305, and in Wales r 31 of sch 1 to SI 2021 No 1460 (W.375). Home Office Circular RPA 264 dated 10 December 1982 reminded returning officers that poll cards could in turn remind voters that polls are being taken together where district and parish or Welsh equivalent elections are being combined. Specific requirements have since superseded this advice in some instances.

It is an offence to distribute imitation poll cards calculated to deceive: see s 94 of the RPA 1983. This can sometimes cause problems as over-zealous agents occasionally produce party literature that copies the style of poll cards or ballot papers, and exhorts the voter to support their candidate(s).

CHAPTER 15
ABSENT VOTES

There are two kinds of absent votes – postal votes and proxy votes. Postal voting has over recent years become one of the most controversial aspects of our electoral system, along with debates over proportional representation, poor turnout, etc. There have been several cases of both alleged and proven corruption and malpractice reported in the media, particularly the prosecutions in Birmingham (2005), in Peterborough (2008), and Bradford (2010). It has been – and will continue to be – a critical area that attracts attention. Accordingly, it is important that all returning officers (and particularly those recently appointed) pay attention to this often demanding and bureaucratic process that twenty years or so ago received no particular scrutiny.

The key change in the formal rules about postal votes was made in 2001 when postal voting was allowed on demand. (The following references to postal votes apply similarly to postal proxy votes, but there are still rule differences affecting applications for ordinary proxy votes, on which see later in this chapter. Proxy voting is not available simply on demand, and one of the requisite reasons for applying must be given.) A process originally started after the First World War to allow the military to vote (and extended in 1948) was seen as a way to counteract falling turnout, and thus adapted to meet the needs of modern lifestyles; those who were too busy to attend polling stations could still vote by choosing to do so by post. The old ideas of having to claim infirmity or absence on business were scrapped. Postal voting applicants now need not give any reason: applications may be granted for either definite or indefinite periods, or just for a particular election.

Although a very worthy idea, the real problem has been adapting an old system into a process suitable for the twenty-first century. It is a classic example of tinkering with the existing rules and producing a result that many experts believe is not "fit for purpose." The Government, however, persist with this approach (much criticised by SOLACE, the AEA and others in the electoral field) to deal with new problems as they occur; there have been important changes in recent regulations, described later in this chapter.

There was a huge expansion in demand for postal votes following the 2001 changes. At the 1997 Parliamentary general election 2.4% of the votes cast nationally were by post – by 2001 this had risen to 5.3%. Several constituencies reported huge increases in postal voting – for example, Stevenage 1250%, North Tyneside 1000%, and Cardiff 700%. In 2004, four regions of England piloted all-postal voting for the European Parliamentary elections (there were a number of pilots at local elections before that year). It was estimated that without postal voting on demand, turnout at the combined 2004 European elections would have been 3% lower.

Following the 2004 experience, on 6 April 2005 the Electoral Commission published Circular EC8/2005 on *Guidance on Fraud for Use at a UK Parliamentary Election (England & Wales)*. On 29 March 2005 they also issued a code of conduct for political parties, candidates and canvassers on the handling of postal vote applications and ballot papers. This has always been welcome by practitioners, but also criticised because of its lack of enforceability. The Queen's Speech in December 2019 identified that the Bill that will introduce voter ID will also ban campaigners from handling postal votes; will introduce a power to limit the number of postal votes a person may hand in; will establish a requirement on those registered for a postal vote to re-apply every three years (currently registration can last indefinitely), and will limit to two the number of people for whom a voter may act as a proxy, regardless of their relationship. While the focus will no doubt be around the voter ID issues, the other issues that the Bill will contain will further support returning officers in dealing with issues around absent voting.

Much consideration has been given to potential fraud problems since 2005; as noted in chapter 2, together with the Association of Chief Police Officers (ACPO), in October 2012 the Commission published revised *Guidance on preventing and detecting electoral malpractice*, which was subsequently revised in 2013. The Electoral Commission also publish an analysis of allegations of electoral malpractice on their website, the most recent of which relate to the 2017 and 2018 elections.

Although almost four million votes (some 15% of the total) were cast by post at the 2005 Parliamentary general election, there has been a levelling off of demand since then, possibly due to the media coverage of electoral fraud (several prosecutions having been widely reported) and also, probably, because there is a finite demand from the electorate for this voting method. Given public concern about the security of postal ballots, the more stringent requirements of the new legislation about postal voting, and the unlikely occurrence of any more all-postal experiments (no longer supported by the Electoral Commission) it would have been surprising if the proportion of votes cast by post at the May 2010 general election had very markedly exceeded the 15% or so recorded in 2005. (The national turnout was 84% at the 1950 general election, the highest since January 1910, and has not been exceeded since.)

The key rules on absent votes are set out in sch 4 to the RPA 2000 and Parts IV and V of the RPR 2001, SI No 341 (as substantially amended). The actual process of sending out and receiving postal votes is intricate and detailed – well beyond the scope of this book to describe – and with the increased demand many more staff are required over a longer period of time.

Strangely, candidates and election agents are now no longer entitled to be present when absent votes are prepared for despatch. They do, however, have a right to attend when the returned envelopes containing the marked ballot papers are opened, so notice must accordingly be given of these occasions (more than one, almost certainly) and times. It will also be helpful to say in advance when absent votes will be despatched, even though the right to be present has been abolished, as candidates and agents will find that information useful for their campaigning.

The requirements for preparing absent votes for despatch take time to complete and should not be under-estimated. Many will outsource the printing of postal vote packs, which are then sent out direct by Royal Mail to voters, but even then, effective contract management requires on-site visits, sampling and proofing. Moreover, the 2001 rule changes extended the deadline for receipt of applications (see r 56 of the RPR 2001), and returning officers must consider what is an adequate number of staff now to employ to cope with the anticipated workload. Close liaison with local postal staff is also essential – they must clearly understand the deadlines of the electoral timetable. As well as Royal Mail it is possible to use either council staff or a commercial delivery firm to deliver postal ballots. Again, there is no longer the former restriction that addresses to which postal ballot papers are to be sent must be within the United Kingdom (though their return within the statutory timescale can be problematic). Return postage is to be prepaid for those sent to United Kingdom addresses only. As to where postal ballot papers are to be sent, see reg 72 of the RPR 2001, SI No 341 as augmented by RPR 2002, SI No 1871, para 12.

There has been past criticism of the performance of Royal Mail in all aspects of the delivery of postal votes. Both SOLACE and AEA representatives have discussed this problem with the Royal Mail, and there is now a guide to best practice – this is called *Managing Postal Voting* and is published by Royal Mail on their website; it seeks to establish a plan of action as well as explaining their "sweeps" of sorting offices. It also includes protocols on all aspects of the postal voting process and working relationships with the Royal Mail.

Note also that it is now possible for voters to deliver by hand, or arrange to have delivered, their completed postal votes on polling day to a polling station as though they are voting there in the usual way (though so long as it is within the relevant constituency it need not be the polling station to which they would have actually gone to vote in person). This provision is contained in reg 79 of the RPR 2001, SI No 341, adding to para 45(1B) of the Parliamentary Elections Rules. Count proceedings have been known to be delayed by the arrival of considerable numbers delivered using this new provision. Indeed, with the advent of the new checking requirements in 2007 some returning officers and electoral administrators seriously doubted the continuation of traditional overnight counts; many had planned to move to a Friday morning start before s 48 of the Constitutional Reform and Governance Act 2010 made this much less likely.

In the aftermath of the 2005 Birmingham postal vote fraud case and other high profile media fraud stories, significant changes were made to the rules to tackle the problems. Section 14 of the Electoral Administration Act 2006 now provides that those wishing to vote by post, proxy or postal proxy must provide both their signature and date of birth when applying (the so-called "personal identifiers"), and empowers the electoral registration officer to check the authenticity of these personal identifiers against other records. Existing absent voters must provide the same personal identifiers to continue to receive postal votes. Fresh signatures are additionally to be required on or before every fifth anniversary of a person being recorded as a postal voter or postal proxy.

This security provision is followed up by the postal voter having to provide a signature and date of birth on a "postal voting statement" (replacing the existing witnessed declaration of identity) when returning the ballot paper. The then DCA were committed from the outset to the principle that checks should be carried out on all these statements. They also recognised, however, that there was a need to be realistic as to what could be achieved within already stretched resources for the May 2007 local elections. Thus, the new regulations included a requirement that not less than 20% of returned postal vote statements must be checked against the original applications. There is discretion for returning officers to carry out a higher level of checking if appropriate. (Note that the check applies to every postal vote opening, and not just to 20% of the total number received; and note also that while it is the electoral registration officer who makes the checks on applications, it is the returning officer who checks the returned votes.)

New offences were introduced in connection with postal and proxy votes, including making a false application for a dead or fictitious person, misdirecting a postal vote, seeking to deprive another of an opportunity to vote, etc. Similarly, there are provisions to make false registration an offence, which could also be the basis of an unlawful application for a postal vote. Where a postal vote applicant asks for the ballot paper to be sent to an address different from the address stated in the application, the reason must be given. In addition, the Absent Voting (Transitional Provisions) (England and Wales) Regulations 2006, SI No 2973 make further stipulations about the steps the electoral registration officer must take in requiring personal identifiers from existing absent voters, and about related matters. The checking rules remained the same for the 2008 local elections. The Electoral Commission published *Checking signatures and dates of birth at postal vote openings* dated 28 October 2010, giving forensic advice about assessing the genuineness of a compared signature by considering its shape, pen-path and fluency.

Another controversial area has been the handling of postal votes by party agents and workers. SOLACE takes a clear position that postal votes should be posted back to the returning officer as a primary route, but understands that people may leave this too late. The practice followed in certain places, however, of party workers collecting these votes when canvassing before polling day is totally unacceptable. It leads to allegations (well-founded or not) of such votes being tampered with, or not returned at all. Several returning officers (Kettering and Southampton are good examples) have produced local protocols agreed with their party agents to prevent this practice altogether. The national protocol *Code of conduct for political parties, candidates, canvassers and campaigners on the handling of postal vote applications and postal ballot papers in England and Wales* published on 3 February 2011 by the Electoral Commission, however, is more tolerant and takes a more permissive line: see paras 20-24. It is not an easy situation to resolve – the practice is not illegal and no-one wishes to deprive an elderly, often infirm, person of their democratic right to the franchise. The joint authors of this book still maintain, nevertheless, that the best practice is to exclude party activists from this type of role. This is to be codified into legislation when the Elections Bill 2022 is enacted.

The Birmingham judgement makes it clear that it is not the electoral registration officer's or returning officer's role to investigate possible fraud: "The returning officer has no duty to investigate electoral offences and no resources to do so either. More to the point … the returning officer has no power to investigate" (para 139 of the judgement).

This is reaffirmed at paras 142 (including some electoral registration officers' functions) and 143 of the judgement. Clearly, however, if the returning officer has concerns about fraudulent applications or receives any allegations about absent voting fraud, these should be reported to the police for further investigation. Thanks to liaison work with the former Association of Chief Police Officers (ACPO, now the National Police Chiefs' Council) most forces have now appointed a single point of contact ("SPOC") for advice relating to elections at either command unit level or force level; jointly with the Electoral Commission *Guidance on policing elections and referendums* was published dated February 2011. See also chapter 28 on integrity and fraud issues.

There have been a couple of cases on what constitutes "delivery" of a -vote by the returning officer to the voter. In *Knight v Nicholls* [2004] EWCA Civ 68 it was alleged that the returning officer was in breach of his duty because a number of postal ballot papers had been received late through the failure of the Royal Mail to delivery promptly. The court did not accept this contention, and held that the returning officer's duty had been complete when he delivered the ballot papers to the Royal Mail. This dictum was approved in *Considine v Didrichsen* [2004] Lawtel Document No AC0107399 (a case arising from an election petition challenging a local election result in Hull), though Mr Justice Jack refined the principle by saying that "the duty to issue postal ballot papers was completed when the paper was correctly addressed to the voter and delivered to the officer's chosen carrier." Unfortunately, in this latter case postal ballots were incorrectly addressed and the decision went against the returning officer, the election being declared void.

Section 22 of the Electoral Registration and Administration Act 2013, by inserting para 7E into sch 4 to RPA 2000, made provision for Regulations to require a registration officer to notify someone that their postal ballot paper has been rejected.

In October 2006, the Council of Europe's Parliamentary Assembly resolved that there is "a growing body of evidence that widespread absent vote fraud is taking place in the UK." They accordingly appointed two officials (a former German justice minister and a

Polish senator) to look into allegations of irregularities in Birmingham, Blackburn, Coventry and London. The then DCA Minister, Bridget Prentice MP, did not welcome this move and stated that robust systems (described earlier in this chapter) had been put in place to deal with fraud. Visits from such officials continued, however, and they came again at the May 2010 general election.

Proxy voting requirements have not been similarly changed in the way that the postal vote rules have altered (except where postal proxies are concerned), and there are still prescribed grounds for applications (eg physical incapacity, service voter, attendance on a course, etc). An elector cannot have more than one proxy at once, even if more than one constituency is involved: see para 6(2) of sch 4 to the RPA 2000. To be a proxy voter, a person must be eighteen, not subject to any legal incapacity, and be from either the Commonwealth or the Republic of Ireland. Except in a specified family relationship, a person cannot be a proxy for more than two electors in the same Parliamentary constituency or electoral area (ie district, borough or parish, etc – it does not mean ward or electoral division): see para 6(6) of sch 4 to the RPA 2000 and s 203(1) of the RPA 1983. Most returning officers have in the past not tried positively to check for compliance with this limit, and have only reacted to it if obliged to do so by its coming obviously to their attention; it is almost impossible daily to check thousands of forms during the very busy pre-polling day period. There is a risk otherwise that an unwilling and quite genuine absent vote applicant might be turned down because unknown to them their proxy has agreed to act in more cases than permitted. Arguably if there is excess, the first two only (plus any permitted family situations) will be valid, though some returning officers consider that the latter take precedence having impliedly revoked the former applications.

To deal with medical emergencies an elector is now allowed to appoint a proxy up to 5pm on polling day if they become physically incapacitated after 5pm on the sixth day before the day of the poll – ie they could not have applied under the normal procedure. The form will need to be attested in the usual way and the application made in person to the electoral registration officer.

In all circumstances, when an electoral registration officer has granted an application to vote by proxy that must be confirmed in writing to the elector, describing the duration of the appointment of the proxy (reg 57(2), RPR 2001). A proxy must also be notified of their appointment. The form of the proxy paper for this purpose is prescribed (reg 57(3), RPR 2001 and form E, sch 3, RPR 2001). Acknowledgements of proxy vote applications have now, in a recent change, become required (reg 57(1) RPR 2001 as amended by the RPR 2005). Thus, the electoral registration officer must write to the elector and notify them whether their application has been accepted or rejected. This gives the elector an opportunity to check that the information they gave on their application has been processed correctly. Also, it gives an opportunity to safeguard against potential fraud, or misunderstanding on the part of the elector. If an elector receives an acknowledgement for a postal vote that they have not requested, or were not aware that they had requested, the receipt of the acknowledgement will give the elector an opportunity to check with the electoral registration officer.

CHAPTER 16
POLLING AGENTS AND TELLERS

Polling agents are provided for in r 30 of the Parliamentary Elections Rules (sch 1 to the RPA 1983). Before polling starts, candidates can appoint polling agents "for the purpose of detecting personation" (voting in person – or by post – as some other person, whether that other person is living, dead or fictitious). There is no limit on the number who can be appointed, and they can be paid or unpaid, but of course candidates are responsible for the actions of their agents. Returning officers must be notified of the names and addresses of those appointed "not later than the second day" (ie valid timetable days) "before the day of the poll": r 30(3).

There is, it seems, an increasing tendency to appoint polling agents today, even if personation is not a prevalent problem. The advantage to candidates (and the agents) is that polling agents are allowed to be present *inside* the actual polling stations themselves. Unless the returning officer allows a greater number by notice, four is the maximum number of polling agents allowed inside a particular polling station, and if more than four have been appointed the returning officer must decide by lot which four are allowed. A person can be a polling agent for more than one candidate, and candidates can be their own polling agents in effect: see r 27(2), (3) and (9), for instance, of sch 2 (and r 27(2), (3) and (11) of sch 3) to the Local Elections (Principal Areas) (England and Wales) Rules 2006, SI No 3304. The equivalent community council provisions in Wales are in r 33 of sch 1 to SI 2021 No 1460 (W. 375). Acting as their own polling agent will not increase the total allowed in a given polling station above four, but candidates are entitled to be present there anyway – see r 30(1)(c). As to who may be lawfully present in a polling station, see the list in chapter 7.

Polling agents must not interfere with voters or the process of their voting. They can, however, require under r 35 of the Parliamentary Elections Rules that the formal questions to voters or proxies be put by the presiding officer; but they are not permitted directly to put them themselves. They must be notified of, and abide by, the requirements of secrecy: r 31(a).

The rules on polling agents are the same in their application to all forms of elections (though in a referendum or parish or community poll, there are no candidates to appoint them even though personation is equally a possibility). For Senedd elections the provisions are contained in r 38 of sch 5 to the National Assembly for Wales (Representation of the People) Order 2007, SI No 236. They can also be appointed for parish and community council elections as for other kinds and have the same rights - see the Local Elections (Parishes and Communities) (England and Wales) Rules 2006, SI No 3305, sch 2, rr 27, 30(1)(d) and 33(1)(b), and in Wales r 33 of sch 1 to SI 2021 No 1460 (W. 375). The only exception to this general rule is to be found in the Local Authorities (Conduct of Referendums) (England) Regulations 2012 SI No 323 (see M in chapter 4). Paragraph 18(1) of the Local Government Act Referendums Rules, comprising sch 3 to these 2012 Regulations, allows – but does not require – the counting officer to appoint "polling observers" to perform for these referendums essentially the same functions as polling agents in other cases. The former DETR (now DLUHC) issued guidance suggesting that the counting officer might invite leading figures of the opposing campaigns to nominate such observers and suggest their attendance at particular stations, but the counting officer is under no obligations to do so. Rule 11, however, of the Regional Assembly and Local Government Referendum Rules (comprising sch 1 to SI 2004 No 1962) makes clear that only the counting officer's staff and Electoral Commission observers may be present at the issue of referendum ballot packs for those polls.

Whereas polling agents have a statutory, if incidental, role to play, tellers do not. They are entirely informal appointments, having no legal status, who are typically asked to stand outside polling stations asking voters for their electoral register numbers. Tellers are allowed in polling *places*, but in that capacity they have no right to enter actual polling *stations*. Tellers will often tend to encroach into polling station entrances if not discouraged, and they must be politely but firmly controlled. Many voters find them intrusive, and are unsympathetic to the general aim of trying to record who has been to vote. Tellers were the subject of Home Office Circular RPA 359 dated 3 December 1991, incorporating useful guidance for returning officers. It is a matter of some regret that political parties do not encourage their staff to take more notice of the current version of the guidance code, and seek to control "aggressive telling".

The Commission's guidance for tellers (there is also a brief summary of *Do's and Don'ts* for tellers) is not mandatory, but provides a useful review of the topic, and states (para 1.4) that "tellers play an important role in elections and referendums." It advises (para 1.7) that tellers may approach voters for information either as they enter or leave the station (traditionally, such approaches were only encouraged on exit, but this was widely ignored) and may – para 1.18 – also wear rosettes with candidates' party names, though not slogans (traditionally, words on rosettes were frowned upon by returning officers, including the present authors). Voters, however, "must never be asked to re-enter the polling station to ascertain their elector number or retrieve a poll card" (para 1.12). Originally the 1991 code did not receive a warm welcome from some returning officers or electoral administrators, but over the years it has come to be much more widely accepted. In para 1.21 the Commission emphasises the importance of local agreements – a useful subject to be addressed in the meetings with agents that returning officers are advised to hold (see (vi) in chapter 8). They also publish similar guidance in Welsh.

CHAPTER 17
PLANNING THE COUNT

An election count is a major public event in itself. It also has (and needs to have) something of the theatre about it. Other than for some by-elections, it may involve the possible presence of some hundreds of people. Counts still frequently take place at night, at the end of an already long and probably physically demanding day. Tension is often high, as are expectations: candidates, agents and supporters have a lot at stake, and so does the returning officer. The whole exercise is very public and visible: if it goes wrong there is likely to be at least serious embarrassment escalating, possibly, to very expensive High Court litigation in the more extreme situations.

So a checklist of things to consider may be helpful – particularly if you plan to use premises not previously used for counts:

(i) *The timing of the count.* More counts than not still take place at night, but it is demanding (particularly in these days of the Working Time Directive) to start a count at or shortly after 10pm following polling for fifteen hours. Separate counting staff can be used, but for you and certain key staff very long hours may be inevitable. At combined polls many of you will be back the next day after only a brief rest. In recent years problems with high volumes of postal votes arriving at the last minute, or with experimental voting arrangements, have increased the problems for returning officers in delivering a reliable and reasonably expeditious set of results from a 10pm start. Although declaring an accurate result is your paramount duty, the expectations of Ministers, local politicians and the like have continued to exert strong pressure to count from the close of poll rather than deferring to the following day, and in deciding what to do you are likely to have to weigh both the practical and the pragmatic.

The timing of the count became quite a *cause célèbre* in the run-up to the May 2010 general election. A number of acting returning officers took the view that the most practicable course was to conduct the count on the Friday morning after polling on the

Thursday. There were a number of crucial factors – time taken to get the ballot boxes in; availability of staff; processing ballots in a combined poll; checking postal votes; cross-border issues with Parliamentary constituents, etc. The clear majority, however, always maintained that they would start the count on Thursday evening. All this started quite a furore in the media, and with some sitting MPs as well as their constituency rivals. Much was made of the great tradition of the count on Thursday evening – "part of the fabric of the nation" – and former co-author David Monks was very unpopular when he pointed out on BBC Radio 4 that the count process was not there to provide entertainment for the media to broadcast!

Some MPs said it was essential to have the count conducted as soon as possible so that a new Government could be formed without delay. Any delay, they claimed, would cause problems in the money markets and further damage the UK economy. In the event it took several days after 6 May to form the Coalition Government, so the merits of this argument may in the event have been somewhat questionable.

Be that as it may, Parliament decided at very short notice to insert an amendment into the Constitutional Reform and Governance Bill requiring all returning officers to take steps to begin counting (not verifying) votes for UK Parliamentary elections within four hours of the close of poll. The Electoral Commission took the view that this was a further duty alongside the already existing duty to make arrangements for counting the votes 'as soon as practicable after the close of poll.' These new provisions only received Royal Assent on 8 April 2010, less than a month before polling day, becoming s 48 of the Act. Returning officers for constituencies where counting did not begin within the time limit were required to publish a statement setting out the steps taken and the time at which counting did begin – this had to be sent to the Electoral Commission within 30 days of the declaration of the result. In fact 45 constituencies (out of 650) did not start counting within the four-hour limit; 23 of these planned for a Friday start, and the others encountered a variety of problems (basically the factors listed above). For more details of all this see Electoral Commission's *Report on the administration of the 2010*

UK General Election, pp 18-20, and Appendix A which listed all the constituencies concerned.

(ii)   *Booking the venue.* Most election dates are predictable, and places big enough to hold   counts are often in short supply. Book the count venue as far ahead as you can. As with   polling stations (see chapter 7), you can requisition some kinds of premises. If the Government is paying, it will question using a private hall at a commercial rate if you could have used a council leisure centre at actual cost (see also chapter 24).

(iii)   *Is the venue suitable*? Think this through carefully, using squared paper or floor measurement if necessary. Is the main room big enough? Is it secure from outside view, which could compromise confidentiality? Can you cope with excited groups crowding round particular areas? Is there circulation space to check people in securely but quickly? Is access for the disabled at least adequate? Can you put the press and media somewhere? Does the building have adequate communications including a private direct telephone line you can use yourself? Can you yourself get into the middle, round the tables etc? Can you put people somewhere safe and under cover (and keep in contact with them) if you have to evacuate for a bomb threat, or the fire alarm goes off?

Then there are other organisational matters. Suppose that 90% of your polling station presiding officers arrive over a twenty-minute peak period. Can they get in by car quickly, park, deliver the ballot boxes, the ballot paper account, and all their 'clobber' quickly?

They're tired: they just want to go home. Can you count them in easily? Have you plenty of help to take their deliveries to the right places systematically? Will you pile all those plastic sacks in a big heap or in a proper order, so that when you have to look for some sack an hour later you can find it quickly? Is there enough space to handle and decide allegedly spoilt votes properly? Is there somewhere you personally can sit down (it's going to be a long night…)? Should you give your staff some refreshment facilities? – Yes, you should.

Some returning officers try to produce a flow chart to show the progress of ballot boxes through the process; checking in, storage pending emptying, being counted, stored when empty, eventual checking out and back to the depot (or wherever). This flow must not be impeded so you need to think carefully about, for example, whether or not to have a public gallery. Space usually dictates, but there are some people who enjoy the tension of the count and dress especially for the occasion. They should have separate points of entrance and exit in the hall, particularly if patronising the bar (see (vii) below).

(iv) *What media arrangements are necessary?* Press and public relations staff can be invaluable at this time, shielding you from needless distraction. Modern technology makes it less physically demanding than once it was, but it is still necessary to make sure that they are covering your event and not expecting it to be conducted for their benefit. At the same time, it is not sensible to be unhelpful or rigid in your approach: they have a job to do too, and this is a television (and social media) age. Responsible broadcasters are not trying to breach the obligations of secrecy: they just want to get the result out first and as fast as possible, and to interview the winner in particular afterwards.

In 'high profile' counts (such as the Prime Minister's constituency) particular effort needs to be made with the media (over 250 turned up at the Rt. Hon. John Major's constituency in Huntingdon in 1997 from all over the world with all their considerable paraphernalia), and it is worthwhile having early briefing meetings with them. Some requests can be unreasonable – eg, wanting to install hidden ceiling cameras "to observe body language" (allegedly) – and they should be resisted firmly but politely. You are in charge as returning officer with a significant task to achieve, and it is not entertainment for the masses whatever television producers might think. It may be reasonable to charge the media for their use of electricity, premises, etc., though to do so may cost more in goodwill than the income justifies. See also chapter 18 on handling the media and related issues concerned with organising the count.

(v) *What security arrangements are necessary?* Take police advice on the security alert situation for the count, and what cover you need in the event of public disorder. Tempers can fray very easily at the end of a long night, especially if people have been in the bar while you and your staff were completing the verification! Have someone at hand who knows the building's alarms and operating systems (and how to get at them) very well. Prepare a contingency plan in case you have to evacuate the building.

Similarly, with high profile counts expect considerable disruption during the week preceding polling day with Special Branch much in evidence searching drains, running names through computers, etc. At Huntingdon in 1997 (when then Prime Minister John Major was a candidate) there were armed police (some more obvious than others) and all ballot boxes coming into the hall were "sniffed" by police dogs. Clearly, all this takes time and needs to be integrated into your arrangements. For example, prior to the 2019 General Election, the National Cyber Security Centre ('NCSC', an organisation of the UK Government that provides advice and support for the public and private sector in how to avoid computer security threats) issued guidance – *Election Security: Notes for Guidance on cyber security issues.* Other guidance has also been issued by the National Counter Terrorism Security Office ('NaCTSO'). It is unfortunately a sign of our times that bespoke security advice has to be produced prior to each major election, and updated to reflect current threats at the time.

(vi) *Issuing admission tickets.* The various rules prescribe who is entitled by law to be present at a count see for example r 44(2) of the Parliamentary Elections Rules in sch 1 to the RPA 1983, and rs 38(2) of both the Local Elections (Principal Areas) and (Parishes and Communities) (England and Wales) Rules 2006, SI Nos 3304 and 3305 respectively (but note that the latter does not include election agents, as they are not provided for in the parish and community election process). The rest need your permission under r 44(3) in each case; everyone will need tickets. Ensure that agents know in advance how many they can have (see chapter 19), and what arrangements you will be making (probably at the last minute) to get them distributed via the agents or whatever. (Carry a few spares in your pocket just in case.)

Note that the former rules allowing candidates' spouses (and latterly civil partners) to attend the count are now replaced by para 85 of Part 5 of sch 1 to the Electoral Administration Act 2006, referring to "one other person chosen by each of them."

(vii) *Bar facilities*. There is no formal objection to there being bar facilities at a count venue, but of course they must be entirely separate from the spaces required for the count access and progress. It is a matter of personal judgement whether or not to have a bar, and practice varies considerably. Many returning officers feel it is not a necessary part of the process, and often the political parties retire to other premises after the count has finished.

Take note of local practice and expectations and the practicalities. In a rural or inner city area, getting counting staff for late night work may be particularly hard. On the other hand, deferring counting to the following day (with the attendant problems of overnight ballot box security) may make many would-be counting staff unavailable. As already stated, agents and candidates generally press for a night count and this is still regarded as the usual practice in the United Kingdom. Some constituencies – eg in Western Scotland, with islands – count the next day as a matter of course because of the time it takes for all the boxes to be brought into a central point. What matters ultimately is not a quick result but a well-ordered and correct result. Stated again, that is your over-riding duty, regardless of pressures from candidates or media, and even from the duty imposed by s 48 of the Constitutional Reform and Governance Act 2010. Furthermore, the decision is one for you to make personally, not for your employing authority.

At the busiest elections it may help and is common practice if a trusted colleague (often one of your deputy returning officers) takes a particular lead for you on count planning and logistics. There is too much to do to leave matters to the last minute.

As to actually conducting the count, see chapter 20.

CHAPTER 18
HANDLING THE MEDIA

Elections are about public choices, so media interest is not only to be expected, it is clearly vital if electors are to be aware of opportunities to vote, how and when to do so, and what the issues and manifestos are. Significant media interest will probably be welcome in the elections office at most times of the year, helpful as it is likely to be in increasing registration and general public awareness without which there cannot be voting anyway.

The period of an actual election, however, can be very different. The timetable is unforgiving. Responding to queries seems to add little, particularly when all the information to be published is prescribed in the process rules and you feel that you have no spare time to be doing anything needless. It follows that doing what you can to anticipate media requests, and to have available the answers to obvious questions even before they are asked, will stand you in good stead. Researchers and reporters are busy too at these times: their deadlines are different in kind from yours, but no less demanding personally in many cases for those who have stories to file in today's 24-hour, instant contact and coverage world. The tone that you set will stand you in good stead if you respect the role they are there to perform; antagonise, and the moment something goes wrong it is likely to result in damaging and even personally spiteful publicity. In that respect handling the media is similar to working with agents as described in chapter 11. A respectful, professional relationship should be expected from both sides, though in the last resort your role as the returning officer means that if you cannot achieve agreement on some matter, you have to make, answer for and be prepared to stand by your decision.

In nearly every council, at least some public relations capacity will be available. It is only sensible to include such staff in your planning, and – most importantly – in your briefings so that they know what is happening, what to expect, and how to answer or fend off many detailed questions which would otherwise be directed to you. Media interest tends to divide into three broad categories.

The first is about general day-to-day news and 'continuity' matters, about election dates, who is standing, where and when the count will be, and so on. The second is much more specific and demanding, centring on polling day itself and in particular media presence at the count. Both these two are obviously legitimate. The third is legitimate too, but in a different way, and in one with which at the time you are likely be less comfortable or accepting. It involves the sort of item which may be seen as newsworthy in the sensational, 'scoop' or human interest sense. If the reporter sees evidence that the postal votes may go out late, or that you are hastily reprinting following an embarrassing misprint, or that the polling station is surrounded by roadworks, that is likely to be followed up. Your tact and diplomacy, and that of your public relations staff, will obviously be crucial here in how you are portrayed. At the same time, the media are also experienced in dealing with people who want to use (or abuse) them to engineer publicity for themselves.

Organising a large count often involves compromises about floor-space and personal convenience. Your first priority is to deliver an accurate result in accordance with the rules, so that it is seen to be fair and accepted as such. That priority must apply alongside other considerations, such as the safety and security of everyone present; the confidentiality of the votes cast; a reasonably efficient and timely progressing towards the outcome of the declaration; proportionate use of resources to do what has to be done; and reasonable facilities for those who have a right to be present or whom you have admitted for other working purposes like security, working the building's systems, and so on. Media representatives will form part of this 'other' category. They will need to be able to do their job effectively, but to do so *within the confines of the rules about secrecy and your paramount duty to conduct the count properly.* There are there to report on events, not to play a direct part in them.

Technology, and the prevalence of social media like Facebook, Instagram and Twitter, has brought benefits to the election count as well as some problems. The latter mainly involve mobile telephones and cameras so small as to be unseen in a crowd, and potentially (if somewhat improbably) capable of transmitting secret information outside the count room. The benefits, however, also lie in the same attributes: television equipment in particular used to be bulky, to involve inordinate cabling, and above all to require high-intensity lighting which made the count room very hot. Today's equipment is more easily deployed and moved, while flat screens and computer graphics make it far easier to put up the results in a manner which can be copied and assimilated by those who want to know. The temptation for those insensitive to the formal demands of the declaration of secrecy is to behave as they normally do with today's technology, contacting friends and commenting on events around them as they happen, without regard to any legal restrictions.

Local media, whom usually you know and who will still be around locally long after the election is over, tend in the authors' experience to adopt a rather different approach from their national counterparts. For a start, the locals are on home territory: they have been there before; they recognise most of the local politicians; and they are part of a pattern of long-term local working and informal relationships which, within reason, they want to maintain. It is rather different when local events temporarily attract national publicity. The occasion is much more likely to be seen from London or a regional centre as a 'one-off' with few inhibitions about treading on local toes. They will be gone tomorrow, and achieving what they want today, now, is all. Their tendency to choose supposedly marginal or high-profile counts, for instance, and then expect the event to be significantly organised around them must be resisted. Sensible give-and-take is one thing; giving a five-minute warning of declaration and a microphone check is obvious; but allowing cameras onto the floor of the count or permitting distracting interviewing near people who are trying to concentrate on counting pencil crosses late at night in artificial light, is (depending on your building) probably not. If you can provide a room, and/or some dedicated interview space or work tables, so much the better – and even minimal facilities like water, tea and coffee will be well received during a long count.

If you have high-profile candidate at your count, the media demands may well exceed anything you thought plausible. David Monks was the acting returning officer where Prime Minister John Major was standing in the 1990s at a time of changing political mood and high security risk. Roger Morris remembers Anthony Crosland standing at Grimsby in the 1970s (another candidate served a writ on him during one declaration), and the frenzied by-election there in 1977 after Crosland's death while Foreign Secretary, when press ticket requests for the count included newspapers from Egypt and Israel, and *The Christian Science Monitor*. Mark Heath in his role as regional returning officer returned Nigel Farage as an MEP in 1999 and thereafter. With the advent of the Brexit Party and all that followed, the media interest at the European Election count and declaration for the South East Region of the UK held in Southampton at its peak comprised over eighty different bodies and groups. The additional pressure of high-profile occasions can be very considerable, a distraction from the closing stages of the election process itself and, importantly, a reason for spending more resources than normal.

Despite wanting to be forewarned and to plan ahead as much as possible, however, you should guard against regarding the media somehow as another problem to be resolved. Media handling is, to be sure, an important consideration and proportionate resources need to be made available in that context just as they do for every other aspect of the election process. The other side of being reported as running a disorganised process is to be reported in a good light, or in the process context hardly reported at all, but that will have to be earned. Mainly it will of course be earned by actually running a 'good election' – but in some measure it will earned by winning a reputation at the editor's desk for knowing what is wanted, being readily available at key times, and helping the media to produce their own professional output in the public interest.

With that in mind, the authors invited Ian MacKellar, a reporter with the *Hunts Post*, to contribute a media perspective on what they want and look for when covering elections. We gratefully acknowledge his willingness to give below his personal outlook, reprinted here from *Running Elections 2013*:

"Which media?

It is easy to forget that there may be more media interested in your elections than care about your routine activities. As well as the regional daily and weekly newspapers that cover the area, regional broadcasters will want to cover at least some of your elections, particularly general elections, and in some cases you will need to make provision for national media.

The level of interest will depend on what hangs on the outcome – could a national Cabinet member lose a seat? Could political control of an authority change hands? Is there a high profile candidate with a realistic chance (Martin Bell, Tatton and 2004 Euros) or a serious single-issue candidate (Richard Taylor, Wyre Forest)? Such issues change the way you need to plan for elections to generate the best electoral outcome. People are more likely to turn out when they think, rightly or wrongly, that their vote has a greater chance than usual of influencing the outcome.

When do you need to help the media?

The two peaks of interest – first, closing of nominations and then election day, including the count and declaration – generate completely different requirements. There could also be interest afterwards, if something has gone wrong – allegations of electoral irregularity in the polling process or expenses, for example, but those have to be dealt with *ad hoc*.

The level of interest in nominations often depends on the election itself – general elections and other national Parliamentary/Assembly polls naturally generate more interest than county/London borough, district, Euro and parish, in that order – and whether or not the journalist covering the process or his or her editor or news editor is interested.

Close of nominations

Tell the media in advance how you are going to notify them of the list of candidates. It is not enough to say that the list will be on your website. It is an opportunity for returning officers to be proactive and perhaps to spark an interest that is not naturally there.

You could, for example, produce a factual briefing document that, as well as the candidates' list, includes information about the current political make-up of the authority and how that would change if each of the parties won all the seats they were contesting, in polls where only one-third of the seats are up for grabs. It could include sitting members who were offering themselves for re-election and those who were not, and the authority's history of political control. Since such history need go back no further than 1974 [the year of local government reorganisation under the Act of 1972], that should not be too onerous. It will also be necessary to list any putative nominations that have been declared invalid and explain why.

Such an approach brings out the amateur psephologist in journalists. They are almost certain to get their analysis round their necks, but it makes an interesting read or broadcast item and might engage the interest of voters who had not otherwise been intending to cast their ballots. It is also sensible to notify the media of withdrawals, which might spark further interest. Once that date is passed, you can sit back until polling day and leave it to the candidates and their agents to feed the media.

The lead up to polling day

Tell the media in good time what arrangements you are proposing to meet their needs, and be responsive to any reasonable suggestions for modifying them. You will need to spell out the rules each time – there are always new journalists, and memories are short. Explain what the arrangements are for polling and for the count. Provide numbers – how many polling stations, staff involved, electorates, distances from the counting station and so on. The media operate 24 hours a day and need something to fill the time before declarations – even weeklies have 24/7 websites that can help make the process feel important to electors.

Polling day

The media may wish to photograph people queuing to vote, arriving at or leaving polling stations. They may wish to film or photograph high-profile candidates, particularly MPs seeking re-election. Try to make those arrangements in advance and ensure presiding officers are aware and co-operative. The hacks will soon be gone.

The count

Within the guidelines for confidentiality be as flexible as you can at the count – it will have been as long a day for them as for you and your staff. Use the public address system (make sure it works properly in advance) to explain the process for the benefit of them and any members of the public who may have taken an interest. When you examine spoiled ballots, take time to explain publicly the difference between a valid ballot and one that is disqualified. When you call the candidates and agents together in advance of a declaration, explain why that is necessary. Even if there is no reason for a re-count, it does no harm to explain that the process is available and how it would work. It all helps to engage the public interest and make people feel they are witnessing an important component of the democratic process.

The declaration

The declaration should be clear, and those making it should know how to use the public address system so that the results are clearly audible. Journalists will be writing them down and will need to do so accurately, so they should not be rushed. It helps also to provide the majorities and turnouts, even though returning officers are not obliged to do so at that stage.

If the declaration is for an election that is regarded by broadcast media as important, consider engaging a professional sound and lighting company, and tell broadcasters that there will be a clean sound-feed and that the event will be professionally lit. This makes life easier for both broadcasters and returning officers, particularly by removing a plethora of microphones and the intense heat of far more lighting than necessary. But bear in mind that print journalists should not have to take second place to broadcasters – their needs are different by equally urgent. If necessary, provide a separate room or area for post-declaration interviews with the candidates. The need to exclude extraneous microphones and lights is even more important here, because all that needs to be set up is cameras, so interviews can be completed in a fraction of the time. Such facilities will be part of the editorial decision-making process about which declarations to cover, particularly during a general election.

After the declaration

Make sure results are posted on an advertised web-site as soon as they are declared, so that journalists tasked with covering more than one count simultaneously can do so seamlessly."

CHAPTER 19
ON POLLING DAY

With all elections, and almost all polls (except parish and community polls), now running from 7am to 10pm, polling day is long. Section 29 of the Commissioners Clauses Act 1847 had a provision that the presiding officer "may close the voting or poll at any time…if one hour have elapsed during which no voting papers have been tendered", but there is no such opportunity today.

Polling station staff should have a direct telephone line number on which to contact your election office. Almost inevitably there will be the usual crop of oversleeping caretakers or staff, locked gates, "no shows", no heating or power, no ballot paper account or whatever. As to who may lawfully be present in a polling station, see the list in chapter 7. For Parliamentary elections, the Electoral Commission publishes a *Handbook for polling station staff*, and there are equivalent publications, regularly updated, for other kinds of elections. There are also many other handbooks and publications supporting the running of various kinds of elections and polling, available via the Commission's website.

How you respond to problems quickly depends on the nature of the problem and the area. Mobile telephones help a lot today – so does carrying a few useful supplies of spares around in the car. Some heavy-duty gaffer tape will prove invaluable if it's wet and windy and some of the posters won't stay up.

Do not underestimate the value or impact of the returning officer personally visiting a polling station to deal with a query or problem, whether raised by election staff or an agent. It is a matter of judgement, but sometimes the most trivial of issues may matter disproportionately to a candidate or agent. If the returning officer has personally been to that polling station, and reviewed the issue, it is much easier to reply – and to close any further debate or discussion down. It also gives the staff serving at that station support and encouragement to know that you, the returning officer, are personally and directly engaged on the issues of the day. Valuable too, of course, are incidental visits, occasioned less by any immediate problem than your desire to support the staff and get the 'feel' of the day around the area being polled.

You will also arrange for others to help you conduct polling station inspections, thereby providing a good level of coverage across all your stations with, we suggest, spare capacity at crucial or higher risk times. Other methods of keeping in touch with your polling stations can be useful: for example SMS or other text mass messaging services can provide an effective way for the returning officer and their election office staff to get a message "out" to all polling station staff instantly. Such systems often are already in place in councils, used by emergency planning (for example). So it is worthwhile finding out what, if any, such systems can be re-purposed for use during elections.

During the day, pacing yourself and your key helpers is vital. The hot meal, the shower, the few minutes of fresh air – whatever works best for you will prove invaluable late at night when you've been up for eighteen hours and still need to work calmly and effectively with your usual sense of judgement.

Even if you have organised several 'openings' beforehand, still allow adequate time to open the postal votes (allowing the rights of inspection, of course). Check the Town Hall letterbox at 10.01pm in case a vote has been hand-delivered at the last minute. It is now possible to return postal votes to any polling station though, in logic, this seems to defeat the original purpose – see RPR 2001, r 79. We suggest you drink no alcohol whatsoever that day, so that no allegations of, or opportunities for, mischief can arise. Wear sober clothing too, and avoid obvious colours that could be alleged to be tacit signals of party support.

It is a good idea to visit a few polling stations yourself as soon as polling opens, particularly including any problem cases. It gives you a feel for the day, and when someone rings up to complain about what's happening at St Joseph's Community Centre or wherever, it's helpful to be able to say that you've been out and about a bit – even if not to that particular location. Most returning officers appoint a number of experienced staff (probably your deputies) to tour round and 'inspect' an allocated number of stations during the day – this is particularly helpful in the larger rural districts. It is recognised DLUHC practice to meet the reasonable costs of polling station inspectors for Parliamentary elections.

Good communications are vital on polling day – if a problem arises time is short and people want to speak to you quickly. Similarly you have little time to respond. Self-evidently all these impressions will contribute much to an overall opinion about whether the whole process is well under control. At the same time lots of issues which seem big and noisy on polling day fade in the calmer climate of the morrow, and are not pursued.

Note that if an alteration is made to an electoral register which takes effect on the day of the poll, the presiding officer must keep a list of voters to whom ballot papers are given in consequence of that change: see r 41 of the Local Elections (Principal Areas) (England and Wales) Rules 2006, SI No 3304 – as they were originally – and r 49 of sch 1 to the now equivalent Local Elections (Communities) (Wales) Rules 2021, SI No 1460 (W. 375).

While you will hope that no presiding officer needs to issue any tendered ballot papers (always coloured, and usually pink in Parliamentary polls), it is helpful to have in mind the four situations (set out here with reference to local elections) in which they may now occur:

1. Where the lists of those having already voted include the person claiming to vote. SI 2006 No. 3304, schedule 2, r 38(1).

2. Where the person is listed as a postal voter but claims not to have applied for a postal vote. (If the person accepts that they did apply for a postal vote, they cannot vote in person, and a tendered ballot paper must not be issued, unless 4. below applies.) Rule 38(2).

3. Where the person is listed as a proxy voter, but claims not to have applied for a proxy vote. (If the person accepts that they did appoint a proxy, they cannot vote in person and a tendered ballot paper must not be issued.) Rule 38(3).

4. Where between 5pm and 10pm on polling day the person is *either* an elector both named on the register and who is on the postal voters list, *or* is someone both named as a proxy and who is on the proxy postal voters list, *and in either case* claims that the postal ballot paper has been lost or has not been received. Rule 38(5).

Tendered ballot paper rules also apply to voters with anonymous entries on the electoral register, who are entitled to answer the official questions to voters in the same way for a tendered vote as they are for an ordinary vote.

There are now six circumstances where tendered votes may be issued at community council elections in Wales, set out in r 46 of sch 1 to SI 2021 No 1460 (W. 375). These are, however, essentially the same as the four situations given above, though more fully set out. Rule 47 prescribes the returning officer's duties accordingly.

It is possible that a poll in progress may have to be abandoned because of the death of a candidate. Section 24 of the Electoral Administration Act 2006 inserted r 65 into the Parliamentary Elections Rules (sch 1 to the RPA 1983): see also on this subject chapter 12. There are other rules for combined or local polls (see for instance r 55 of sch 2 to the Local Elections (Principal Areas) (England and Wales) Rules 2006, SI No 3304, the equivalent r 55 in the Local Elections (Parishes and Communities) (England and Wales) Rules 2006, SI No 3305) as originally made, and in Wales r 71 in sch 1 to SI 2021 No 1460 (W. 375). It would be useful to have prepared instructions ready to distribute in the event of a death: thankfully this seldom occurs, but if it does happen the process is likely to be unfamiliar, and additional and distressing confusion may result. The rules and requirements differ from those applicable if a poll has to be adjourned or abandoned for reasons of riot.

It was formerly the law that only voters who had been *issued* with a ballot paper before 10pm could vote, and that even if there were a queue inside the actual polling station no further ballot papers could be issued after that exact time: see the Islington West Division Case, *Medhurst v Lough and Gasquet* (1901) 17 TLR 210.

On 6 May 2010 there were some very high profile media reports of queues forming at polling stations, and of some people being turned away at 10pm without being able to vote. These problems were not extensive (but still very serious) occurring, according to the Electoral Commission, at 27 polling stations across 16 constituencies. The Electoral Commission estimated that probably in excess of 1,200 people appeared to have been affected, and speedily produced a special report on these issues, published on 20 May 2010. The problems occurred mainly in some wards of the larger cities – Birmingham, Sheffield, Liverpool, and some London Boroughs, etc.

More than three centuries earlier, in *Ashby v White* (1703) 2 Ld. Raym. 938, Holt CJ, in a judgement later upheld by the House of Lords, decided that the plaintiff had a property in his right to vote, that to deprive him of it was a great injury, and that he had an action to enforce his right. While the context has changed, it is well to note the importance that the law has always attached to the ability to exercise a right to vote. That right was underlined by s 19 of the Electoral Registration and Administration Act 2013, which inserted r 37(7) into the 1983 Parliamentary Elections Rules, providing that an elector who, at the close of the poll is either in the polling station or in a queue outside it "for the purpose of voting" may still proceed to vote despite the closure.

At the close of polling, in addition to whatever seal(s) the presiding officer attaches, polling agents may affix their own seals if they wish: see r 43(1) of the Parliamentary Elections Rules (sch 1 to the RPA 1983). There are equivalent provisions for other elections: see for instance r 43(1) of sch 2 to both the Local Elections (Principal Areas) (England and Wales) Rules 2006, SI No 3304 and their parish and community elections equivalents, SIs 2006 No 3305 and 2021 No 1460 (W. 375). In practice 'seals' today are often tough plastic locking strips.

The stories of what returning officers find at polling stations are now the stuff of legend and memoirs… staff who are either missing or sunbathing…aerobic classes taking place in the school hall with the polling table being pushed to one side…the polling station staff openly watching *Eastenders* on television, and ignoring waiting voters… They are all part of being a returning officer!

CHAPTER 20
CONDUCTING THE COUNT

Plainly the thoroughness and outcome of your planning (see chapter 17) will predicate the conduct of the count itself. The factors that need to be thought about in forward planning need not be repeated here.

The big counts – particularly on general election night – are part of the traditional British election scene, and often seem as much pieces of theatre as repetitive, old-fashioned counting. However much we now talk about consulting the public and sending them our well-honed community strategies, here with the aid of radio, television, social media and the internet we can witness for ourselves the verdicts of the people of Blyth, Birmingham and Bognor on the government of the day: a win here, a lost deposit or someone dressed as a chicken there. Being part of this sort of atmosphere helps attract the numbers of staff you need, and provides a surge of adrenalin to offset the fatigue of a long day. But it also holds the dangers of being so visibly on public show in your directing and management of events, when tensions are high and tired people with much at stake behave and react differently from the individuals you normally know.

Section 48 of the Constitutional Reform and Governance Act 2010 required general election counts ordinarily to begin with four hours of the close of poll (see chapter 17 and below). (This may be contrasted with the requirement for the 1945 general election when, after polling on 5 July, counting was delayed for three weeks till 26 July to allow for the collection and counting of the overseas forces' votes!)

Do bear in mind, however, how critical it is to have an accurate verification figure. Knowing with certainty the number of issued ballot papers you have for a constituency or ward can pay great dividends when it comes to tallying back after you have sorted the votes into candidates/parties and doubtful ballot papers. At that point, if you have a close count, the accuracy of the verification regardless of the provisional majority can secure an acceptance of the result. With that in mind, you may need to take a view as to compliance with section 48 as against taking extra time to get the verification figure as accurate as you need it to be. Bear in mind that the consequence of non-compliance with section 48 is a requirement to tell the Electoral Commission why you took longer than four hours. Balanced against delivering an accurate result and thereby implementing the will of the electorate, for many that is a no-brainer which takes precedence.

Try to get counting staff in place in good time, keeping a reserve or two in case of need. Consider if you also need a 'runner' – a helper with no other duties who can respond immediately to some need arising which would distract you or your regular staff.

Smartphones and similar devices can be a nuisance at counts – they can be carried, but returning officers should insist that they be switched off (and not merely switched to 'silent'), and should be firm with anyone seen using one in the room(s) where the actual counting is taking place. The potential for a breach, or a perceived breach, of the secrecy requirement is obvious. The RPA 1983, setting out the requirement for the declaration of secrecy, was amended by para 14 of Part 2 of sch 10 to the Parliamentary Voting System and Constituencies Act 2011.

Keep an eye on the layout you planned (see chapter 17). It's easy for a ballot box to be accidentally put on the wrong pile unopened if your handling process doesn't try to make that unlikely. Getting this count right is an acutely personal responsibility, but you have also to be dependent on others. Brief them well; guard against obvious mistakes; but then show trust and confidence in them too.

How many counting assistants can you employ? Naturally this depends on how large the counting task to be done, your view on the probability of a very high or low turnout, and so on. You will also need an additional number of counting supervisors and overall help at the centre where you and others will be directing operations, checking ballot papers accounts and matching them with verified totals from the individual ballot boxes, and later deciding on allegedly spoilt votes, and so on. If the election costs are to be recharged or recovered from elsewhere, particularly from the DLUHC's Elections Unit, the costs of conducting the count will have to be contained within the headings allowed (see chapter 22).

The number of counting assistants, ie actual counters at the tables, not including the supervisory or central staff, determines by law the minimum number of counting agents you must allow the candidates to have present. Counting agents are also loosely called "scrutineers".

Rule 30(2) of the Parliamentary Elections Rules, sch 1 to the RPA 1983, provides that the returning officer must afford each candidate the same number of counting agents, and that that number "shall not (except in special circumstances) be less than the number obtained by dividing the number of clerks employed on the counting by the number of candidates." Similar provisions apply for the Senedd elections: see r 38 of sch 5 to the National Assembly for Wales (Representation of the People) Order 2007, SI No 236 (as amended by art 18(3) of SI 2016 No 272).

If there are several candidates, and some with few supporters compared with the candidates of nationally known political parties, such candidates may not need or be able to take up their quota of places. What is required is equality of opportunity, not of outcome, so once the deadline for appointing counting agents has passed (not later than the second election timetable day before the poll – see r 30(3)), any untaken allocation of places can be offered even-handedly to other candidates (most mainstream parties, however, usually take their full allocation). This is done under the returning officer's general discretion in the last words of r 44(1), as technically it is then too late for original regular appointments (although appointment has to be simply "before the commencement of the poll" (r 30(1)). Written notice of appointments has been given earlier under r 30(3).

For mayoral referendums, para 18(2) of the Local Government Act Referendums Rules (ie sch 3 to the Local Authorities (Conduct of Referendums) (England) Regulations 2012, SI No 323) requires (unlike the permissive provision of para 18(1) for polling observers referred to in chapter 16) that the counting officer appoint people as "counting observers" at the count. This is because the usual election scrutineers will obviously not be there. If the referendum is the result of petition, its organisers may nominate counting observers in writing to the counting officer no later than the fifth day before polling day. The counting officer retains the usual powers to restrict numbers etc., and must use his or her discretion to meet the compulsory requirement of reg 13(1). The phrase used for regional and local referendums is "counting agents", however – see r 23 of the Regional Assembly and Local Government Referendum Rules comprising sch 1 to SI 2004 No 1962, and also r 18(1)(b) of the Referendum Rules comprising Part I of sch 2 to the Parliamentary Voting System and Constituencies Act 2011.

Once you have a provisional result, you should consult the election agents (privately and together) on the figures. In practice candidates are often present too, but your formal dealings are with the agents they have appointed. The agents should have a chance to check the figures, and express a view whether they accept the outcome from an arithmetical or formal standpoint.

Checking that the figures add up will be easier if they already know the turnout percentage. There is no objection to giving this out within the count room (ie publicly to those present, but not broadcast outside the count). At that stage it can compromise neither the eventual outcome nor the personal secrecy of the poll.

What about re-counts? This is in the returning officer's sole discretion, but agents need to understand your decision and reasoning. On the basis that you will choose to undertake recounts until you have a robust result in which you have confidence – and then and only then will you offer a provisional result to the candidates and agents – bear in mind that any request for a recount must be reasonable, ie have genuine reason underpinning the request. A request such as "It is close; I want a recount" will not pass the legislative test. The response to a request depends on the circumstances. Totals need not be exactly the same if differences are minor and wholly inconsequential. It is not appropriate to recount to ascertain whether or not a deposit is lost if the main outcome is clear beyond doubt. But there's also a tactical – and tactful – issue here, and which returning officers will need to take into account. A result should not be finally declared without a warning to the agents, even if one of them is still disputing it.

An alternative to a re-count which may be of tactical value is a "bundle check" where the papers are quickly re-examined stacked in their trays etc. for each candidate. Election agents will sometimes accept this as an alternative to a time-consuming full recount: the decision, however, is yours as returning officer.

Doubtful votes should be put to one side for the returning/counting officer (or appointed deputies) to adjudicate on them. Some papers can require very difficult, marginal decisions. For a modern case at Burnley on counting ballot papers, and giving effect to the three kinds of marks mentioned in r 47(3) of the Conduct Rules comprising sch 3 to SI 2006 No 3304, see *Pilling v Reynolds* [2008] All E R (D) 54; [2008] EWHC 316. The Electoral Commission also publishes guidance on doubtful papers for different kinds of elections and polls. We recommend that such guidance is treated as authoritative, and is followed.

Be prepared also for a tied vote, especially in local elections where the numbers of votes cast are smaller. In the Ballot Act 1872, s 2, returning officers were disbarred from voting at county and borough elections but, ironically in the legislation which introduced the secret ballot, could give an additional vote if it would thereby entitle any otherwise tied candidate to be declared elected! Today the requirement is not to give an invidious casting vote but to preside over the drawing of lots by the tied candidates. Coins, dice, slips of paper etc. are all acceptable, but at such a tense moment it is important that the process is seen as even-handed and fair. Years ago in Northampton, the predecessor of one of the present authors used a cardboard pepperpot; 'the pepperpot election' duly passed into local legend. Make sure that you draw lots in a clearly fair and transparent way, with (if possible) witnesses of standing present, and that you record what you did and the outcome. It is not, however, necessary to have the tied candidates present when you draw lots – you have to do this "forthwith" – but it is obviously desirable that they should be present and fully briefed about what you intend to do if possible.

It may occur, particularly with parish and community council elections, that not both or all of the candidates involved in a tied vote are present. The returning officer must decide between them "forthwith" by lot (r 49 of both sch 2 and sch 3 in each case to SIs 2006 Nos 3304 and 3305, and for community elections in Wales r 62(2) of sch 1 to SI 2021 No 1460 (w. 375)), so must proceed without undue delay. In such a case it is important to ensure that those present see what is happening, so that the drawing of the lots is witnessed and the outcome clear. Then the result can be declared in the usual way. There is no requirement in any election for any candidate or agent, or indeed counting agent, to be present as the count progresses or the result is declared; the law merely prescribes the right to be present.

The actual declaration should be conducted openly visibly and audibly: sometimes candidates wish to gather behind the declarer, or television producers want a nod before you start. All of this is down to common sense, and recognition that this is an event of considerable public interest, the image of which you want to foster, not worsen. See also chapter 18 on handling the media.

It is not necessary to say "I the undersigned" in the ponderous way of municipal legend. Read the result in a sensible but objective way – and consider giving a returning officer in a Parliamentary election (ie a high sheriff or a mayor, distinguished from the *acting* returning officer) a prepared text to read so that they do not have to wrestle with a stylised formal- public-notice kind of declaration. It is now common, but is not obligatory, to add each candidate's party description after announcing their name. Speeches from candidates generally follow and it must be fairly said that, virtually as a matter of course, they all remember to thank the returning officer and staff for their hard work. Again, as to length of speeches, order, etc. much of this is down to common sense, with the victor always speaking first.

In list elections there may be a large number of candidates, and it is simply impossible for them all to speak. If you can, it is best to come to an understanding with agents well prior to the actual declaration.

Counting staff should not be released until you are sure you are ready to declare. Apart from reasonable time for refreshments, the count has to be continuous, but r 45(6) of the Parliamentary Elections Rules does give authority to agree with the agents that the hours between 7pm and the following 9am can be excluded (this remains unaltered despite the requirement in s 48 of the Constitutional Reform and Governance Act 2010 that Parliamentary counts ordinarily begin within four hours of the polls closing, and "for the purposes of this exception the agreement of a candidate or his election agent shall be as effective as the agreement of his counting agents"). There are similar rules for other kinds of count, eg rr 45(8) in each case of sch 2 to SIs 2006 Nos 3304 and 3305 for local and parish elections, and rr 45(12) and (11) respectively in sch 3 (combined elections). For Wales community council elections see r 55(4) to SI 2021 No 1460 (W.375). Sometimes sheer fatigue on everyone's part forces a pause after three recounts or whatever: securing the count room in a sealed state at this point is vital so that events can resume later without allegations of impropriety having occurred while the candidates and counting agents were absent.

Earlier in this chapter we have referred to the Parliamentary Elections Rules, but there are equivalents elsewhere for other kinds of elections: see for instance for the appointment of polling and counting agents rules 27(4) in each case of both sch 2 and sch 3 to the Local Elections (Principal Areas) (England and Wales) Rules 2006, SI No 3304; the Local Elections (Parishes and Communities) (England and Wales) Rules 2006, SI No 3305; and for Wales community councils r 33 of sch 1 to SI 2021 No 1460 (W. 375). Mayor of London and London Assembly elections are deemed local elections, but with some modifications not relevant here: see s 17 of, and sch 3 to, the Greater London Authority Act 1999. See also on the Senedd s 13 of the Government of Wales Act 2006; both paras 9 of Part 2, and para 32 of Part 3, of sch 4; and r 38(2)-(12) of sch 5, to the National Assembly for Wales (Representation of the People) Order 2007, SI No 236 (as variously amended).

At a local election for which you are the proper officer to accept the declaration of acceptance of office (see s 83(1) of the Local Government Act 1972), it is helpful to have the declaration forms or book written up as far as possible beforehand so that you can insert the required full names and signatures. Doing that will save chasing people later, though many still follow this practice. It will also reduce the problems of queuing when the bulk of the individual results are declared over a short space of time. In England the Local Elections (Declaration of Acceptance of Office) Order 2012, SI No 1465 prescribes the form to be used. The Welsh equivalent is SI 2004 No 1508. For the Mayor of London and the Greater London Authority see SI 2002 No 1044, revoking SI 2000 No 308.

At elections for which deposits are required, be ready to return deposits which have not been forfeited – or else do it the following day, which is what the law requires (see r 53 of the Parliamentary Elections Rules, sch 1 to the RPA 1983). As to the return or forfeiture of deposits in mayoral elections, see r 49 of the Mayoral Elections Rules (sch 1 to SI 2002 No 185), and for the Mayor of London, r 51 of the Mayoral Election Rules (sch 3 to SI 2000 No 427, as amended). (Note the different but confusingly similar titles of these Rules.)

Note the provisions of what are now rr 60-65 of the Parliamentary Elections Rules (added by s 24 of the Electoral Administration Act 2006) about polls abandoned where a candidate dies, referred to in chapter 12. In the case of r 61(4) the returning officer will not return the writ at that time, but retain it pending the outcome of a re-run election.

At general Parliamentary elections it is your responsibility to return the writ as acting returning officer, unless the returning officer elects to do so (see section B, chapter 4). The writ must be endorsed with the successful candidate's full name and title (such as Rt Hon), as the Clerk of the Crown (who receives the writ) takes this exactly for entry into the register at the Crown Office. The details given in the nomination papers will not necessarily suffice (where forenames, for instance, may be abbreviated) so it is, again, worthwhile checking with the actual victor or their agent. The returning officer must sign the writ personally and it is worthwhile taking a photocopy before dispatch. There is a special envelope provided for it, which will be collected and should reach the Clerk of the Crown before midnight on the Sunday following the election (the Royal Mail will collect this from the returning officer personally – it does not go through the ordinary post – and one of their authorised personnel may attend towards the end of the count, or the following morning). Finally with regard to the return of the writ, you are usually instructed to write your home/mobile/holiday telephone number by your name in case the Clerk's office wants to speak to you urgently, presumably because they cannot read your writing – so make it legible!

So how long should all this take? Why do some counts take just over an hour and some seven hours or even longer? Clearly, the time taken to gather in all the ballot boxes varies between compact city areas and large rural constituencies. Without doubt, however, there are certain constituencies where substantial short-cuts are taken with established procedure in an effort to be the first result declared. Such short-cuts could never be recommended in any text dealing with running elections and, as we pointed out at the end of chapter 17, an accurate result is the aim, not a mistaken outcome however rapidly achieved. Indeed, it is well worth taking another twenty minutes or so checking the figures, even at 4.30 or 5am, to complete the task properly rather than face the prospect of an election petition. There are enough pitfalls in the count process without needlessly adding a time problem; moreover, civic pride and kudos in declaring the first result on live television will soon dissipate in the recriminations of petition litigation.

CHAPTER 21
WHEN THE ELECTION IS OVER

Once the election is over there is much mopping up to do, despite the probable feeling of fatigue and anti-climax that follows a period of intense activity or tension.

A priority is the payment of all election staff, together with their expenses. The HMRC RTI ('Real Time Information') requirements have also to be addressed, as do any pension consequences for staff who opt into the scheme the returning officer must provide. So too is getting in, and then paying, the invoices for room and equipment hire, and so on. The results have to be posted on-line and physically. Information is often needed by Government or the Electoral Commission; the media may have follow-up queries, and earlier posters – such as notices of election and notices of poll – have to be taken down.

If deposits are involved and have not been forfeited, they must be returned as soon as practicable after the counting is completed. Ordinarily return by "not later than the next day" is required – see r 53 of the Parliamentary Elections Rules, sch 1 to the RPA 1983. Candidates/agents should take your cheque, though some returning officers retain banker's drafts *in situ* in their safes and return these; this avoids a fee from the bank. Online payments are of course increasingly prevalent now. Forfeited deposits should be forwarded within fourteen days to the DLUHC's Elections Unit – again, they will accept acting returning officer cheques.

It is a good idea to remind agents of the date by which they need to file returns of candidates' expenses with you. Councillors also need to be reminded of the rules about donations to them contained in s 7 of, and sch 7 to, the Political Parties, Elections and Referendums Act 2000. In England, the limits of candidates' election expenses were most recently varied by SI 2020 No 1634 (applicable to local elections other than for the GLA), and in Wales similarly by SI 2021 No 1285 (W.324).

The law helps to move things along by providing (with equivalent provisions for other kinds of elections) in s 78 of the RPA 1983 that claims against candidate or agents not sent to the relevant agent within twenty-one days of the day of declaration of the result "shall be barred and not paid." (Section 79 provides a disputed claims procedure.)

Returns are due in to the returning officer within thirty-five days of the day of declaration under s 81, to be accompanied by a declaration as required by s 82 of, and sch 3 to, the RPA 1983. The returning officer must publish a notice within ten days of the time allowed for receiving expenses returns, advertising facilities for inspection (or indeed default if no return has been received), and must copy the notice to each of the election agents. Notices must be published in at least two newspapers circulating in the constituency. Returns are open to inspection for two years: see ss 88-89 of the RPA 1983. (As to the level of permitted expenses, see s 76 of the 1983 Act.) Once again these requirements are essentially structured in the same way for all elections, but there are some differences in particular cases – see for example the Secretary of State's power to vary permitted expense levels in art 48 of the National Assembly for Wales (Representation of the People) Order 2007, SI No 236.

The duty is to receive returns, not to prepare them or advise upon their content; try to avoid favouring some candidates with your comments and assistance by maintaining a neutral role.

Section 87A of the RPA 1983, inserted by the Political Parties, Elections and Referendums Act 2000, requires the returning officer at a Parliamentary or Mayor of London election to send to the Electoral Commission "as soon as reasonably practicable" a copy of any return or declaration received under ss 75, 81 or 82 of the 1983 Act. See also para 39 of Home Office Circular RPA 436 dated 6 February 2001.

SI 2006 No 2910 inserted Part 7 into the much-amended original RPR 2001, SI No 341. This comprises regs 116-120, and entitles those authorised (r 117) to demand marked copies of the electoral register or voters lists after both Parliamentary and local elections.

The fees (and reg 120) were amended by reg 4 of SI 2008 No 1901. Part 7 was applied also to Senedd elections by Part 8, added subsequently by reg 2 of SI 2007 No 1368.

Note that when a returning officer passes to a local authority proper officer the election documents after a count is completed, they must be retained for six months: see rr 52-54 of both the Local Elections (Principal Areas) (England and Wales) Rules 2006, SI No 3304; the Local Elections (Parishes and Communities) (England and Wales) Rules 2006, SI No 3305; and – in this case retention for a year by the registration officer – r 69 of sch 1 to the Local Elections (Communities) (Wales) Rules 2021.

As to the returning officer's personal accounts, see chapter 24.

Note that the Electoral Administration Act 2006, s 41 introduced new rules regarding the retention of documents after a Parliamentary election. These are be retained by the registration officer (not sent to the Clerk of the Crown, as used to be the requirement), and the existing provisions are modified to facilitate later inspection.

CHAPTER 22
ELECTION FEES AND STAFF PAYMENTS

The 2011 edition of this book said –

"It is both novel and pleasant to start a chapter of this book with a welcome to a new system that makes electoral administration more straightforward! The financing of elections had been one of the more arcane areas of managing them, and the need for reform was recognised on all sides. A new system was introduced for the June 2009 European Parliamentary elections, and a similar scheme apparently operated well for the May 2010 general election. The basis in primary legislation for these changes is section 68 of the Electoral Administration Act 2006."

This system continues to evolve and develop, and returning officers should be aware that developments are still being made. There remains some concern that the process is still overly bureaucratic. While the assumptions underpinning the new approach continue to be refined, a balance needs to be struck.

The DLUHC undertook a wide ranging review of the elections funding model used for national polls in 2013-14. This involved extensive consultation with stakeholders and led to a number of significant changes. These included:

• a new methodology for calculating funding allocations to returning officers;

• a more flexible and proportionate approach to scrutiny; and

• a reduced deadline for returning officers to submit their expenses claims.

The changes came into effect at the 2014 European Parliamentary elections. The new approach takes the actual settled expenditure at the previous poll of the same type (in this first case the 2009 European Parliamentary elections) and adjusts it for price inflation, electorate size, registered postal voters, and combination, to create a more accurate estimate of expected cost. The new scrutiny approach sought to reduce the administrative burden on returning officers, while maintaining claimed expenditure.

Three levels of scrutiny were introduced, each requiring a different level of supporting documentation to be provided with a claim. Returning officers are assigned a scrutiny category through a combination of risk based and random allocation. Where a returning officer claims for more than their maximum recoverable amount, their claim is automatically moved to the highest scrutiny category.

At the heart of the approach is that each acting returning officer (ARO) is allocated a "maximum recoverable amount" for each Parliamentary constituency. Within that maximum amount it is possible to allocate resources, provided that they are necessary for the efficient and effective conduct of the election. The amounts are decided by using detailed assumptions for everything from polling station costs to staff pay rates based on data provided by electoral administrators, including accounts from previous elections. The most recent Order is the Parliamentary Elections (Returning Officers' Charges) Order 2019, SI No 1454. The Order itself is a much more readable and intelligible document; gone now are the former three divisions with "maximum recoverable amounts" and costs for which there is no maximum. There is only one sum that is outside this local discretion: unsurprisingly, that is the ARO's personal fee for running the election, which is fixed by the Order. Similar orders are made prior to other elections or polls funded by Government.

Also of relevance are the Guidance Notes to the Fees and Charges Order produced by the DLUHC. They set out the underpinning detail behind the Order, and also the process.

Crucially, it is the returning officer who signs off the paperwork submitted to the Electoral Claims Unit (ECU) of the DLUHC regarding fees and charges for a Government funded election or poll. Returning Officers should ensure that they review, and are content with, what is submitted on their behalf/in their name by the election staff as it is they who are personally responsible and accountable for what is claimed.

To expand on this, from the 2019 general election, ARO fees were generally in the region of £2,500/4,500 per constituency (though in Wales, most were below £3,000). The other costs, the second figures, were usually over £100,000 and in some cases approached £200,000 (large rural areas, etc).

The Government now publish the costs of each election after the event. The *Costs of the 2015 UK Parliamentary General Election* was published in June 2018. For that election, the overall cost to central government was £14,732,548. Of that, £2.44 million was paid to returning officers for their services (ie their fees), £70.44 million was for returning officers' expenses (the costs of running the poll), £0.24 million for postal vote 'sweeps', and £41.61 million for delivery of candidate mailings. In 2017, the overall cost was about £141m, with fees and expenses around £98m and £42.5m for delivering election literature. Each postal vote was estimated to cost £2.15, and each polling station vote £1.22. Final figures for the December 2019 general election are awaited.

The legislative regime – and the approach of the DLUHC – is that elections should be run within the "maximum recoverable amounts" allocated. Excess spending above the local "maximum recoverable amount" can be recovered, but only if it can be shown that it was reasonable to incur these costs, and it is always wise to pre-warn electoral officials in Whitehall if such additional spend is foreseeable.

Prior to the election, the DLUHC pays an initial advance to each returning officer of up to 75% of the allocation set out in legislation. Further advances can be made at the DLUHC's discretion up to a further 15% of the overall MRA. These are made to cover unexpected and/or higher costs which cannot be covered by the initial advance.

In circumstances where polls are subject to combination, the costs of the shared aspects are divided equally between each of the polls. Combination of polls is factored into the calculation of the funding allocations for returning officers. For example, The Parliamentary

Elections (Returning Officers' Charges) Order 2015, SI No 476 specified different maximum recoverable amounts for constituencies that were subject to combination and those that were not.

The Elections Claims Unit ('ECU') is a team within government that is responsible for the administration of the scrutiny process and settlement of claims. Returning officers submit their election claims to the ECU. The ECU is then responsible for checking that costs have been accounted for correctly, that the necessary supporting evidence has been supplied and that the items claimed are reimbursable. As part of this process the ECU may request additional information or evidence from the returning officer, and may query items of expenditure. Once a claim has been scrutinised and all queries have been resolved, the ECU is responsible for raising the payment of the remaining balance to the returning officer.

Any excessive or improper expenditure is the personal liability of the ARO, but thankfully such occurrences are rare, though not unknown! AROs have in the past been pursued for the costs of (apparently) excessive floral decoration of the stage (from whence the results were announced), and for purchases of alcohol for themselves/their mayor/their staffs. It used to be a frequent experience that very small sums indeed would be queried and pursued out of proportion to the costs of doing so.

The use of electronic spreadsheet forms for completing claims does not mean that hard copy documentation is now unnecessary, but it should help the overall process and make the submission of claims more straightforward.

The media do from time to time investigate the fees paid to AROs. This is against a background of ever-increasing press interest in chief executives' salaries and pensions, given the financial pressures in the public sector.

The technicalities about the ARO being an entirely separate position or office, with personal responsibilities, were immediately lost in the welter of criticism for supposed election night chaos and failure.

Thus *The Sunday Telegraph* on 6 June 2010 ran the headline *"Officials get bonuses despite the fiasco of election night"*. The gist of the report was that *"at least 6 officials (AROs) responsible for the chaos that left hundreds unable to vote have collected substantial bonuses for their work on polling day"*. The article clearly recognised that separate fees are paid for electoral work, but portrayed sums of up to £14,000 or £25,000 (multiple constituencies in larger cities mean a cumulative fee) on top of £200,000-plus salaries as ill-deserved and unacceptable. Indeed, the article reported that several AROs were considering whether or not to take their fee.

The Times on 1 December 2019 ran with *"Salary boost makes returning officers the winners in general elections: A bumper five years for elections have earned highly paid council chiefs tens of thousands of pounds in extra payments"*

The message of all this for the future is that this can be a volatile public issue, and that AROs now need to be extremely careful in their dealings with the media in an area that used to attract virtually no attention whatsoever.

For local elections the fees scales and payments or costs limits are set by the local authority which employs the returning officer. There is a range of local discretion, as is the case with local authority pay rates generally. This is usually done on a county basis (or equivalent), so that local authorities have the same fees as in neighbouring areas and do not compete with one another for staff.

Election staff do not receive large sums, so it is only fair not to delay their payment. Income tax is deducted by the returning officer at source, as HMRC Real Time Information ('RTI') now applies to elections. Returning officers use various methods of financial administration. To sign literally hundreds of cheques personally is very time-consuming. It is possible to authorise a couple of deputies to do this; it is also possible to use the council's finance department to make payments out of the election account by requisition. This latter process can also complement any later audit – or you can run a completely separate and independent payroll with suitable external expertise.

Given that returning officers now need to manage the RTI HMRC taxation requirements as well as provide pensions, many now need to have a resource that takes care of those matters as well as payroll issues.

Employment as or by a returning officer for election purposes is disregarded for national insurance purposes: see the Social Security (Categorisation of Earners) Regulations 1978 SI No 1689 (as amended in relation to civil partnership by SI 2005 No 3133). (National insurance payments should, however, be deducted from electoral registration work (such as annual register canvassing), which is outside this definition.) Chapter 5 refers to which fees received by returning officers are pensionable and which are not. Since 2010 the Government have changed previous practice by declining to define new kinds of elections and polls as pensionable. None of the fees for the 2011 AV referendum, the 2011 Welsh referendum, the EU referendum in 2016 and the police and crime commissioner elections have accordingly been pensionable. Nor are elections to the eight combined authorities.

CLG's response on the issue clarifies their view in relation to pensionability generally, and it is therefore an important matter of which returning officers should be aware, as the current law may change in relation to future elections and polls. In response to correspondence with the Electoral Commission, CLG stated that:

"I confirm that such fees are not covered by the Local Government Pension Scheme (Miscellaneous) Regulations 2012 which were laid on 1st August. This accords with the recent decision made by DCLG Ministers on this matter. They are not persuaded of the case for making fees for Counting Officer duties pensionable, as they believe it is inappropriate to increase public funding for senior officers' pensions in this way. It would not be consistent with a need to tackle the deficit and make savings across the publish sector, nor would the Government's broader reforms of public sector pensions."

In relation to fees for local elections, recent events have highlighted both a gap in the legislation which has caused some concerns, but also other changes which have made the position of returning officers receiving fees for the conduct of local elections more liable to public scrutiny and, therefore, warranting more care and attention.

In relation to Parliamentary elections, RPA s 29 provides that a returning officer is entitled to recover his or her charges in respect of services rendered or expenses incurred for or in connection with a Parliamentary election.

In relation to county, county borough, district or London Borough elections, RPA 1983 s 36(4) provides that all expenditure properly incurred by a returning officer in relation to the holding of such elections shall, providing it does not exceed a scale of fees set for that purpose (referred to later), be paid by the council. There is no reference to payment of fees in s 36(4), but it is however worth noting that –

1. Under RPA s 35, there is a statutory duty on councils to appoint a returning officer. Under s 112 of the Local Government Act 1972 a council is also empowered to appoint such officers as thought necessary for the proper discharge of functions, and officers appointed must be paid such reasonable remuneration as the appointing authority thinks fit.

2. Under s 111 of the Local Government Act 1972 a local authority has the power to do anything (whether or not involving expenditure) calculated or facilitated or conducive or incidental to the discharge of any of their functions.

There is accordingly both a legal duty to appoint a returning officer, and a power for councils to pay that returning officer.

In terms of transparency, s 38 of the Localism Act 2011 stated that a relevant authority must prepare a pay policy statement for the financial year 2012-13 and for each subsequent financial year. Section 40 provides that authorities must have regard to any guidance issued or approved by the Secretary of State; the issued guidance states that as well as senior salaries, authorities must also make clear what approach they take to the award of other elements of senior remuneration, including any policy to award additional fees for chief officers for their local election duties. The guidance recognises that some authorities have taken the local decision to include fees within a chief officer's overall salary, while others pay separate fees. Authorities are required to make it clear in their pay policy statement which approach applies and if separate fees are paid, describe their approach to setting and publishing these. So, regardless of what an authority does and how it does it, transparency is now required.

While there is a range of approaches, it is clear that one of the benefits of using a scale of fees, as referred to in s 36 of RPA 1983 is that that scale can be applied across a range of authorities (for instance, in Hampshire it covers all of the county's principal local authorities and the Isle of Wight). The basis upon which Hampshire (and indeed many other areas) works is predominantly to aid transparency as well as independence – particularly in relation to local returning officer fees. In Hampshire, a committee determines the scale of fees, which is then published on each of the local authorities' websites. Authorities have passed the necessary resolutions to agree to abide by the local fee scale, and thus the fee scale is not set by the councils (or indeed the returning officer in their substantive post) but is set 'independently' of the local authority, but in a very transparent manner. This also provides a further benefit in that in situations where there is a heavy demand for staff to run elections, there is no leap-frogging by paying an additional sum to get poll clerks in Authority A at the expense of Authority B.

The fundamental principle, however, is this – whatever process is adopted for the setting of the local returning officer's fees for local council elections needs to be transparent, above board and entirely scrupulous; it is a matter that has attracted recent attention both publicly and politically, and newly appointed returning officers should be wary of inheriting or adopting an existing fee structure without ensuring that it is sound, robust and lawful.

CHAPTER 23
ELECTION PETITIONS

The only method to challenge an election result is by way of petition which is commenced, rather like issuing a High Court writ, at the end of the electoral process. Alternatively, if an election process or decision is to be questioned while the course of that process continues, such a challenge will have to be made by way of judicial review, probably seeking a declaration or otherwise to invalidate a decision.

The petition process is highly complex, expensive (as with all High Court litigation), and not often used. The number of petitions launched varies from year to year but is usually very small. There were, for instance, some eight election petitions commenced in the High Court after the 2006 local elections. For example, in Birmingham, the High Court (in August 2006) decided to unseat a BNP councillor after it was found that she had wrongly been declared elected following an error at the count. The Court declared that the Labour candidate should in fact serve in the Kingstanding Ward. In this case a batch of votes was double-counted, and although the mistake was quickly noticed the result had already been announced and could not be changed except by the Court, after a petition had been filed. The general rule is that once the result of an election has been declared, if it is to be questioned the procedure will have to be by way of election petition.

Following the 2008 local elections the High Court received only three petitions, although none related to electoral malpractice. A petition in Warrington was not valid because the petitioners failed to pay the surety (£2,500) into court within the three-day time limit following presentation of the petition. Two further petitions continued. The first related to a close result at Stoke-on-Trent, and the second to incidents in Bradford where a candidate made allegations that the police had unlawfully detained him, preventing him from canvassing. There were also allegations in this latter petition against the returning officer, claiming that the candidate had been denied access to certain paperwork relating to postal votes.

Two petitions were issued challenging results at the May 2010 general election. One related to allegedly false statements considering a candidate's personal character in the Oldham East and Saddleworth constituency. The other alleged maladministration by the ARO for Fermanagh and South Tyrone, involving supposedly inaccurate verification of fifteen ballot boxes at the count. Two further petitions related to local elections at Waltham Forest (error in vote counting alleged), and Croydon (voters allegedly having been allegedly denied their vote after queuing at the close of poll, 10pm).

In the *Oldham East and Saddleworth* case ([2010] EWHC 2702), the election court found in November 2010 against the former Labour Government Minister Phil Woolas, and ordered a re-run of the election. (Mr Woolas had won by 102 votes after two re-counts.) The court found under s 106 of the RPA 1983 that he had knowingly printed untruths about his Liberal Democrat opponent Elwyn Watkins, and he was also barred from both standing for any elected public office and voting in general and local elections for three years. Attempts to secure judicial review by Mr Woolas failed. In the Fermanagh and South Tyrone case Rodney Connor, who was defeated by just four votes after three re-counts, had himself retired earlier in 2010 as the Chief Executive of Fermanagh District Council. The Speaker reported to the Commons on 25 October 2010 that Mr Connor's petition had failed.

At a Parliamentary election, the petition can be presented either by a voter, a candidate or someone claiming to be a candidate. The respondent is either the candidate declared elected or, if the conduct of the returning officer is impugned, the returning officer.

A returning officer is an officer of the state performing public functions, who is not acting in a personal capacity when performing the duties or being served with an election petition. Valid service of an election petition, however, can be made through an authority's usual internal arrangements where the returning officer is chief executive (or presumably by extension, any other postholder): see *Scarth v Amin and Reeves* [2008] EWHC 2886; [2009] PTSR 827. This does not of course contradict the individual accountability or responsibility of the returning officer role; the distinction is between the returning officer as a private individual and as someone holding a public office or position.

The detailed procedure is the subject of Part III of the RPA 1983, ss 136-157 of which provides the procedure on all election petitions. Twenty-one days after return of the writ is the normal time limit for presenting petitions: s 122(1) of the RPA 1983. It is not necessary to review that procedure in detail here (but note the surety for Parliamentary elections is £5,000): see the Election Petition Rules 1960, SI No 543, as amended by SIs 1985 no 1278, SI 1999 No 1352 and SI 2003 No 972. As to special cases to be determined by the High Court, see s 146.

The Parliamentary election procedures apply similarly, apart from one or two modifications, to the Senedd. See Part 4 of the National Assembly for Wales (Representation of the People) Order 2007, SI No 236.

Local government election petitions share much of the same statutory background under ss 127-128 of the RPA 1983. Apart from candidates or claimed candidates, however, four local government electors, not just one as in the earlier cases, are necessary: s 128(1). The time limit is again twenty-one days "after the day on which the election was held" (s 129(1)), ie not the day of declaration of the result.

Another process sometimes used in local elections is to involve the county court in an inspection of documents. Under r 53(1) of the Local Elections (Principal Areas)(England and Wales) Rules 2006, SI No 3304 the county court may order the production of certain election documents if satisfied "by evidence on oath that the order is required for the purpose of instituting or maintaining a prosecution for an offence in relation to ballot papers, or for the purpose of an election petition." The equivalent r 53(1) of the Local Elections (Parishes and Communities) (England and Wales) Rules 2006, SI No 3305 is in the same terms, as is the similar r 67(2) of sch 2 to the Local Elections (Communities) (Wales) Rules 2021, SI No 1460 (W.375).

With regard to mayoral referendums similar provisions are set out in the Local Authorities (Conduct of Referendums) (England) Regulations 2007, SI No 2089 (see M in chapter 4), broadly substituting "referendum petition" in place of "election petition". For the questioning of mayoral elections see reg 5 of the Local Authorities (Mayoral Elections) (England and Wales) Regulations 2007, SI No 1024. Schedule 6 of the Local Authorities (Conduct of Referendum) (Wales) Regulations 2004, SI No 870, modifies the Election Petition Rules 1960 in that context.

For an example of a judicial review of an election petition process, see *Aehmed v Afzal* [2009] EKHC 1757.

Needless to say, if a petition results in action in the High Court it is very serious with considerable ramifications – hence the need for insurance. High Court litigation can easily run up six-figure bills, and it is simply essential to take advice at an early stage on such matters. Fortunately, underlining the high quality of electoral administration in this country, such petitions are rare, but never to be ignored!

Although the case refers to the Northern Ireland Assembly, it is useful to note the House of Lords' approach to holding an election outside the statutory period (which they confirmed as valid): see *Robinson v Secretary of State for Northern Ireland* [2002] *The Times,* 26 July.

It was provided in para 23 of sch 1 to the Parliamentary Voting System and Constituencies Act 2011 that the AV referendum of 5 May 2011 could only be challenged by way of judicial review, and not election petition. In s 9HE(1)(b) of the Local Government Act 2000 (inserted by Part 1 of sch 2 to the Localism Act 2011) the Secretary of State is given power about "the questioning of elections for the return of elected mayors and the consequences of irregularities." There must be prior consultation with the Electoral Commission, but such Regulations may modify or except provisions either of, or made under, the Representation of the People Acts – so allowing statute in principle to be amended or disregarded by statutory instrument.

A similar approach is set out in relation to referendums about neighbourhood development orders (see R in chapter 4) in s 61N(3) of the Town and Country Planning Act 1990, inserted by s 116 of and sch 9 to the Localism Act 2011 – challenge may only be by way of judicial review within six weeks of the date of declaration of the referendum result.

CHAPTER 24
THE RETURNING OFFICER'S ACCOUNTS

We have referred in chapters 21 and 22 to paying the bills, paying the staff and yourself, and to settling the election accounts generally and reclaiming the cost if the expense is borne by the DLUHC or elsewhere. How should a returning officer or equivalent hold money paid to him or her for defraying the costs of running the election?

Such monies belong, of course, neither to the returning officer personally nor to the employing authority, but he or she is personally liable to account for them. It is best that they be kept in a separate account distinguished from all other funds held for any other purpose, though some returning officers utilise their own Council's bank accounts, and have separate statements.

Opinion varies as to whether you should have separate account for different kinds of elections. This has advantages, but the purity of separation is difficult to maintain when polls are so frequently combined nowadays (see chapter 25). It is not unlawful or inappropriate to maintain only one election account, but equally bank costs or bank interest may then have to be apportioned, with similar difficulty. Ultimately this is a personal responsibility and decision, and you must make a pragmatic choice. A possible compromise might be to keep separate DLUHC or other recharged elections from ones paid by your employing authority, but there is no perfect and tidy solution.

What is absolutely critical is that the returning officer puts in place a regime that is accountable and transparent enough to both benefit from but also suffer considerable scrutiny. The assumption should be, and rightly so too, that in handling what are comparatively large sums of public money, the processes behind that are likely be subject to both independent and public scrutiny. The returning officer should, therefore, make use of whatever resources are available, whether that is the council's own internal audit regime and/or other appropriate processes, to put in place open and transparent systems for managing these matters.

The DLUHC will advance a substantial sum by way of advance (see chapter 22) to most operating costs at the start of a Parliamentary election process for which they ultimately pay the costs (though not general office overheads outside permitted headings). If that money is not held for long periods, it will not be expected to earn interest, but any so received is liable to be accounted for.

Parliamentary accounts have to be submitted to the DLUHC for inspection, and approval obtained within twelve months - the Electoral Claims Unit which undertakes this work (see chapter 22). The Unit often raises queries on various payments and their allocation within the accounts. Thus, for example, if you seek to recover loss of hiring fees for a public hall being used for the count, you can expect plenty of questions about how you assess loss of bar takings (and, even then, they may well not be reimbursed). Following the European Parliamentary elections of 1999 more guidance was agreed between the (then responsible) Home Office and SOLACE/AEA on what is chargeable and what is unacceptable. Nevertheless, preparation and final acceptance of the accounts is never a rapid process; it can run into months, and in the past more typically years. The DLUHC are now rightly much more vigilant about the time limit.

For the police and crime commissioner elections on 15 November 2012 the Home Office decided to follow a similar approach. See the Police and Crime Commissioner Elections (Returning Officers' Accounts) Regulations 2012, SI No 2088 (as most recently amended by SIs 2016 No 488 and 2021 No 179), and the accompanying Police and Crime Commissioner Elections (Local Returning Officers' and Police Area Returning Officers' Charges) Order 2021, SI No 390. In addition, a shorter timeframe was allowed for the return of the accounts: eight months from the date of declaration under reg 4 of SI No 2088. Practitioners expressed considerable concern in relation to this requirement.

For Wales the Senedd Cymru (Returning Officers' Charges) Order 2021 is SI No 315 (W.80). The Explanatory Memorandum dated 19

March 2021 to the Senedd Cymru (Returning Officers' Accounts) Regulations 2021 explains that "This Explanatory Memorandum has been prepared by the Local Government Department. This instrument is not subject to any procedure and therefore is not required to be laid before the Senedd. It is simply required to be made (signed), brought into force and published."

In 2005 the then DCA issued the Returning Officers' Accounts (Parliamentary Elections) (England and Wales) Regulations 2005, replacing those of 1991. (This was a ministerial, not a Parliamentary, order and accordingly it did not carry a statutory instrument number.) These regulations were supplemented by the *Acting Returning Officers' Expenses Guidance Notes*, originally distributed by email on 18 February 2005 and referred to in para 3 of the DCA's *EPR Newsletter* for March 2005 (issue 2/05). Specific guidance on the Fees and Charges Order is now issued by the DLUHC prior to each general election.

Free banking for such occasions may well not be available today: such costs must be obtained from the employing authority if not able to be set against interest received, as usually they cannot be recovered by recharge. Today's rules mean that returning officers will expect to have to produce appropriate documentation to open accounts. A good way of styling them is to combine your own or your authority's or constituency's name with "election account", so that its purpose is plain to see, and mistakes are less likely to occur.

Obviously the accounts you hold are not part of your authority's resources either, but it is good practice to include them in the authority's general audit plan, to guard against problems and to underline a feeling of transparency about how you handle, and account for, large sums of what is still public money. Remember too the "accountability of officers" provisions of s 115 of the Local Government Act 1972.

CHAPTER 25
COMBINED ELECTIONS

Combined elections have become the norm rather than the exception of earlier years. There is an (often unhappy) expectation among both returning officers and electoral administrators that major national elections will be combined with local polls. There may be some complaint as to increased workload and confusion over timetables, but even after consultation (for example as to whether the 2009 European Parliamentary elections should be combined) the eventual outcome is virtually always combination. Why is this?

One announcement of a combined poll volunteered some answers to this question. This was made on behalf of then recently elected Coalition Government on 5 July 2010 by the Deputy Prime Minister, Nick Clegg MP. In the House of Commons, he announced details of his Government's proposals to introduce a Bill to provide for a referendum on the alternative vote system (AV), and said:

".........by giving people a choice over their electoral system, we give that system a new legitimacy. Surely, when dissatisfaction with politics is so great, one of our first acts must be to give people their own say over something as fundamental as how they elect their MPs. The question will be simple, asking people whether they want to adopt the alternative vote, yes or no; and the precise wording will be tested by the Electoral Commission.

As for the date of the referendum, in making that decision we have been driven by three key considerations. The first is that all parties fought the general election on an absolute pledge to move fast to fix our political system, so we must get on and do that without delay; secondly, it is important to avoid asking people to keep returning to the ballot box; and finally, in these straitened times we must keep costs as low as possible. That is why the Prime Minister and I have decided that the date for the referendum on the Bill will be 5 May 2011, the same day as the elections to the devolved legislatures in Scotland, Wales and Northern Ireland, and local elections in England. That will save an estimated £17 million. I know that some hon. Members have concerns over that date, but I believe the people will easily be able to distinguish between the different issues on which they will be asked to vote on the same day".

The Opposition in Parliament objected to this combination date, saying that there had been no consultation and no precedent. The four previous national referendums held in the UK (the EEC referendum of 1975 and the more recent Northern Ireland, Scottish and Welsh referendums) had not been held on the same days as other elections.

Of course, this was the policy of a Coalition Government that had itself been elected following a combined poll on 6 May 2010. Local government elections were already scheduled to take place on that day in many parts of England – indeed, a total of 4,178 seats in 2,940 wards of 164 local authorities were contested. 649 Parliamentary constituencies were contested that day; following the death during the election period of a candidate nominated in the North Yorkshire constituency of Thirsk and Malton, however, the election timetable was suspended there and the poll postponed until 27 May.

Interestingly, when it came to the first police and crime commissioner elections, these were delayed from the original date of May 2012 to November 2012. Many, including some MPs in Parliament, had suggested that it would be better to combine them with planned elections in May 2013, but the Government opted for 15 November 2012, one reason cited being that it would be better to keep them separate from 'normal' and hence 'political' elections.

On 7 October 2008, the then Local Government Minister, John Healy MP, announced in the House of Commons that the Government would use the power in s 60 of the Local Government and Public Involvement in Health Act 2007 (inserting s 37(2A) into the RPA 1983) to move the 2009 local elections in England to the same date as the European Parliamentary elections; ie from 7 May to 4 June. This followed an extensive consultation period (organised by the then CLG not MoJ) with some 278 representations received (including from SOLACE). Over 75% of these responses were in favour of the change. Mr Healy said "Like in 2004, holding local elections alongside two separate elections within a month will be more convenient for voters, less costly for the taxpayer and more efficient for electoral administrators."

Perhaps all one can take from these examples is that decisions on combining by Government may not be consistently applied across the years across different types of elections.

The local elections in that year were mainly county councils in two-tier areas; there were also some unitary council elections (such as Bristol, Central Bedfordshire and Shropshire) as well as mayoral elections (such as Doncaster and Hartlepool). Combination supposedly increases turnout. In 2004 the turnout for the European Parliamentary election increased from the 24% of 1999 to 34.5%. In 2009 it was again 34.5% (the overall EU turnout was 43%). The 2010 general election saw a 65.1% turnout, the third lowest since 1945.

Not everyone, however, favours combination. In 2007, there were considerable problems in Scotland during their combined Parliamentary and local elections. The Electoral Commission commissioned a thorough review from a Canadian elections expert, Ron Gould. (Their remit did not then include Scottish local government elections, though it does now.) One of his key findings was that combined elections are a disservice to local government and its candidates. He found that separate elections better enable voters both to engage with the campaigns in a worthwhile way and to make an informed decision. This resulted in the Scottish Parliament passing legislation 'decoupling' the two forms of election. Many administrators in particular, would argue that such considerations apply equally well south of the Scottish border.

Combining elections is primarily the subject of ss 15-17 of the RPA 1985. Under s 15 where either a Parliamentary or European election falls on the same day as an "ordinary local government election", or a Parliamentary and European so come together, "they shall be taken together." An "ordinary local government election" includes parishes and communities: s 203(1) of the RPA 1983. Where a regional assembly referendum and a local government referendum in the same area fall on the same day, they also must be combined: see para 4 of the Regional Assembly and Local Government Order 2004, SI No 1962. Similarly where a Senedd election and a Welsh local government election fall on the same day, they too must be combined: see art 16(1) of the National Assembly for Wales (Representation of the People) Order 2007, SI No 263, and the rules and modifications made by sch 4 thereto. For combinations involving police and crime commissioner elections, see sch 4 to the Police and Crime Commissioner Elections Order 2012, SI No 1917.

Election polls for related areas not definitely required to be taken together (for example a district council by-election in England falling on the day of either the main county elections or of a county by-election) "may nevertheless be so taken if the returning officer for each election thinks fit": s 15(2), ie there may be more than one returning officer involved.

Section 17, which substituted s 36(3) of the RPA 1983, provides that the main district council elections and parish elections, or such by-elections, shall be taken together, and allows regulations to provide for the procedural differences accordingly required. Section 36(3) of the RPA 1983 has since been further amended to remove the references to Welsh district and community councils: see sch 18 to the Local Government (Wales) Act 1994. Modifications for combined polls in main local government, parish and community elections are provided in each case by sch 3 to the Local Elections (Principal Areas)(England and Wales) Rules 2006 and the Local Elections (Parishes and Communities) (England and Wales) Rules 2006, SIs Nos 3304 and 3305.

What sort of matters does "taking together" involve? The principal issues surround poll cards, public notices, whether or not to use one ballot box (or if a busy station requires more than one box, whether votes for different elections are put into the same box), and at the counts how different votes are separated and ballot box totals verified, and so on. Different types of electoral issues arise with combined polls. Section 3A of the RPA 1983 provides that "For the purposes of this section electoral areas are related if they are coterminous or if one is situate within the other." There are usually no geographical problems when the electoral areas being combined lie within the same authority area. As we have noted above in relation to postal votes, there can be tricky points to resolve, however, when electoral areas cross authority boundaries, which they often do at general elections, and possibly following boundary reviews. These could give rise to the somewhat unusual (virtually Gilbertian!) question "Who is the returning officer?" To answer this, see reg 4 of the Representation of the People (Combination of Polls) (England and Wales) Regulations 2004, SI No 294. Where it is mandatory for the elections to be combined, the acting returning officer for the relevant Parliamentary constituency is responsible in overlapping areas. Where the combination is discretionary for a general and local election the acting returning officer of the constituency and the council have to agree who is to carry out the various duties – normally, the acting returning officer takes precedence.

The franchise may not be identical for different election or poll types. At combined elections, most electors will be able to vote in both or all cases, but some will only be able to vote in one (see chapter 3 as to the marking of names in the electoral register).

This technical rule was partially responsible for the 'delays' and 'turning away' of voters at certain constituencies in the 2010 general election. In particular, EU voters who were allowed to vote in their local elections were ineligible to vote in the Parliamentary election. This caused some delays at polling station tables where votes were being issued, as these inaccessible rules were being explained, sometimes to people whose command both of English and of arcane electoral legislation was limited. In these circumstances, queues soon built up; tempers began to fray; polling staff were abused; the media had yet another story with which to berate the public sector; and so on. The consequences of rules like this necessitate proper attention being paid to the numbers of electors assigned to particular polling stations, and also to ensuring adequate staffing.

CHAPTER 26
PERFORMANCE MANAGEMENT; AND THE DUTY TO ENCOURAGE DEMOCRATIC PARTICIPATION

The Coalition government elected in May 2010 took a rather different view of performance management in local government from its predecessors. Thus, the new Secretary of State for Communities and Local Government, Eric Pickles MP, took a very early decision to scrap the comprehensive area assessment. Soon after, the Audit Commission (now abolished) announced that it would not be producing the scores for Use of Resources assessment, etc and revised their approach to auditing councils.

Strangely, though not unexpectedly, performance management and the setting of performance standards reached the world of electoral administration well after their introduction in other parts of the public sector. They are, however, the province of the Electoral Commission, not the Government.

Section 67 of the Electoral Administration Act 2006 provides the Electoral Commission with a permissive power (inserted as s 9A of the Political Parties, Elections and Referendums Act 2000) to define and publish performance standards for the administration of elections by returning officers and electoral registration officers. ('EROs'). This power is not directly applicable to Northern Ireland – and neither incidentally does it apply to Scottish local government elections (the Commission's remit does not include the latter).

In preparation for the new Performance Standards, the Electoral Commission decided to develop a clear vision for what it considered to be quality electoral services, which would then form the basis for performance standards. That vision remains in place and identifies four main themes that support the delivery of quality electoral services:

- Integrity – a secure process for registration and voting;
- User focus – an easy and accessible process for candidates and

electors;
- Professionalism – a clear and consistent approach to delivery;
- Value for money – efficient and effective service delivery.

Each of these themes is reflected within the performance standards.

Those new to the topic are advised to review the section on the Electoral Commission's website relating to performance standards, where they will find not only the background to the performance standards, but the current standards for EROs, and the performance standards for returning officers.

These are respectively:

https://www.electoralcommission.org.uk/i-am-a/electoral-administrator/electoral-registration-officer/performance-standards-electoral-registration-officers

and

https://www.electoralcommission.org.uk/i-am-a/electoral-administrator/electoral-registration-officer/performance-standards-returning-officers

The standards aim to ensure, for example, that EROs put in place clearly documented strategies, plans and methods that can be easily followed by staff and can be evaluated and scrutinised.

While the previous version had ten performance standards for EROs, the latest version focusses on the two key outcomes of participation and accuracy of the register. The standards are grouped into these two areas representing the most important areas on which EROs should focus in carrying out their registration duties. The Commission assesses performance by:

- Publishing a set of detailed standards and specifying the evidence required to meet the standards;

- Issuing a direction to EROs to assess whether or not they have met the standards; and

- Conducting a detailed verification and moderation of evidence from a sample of EROs across Great Britain, leading to changes where assessments are not supported by evidence.

In relation to performance standards for returning officers, the framework has been developed around key outcomes with the focus on the voter and those who want to stand for election, and in particular whether ROs are taking the necessary steps to deliver the following outcomes:

"• Voters are able to vote easily and know that their vote will be counted in the way they intended

• It is easy for people who want to stand for election to find out how to get involved, what the rules are, and what they have to do to comply with these rules, and they can have confidence in the management of the process and the result".

The aim of the standards is to focus on outcomes rather than completion of a process. Some process measurements, however, are clearly still valuable and important.

The 2016 framework therefore monitors returning officers' processes in the following areas:

- Voters;
- Those standing in the poll;
- Co-ordination and management of the poll.

The previous version had ten performance standards for returning officers which included 37 requirements in total. The latest iteration focusses on the three key outcomes with a smaller number of requirements to demonstrate delivery.

As already stated, the performance standards find their authority within primary legislation, and those new to the ERO and/or returning officer roles should review the Commission's website to ensure they are familiar with the requirements. Put briefly, there is nothing within either sets of standards that any ERO or returning officer should not be aspiring to deliver. It is also wise to review any reports produced by the Commission on compliance. As well as reflecting on one's own performance, there is much to be gleaned by seeing the national picture. If others are performing better, why?

In terms of outcomes, the most recent report from the Electoral Commission in relation to electoral registration related to the progress with the canvass (July-September 2021). A report giving analysis of electoral registration data dated 2020 is also available. An additional report assessed the performance of returning officers at the May 2015 polls. All these reports are also available on the Commission's website.

One of the difficulties of the performance management regime, particularly in its first iteration, was that it was largely built around the collation of data and information, and hence was often passed to the electoral services office for completion and, therefore, the level of involvement and/or participation of returning officers in particular was perhaps less than the Commission might have desired. As the approach has evolved, it has moved away from that, but it is strongly recommended that both returning officers and EROs should be fully aware of both the submissions, being ultimately being responsible signing them off to the Commission in relation to performance, but also for the findings. First, these are matters for which returning officers and EROs are responsible, and as such they will want to ensure that everything for which they are held accountable for (even in print) is correct. Secondly, returning officers and EROs will, of course, want to ensure that their services are delivered to the highest standards, and hence will want to identify areas where they can improve, and can highlight best practice.

There is a degree of concern from practitioners that the standards enable there to be adverse criticism of those who meet the legal performance requirements placed on them by Parliament, but fail to achieve a higher standard or requirement expected by the Electoral Commission. The Commission do recognise this issue in the way that it presents the information, acknowledging that some returning officers have shown they have performed beyond the requirements of the standards, and demonstrated creativity and innovation (rather than setting a bar of acceptability above that required by the standard and/or law).

Performance standards will no doubt continue to evolve, and will move beyond the statutory minimum requirements – perhaps moving into areas where objective measurability is harder, but where the impact may be more significant.

Section 18 of the Electoral Registration and Administration Act 2013 amended the RPA 1983 by adding a new provision, s 29A, which allows the Secretary of State, on a recommendation by the Electoral Commission, to withhold or reduce a returning officer's fee for reasons of poor performance. Section 29A(3) sets out the factors to which the Commission must have regard when making such a recommendation, one of which is an assessment of their performance against the performance standards.

Returning officers and EROs, in their substantive roles, will not be strangers to the world of performance standards. The proliferation of performance standards within the public sector has significantly reduced over the last few years, but all will be familiar with both their use and approaches to them. Returning officers and EROs can use them, of course, to make sure that they service they deliver is of a high standard, and in many cases that is what all of us in our 'day job' would seek to use performance standards to achieve. The ongoing ability to review, refine and improve the performance standards is welcomed.

The wise returning officer will, however, for all the reasons set out in this chapter, want to keep an eye, both on their performance against the standards, and also how they are performing against others. It is clear that Parliament intends to use the performance standards as a way of taking action where they feel that returning officers' performance has not been satisfactory. Whether, of course, their view on performance and the evidence from the performance standards validate that approach, remains to be seen.

Suppose that electoral or registration work is considered or alleged to be sub-standard? The implications where a returning officer is seen to have made a serious misjudgement or mistake in an election process have sometimes caused difficulties. The responsibility and accountability rest with the returning officer personally (a key reason for carrying adequate insurance as discussed in chapter 9). Their employing authority has no direct powers or standing to interfere in that process, whether the elections be Parliamentary or local — yet the authority originally made the relevant statutory or proper officer appointment, and have certain rights thereby. (See the concluding pages of chapter 5.) Local political pressure is likely to be intense, the more so if the alleged failure has been a very public one.

The authors have advised on a variety of problems and incidents over the years. When "things go wrong" in the electoral process the outcome can quickly be very intense public pressure on returning officers and others.

The media (and probably your members) will not be much interested in technical excuses about the lack of time to print ballot papers; to send out and check postal votes; and the difficulty in recruiting staff and so forth. After the event these sorts of comments are presented by the media as rather tepid and forlorn, even if you believe them to be accurate and reasonable (which they probably are!).

The administration of the postal voting process now seems to cause problems every year; a couple of years ago one northern authority wanted to have an extraordinary full Council meeting to instruct the returning officer on security and integrity issues. This is entirely inappropriate: the rules dealing with all types of absent voting are prescribed in legislation – they cannot be varied locally, and their administration and application is entirely a matter for the ERO and/or returning officer. It is worth noting that eventually the members of that authority accepted this situation; the proposed extraordinary meeting did not take place, despite the postal vote problems there had been.

It may assist to re-affirm clearly that an employing authority has no right to interfere, obstruct or give any kind of instruction to a returning (or counting) officer. Indeed, the law gives returning officers certain rights to obtain the resources needed for the job (for example, s 35(6) of the RPA 1983 in relation to staffing the GLA elections). If the returning officer's decision is to be formally questioned during the election process, that will be by way of judicial review; and if the outcome of the election is to be questioned that will be by way of election petition as provided by the RPA 1983 (see chapter 23).

Nevertheless the employing authority has, as in any employment contract, the right to be satisfied that its employee is a fit, proper and competent person for the role and the right to take appropriate action if it appears that that is not, or may not, be the case. Such action, however, will be taken within the scope and terms (express or implied) of the employment contract, and not under the provisions of election law. The statutory protection, where enjoyed by the postholder, will mean that an independent hearing will be needed before any disciplinary action can be lawfully taken by the authority, and if that hearing is conducted as a surrogate election law challenge it is likely to fall foul of s 120(1) or s 127 of the RPA 1983.

There have traditionally been provisions saving elections from being declared void for minor mistakes or irregularities which have not materially affected the course or conduct of events (such as s 23(3) of the RPA 1983 in relation to Parliamentary elections, s 35(5) in relation to local government elections, and s 50 in relation to misdescriptions). Section 46(1) of the Electoral Administration Act 2006 now gives returning officers a welcome and more explicit power to correct procedural errors (though they may not "under subsection (1) re-count the votes given at an election after the result has been declared.") See chapter 33 for further consideration of s 46.

The consolidating Local Elections (Principal Areas) (England and Wales) Rules 2006 and the Local Elections (Parish and Communities) (England and Wales) Rules 2006, SIs Nos 3304 and 3305 respectively, each contain in r 10 of sch 2 a provision allowing the correction of minor errors in a nomination paper up to the point of publication of the statement of persons nominated. Section 11 of, supplemented by para 38 of Part 2 of sch 1 to, the 2006 Act adds ss (3A)-(3E) into s 13B of the 1983 Act about correcting electoral register errors on the day of the poll. (Both SIs 2006 Nos 3304 and 3305 contain r 41 requiring presiding officers to keep a list of people to whom they issue ballot papers as a result of a register alteration taking effect on the day of the poll.)

Where an acting returning officer for a Parliamentary election is guilty of an act or omission in breach of official duty, but remedies that act or omission in full by taking steps pursuant to s 46, no offence is committed under s 63 of the 1983 Act.

Section 46 and its application have yet to be fully examined by the courts. Its precise scope and application must, until then, remain unclear, but it is certainly the view of experienced returning officers that it should be a shield, not a sword. It is no replacement for meticulous care and attention to detail but, as the cliché goes, to err is human. One example of the operation of s 46 was at a local election some years ago in the south east of England. By mistake, the returning officer had included a non-registered description for a candidate in the statement of persons nominated. It was noticed just before postal votes were being dispatched, and the particular candidate – acting as his own agent – was notified by letter. He was told both of the error and of the returning officer's intention that his candidature be either 'independent' or left blank. The returning officer received no prompt response (but some abuse much later) and, therefore, decided to proceed with the 'blank' option. The candidate was not elected and, apart from some personal abuse, the matter was concluded with that outcome.

More recently a returning officer mis-spoke at the point of declaring the result and mistakenly announced the wrong candidate as elected. However, realising their error at once and without the need to recount the votes, s 46 enabled them to turn back to the microphone and correct their error. While this is a mistake that is certainly best to avoid, the law is helpful in addressing such matters.

The 2006 Act also contained an important new provision (s 69) to empower what are termed "local electoral officers" "to encourage the participation of electors in the electoral process."

Returning officers have tried various innovative measures to encourage registration and participation in the electoral process. One of the authors serving as returning officer in a large district area put large striking colourful adverts on the side of the Council's numerous refuse vehicle fleet, encouraging early registration and voting on polling day. This campaign was funded by direct grant from the then MoJ. Since the Government's *Spending Review* of October 2010, it would seem highly improbable that further substantial funding from central government will be available.

There had previously been some uncertainty as to whether a local electoral officer (a collective term defined by s 69(8) as either an electoral registration officer or a returning officer at a Parliamentary or local election), has the power actively to encourage people to register for and/or vote at an election. Section 69 ended that uncertainty. It also complemented the work of the Electoral Commission, which has run its own campaigns to increase participation. It does not of course remove or alter the existing powers of local authorities themselves (as opposed to their local electoral officers) to do similar things using powers such as those in s 142 of the Local Government Act 1972 or, perhaps, s 2(1) (b) of the Local Government Act 2000 (the social well-being power), and now ss 1 and 2 of the Local Democracy, Economic Development and Construction Act 2009 referred to above. In the current financial climate, however, funding is the key issue.

To assist with the s 69 statutory power the Electoral Commission launched a Participation Toolkit. The toolkit was an online resource (called the Do Politics Centre) available through its website containing practical materials, advice and guidance for practitioners aiming to increase electoral awareness and registration. All materials are free to access and include good practice case studies, event plans, campaign techniques and templates for communication materials. The Commission's site is regularly updated to reflect new innovations and developments. That original website has now been replaced: see www.electoralcommission.org.uk now.

CHAPTER 27
CHANGES OF AREAS

A. Parliamentary Constituencies
B. Local Government Areas
C. Local Government Electoral Boundaries
D. Parishes and Communities

The law on changing areas is complex, and keeping up to date with boundary issues of various kinds easily becomes a treadmill. The provisions have inevitable implications for election law as such: they are not central to this book, but an outline of the main areas may be helpful. The key theme running through all this work is one of numerical equality to make votes so far as possible of equal weight – thus Parliamentary constituencies are reviewed to reach an average figure, sometimes referred to as the electoral quotient, often difficult with the easy movement of population in the United Kingdom – eg the considerable exodus from inner city areas in recent years, and the growth of new towns such as Cambourne and Milton Keynes.

A. PARLIAMENTARY CONSTITUENCIES

Parliamentary constituency boundaries (at the beginning of 2020 there are 650, as set out in B of chapter 4) are ultimately fixed by statutory instrument approved by Parliament on the recommendations of the Secretary of State. Those recommendations in turn have traditionally been formed following a statutory procedure including a public hearing process, known as a "local inquiry". The Parliamentary Voting System and Constituencies Act 2011, however, has made very significant changes to the way in which constituencies are determined.

Section 2 of the Parliamentary Constituencies Act 1986 established separate Boundary Commissions for England and Wales. (The 1986 Act was supplemented by the Boundary Commissions Act 1992.) It had been intended that these boundary functions would be transferred to the Electoral Commission under the Political Parties,

Elections and Referendums Act 2000, but that was repealed by s 61 of the Local Democracy, Economic Development and Construction Act 2009. The Parliamentary Constituencies Act 2020 significantly amended the provisions.

Boundary Commission reports must now be submitted to the Speaker of the house of Commons (instead of the Secretary of State) under s 3 of the 1986 Act as amended. Modifications are the subject of s 4A of the 1986 Act, while s 4 of the 2020 Act further amends s 5 of the 1986 Act relating to publicity and consultation.

The 2011 Act proposed to reduce the number of Parliamentary constituencies to just 600, and substituted a new sch 2 into the 1986 Act. In s 5 of the 2020 Act this total of 600 is amended back to 650. The United Kingdom "electoral quota" had been established in 2011 by dividing the number of Parliamentary electors registered on the review date by 598 (ie omitting the two Scottish constituencies of Orkney and Shetland and Na h-Eilanan an Iar). The electorates of each of the 598 constituencies were required to be no less than 95%, and not more than 105% of the quota (r 2(1), though there may be exceptions for both very extensive constituencies and those in Northern Ireland. The assumptions to be made, and the method of allocation, were set out in the rest of sch 2.

That calculation is now varied by the 2020 Act, which in s 7 adds the Ynys Mon constituency of Anglesey as a "protected constituency." Each other constituency must be wholly within one of England, Northern Ireland, Scotland and Wales, the allocation method being the subject of r 8. It should be noted that under r 9(3), for the purposes of this schedule "local government boundaries" in England means only the boundaries of counties and London boroughs, and in Wales the boundaries of counties and county boroughs.

Immediately after the Act was passed the Boundary Commissions commenced the task of devising a new set of 600 constituencies to be in place eighteen months before the then next scheduled general election in May 2015. They were close to the end of that process – with revised recommendations that could have given the

Conservatives a lead over Labour of up to 20 more seats than they had won in 2010 – when it was halted by Parliament. The Liberal Democrats had decided to oppose their Coalition partners on this issue because of disagreement over House of Lords reform. Labour, with the other opposition parties, joined them in voting for a five-year delay in implementing the 2011 legislation.

The Conservative party's 2017 manifesto, like that in 2015, continued with its commitment to continuing the current boundary review, 'enshrining the principle of equal seats, while reducing the number of MPs to 600'.

In May 2018 the government said it was committed to continue with the then-current Boundary Commissions' reviews and when the Commission reported back, the government would consider carefully how to proceed. Subsequently a review is being carried out in England by the Boundary Commission, now intended for 2023 under s 9 of the 2020 Act, with secondary consultation to be carried out between February and April 2022.

Parliamentary constituencies have previously been the building blocks for both former European Parliamentary regions and what are now Senedd regions: see sch 1 to the European Parliamentary Elections Act 2002 and s 2 of the Government of Wales Act 2006. Under the 2011 Act they also remain so, but s 13 of the Act made consequential provisions and altered the definition of Senedd constituencies in s 2(1) of the Government of Wales Act 2006.

B. LOCAL GOVERNMENT AREAS

The Local Democracy, Economic Development and Construction Act 2009 established the Local Government Boundary Commission for England: s 55. This is the fourth Boundary Commission or Boundary Committee for local government that has existed in the last decade; the current body results from a change from the original intention when the Electoral Commission was created, and is a separate body corporate independent of the Commission that "is not to be regarded as a servant or agent of the Crown." It is important to distinguish changes of local council areas, or the abolition of particular councils, from electoral changes within existing council areas.

Section 8 of the Local Government and Public Involvement in Health Act 2007 was amended by sch 4 to the 2009 Act to refer now to the Local Government Boundary Commission. Under s 8 reviews may take place of local government areas; the procedures for reviews, consultation and implementation are set out in ss 8-16 of the 2007 Act. The enacted provisions envisaged structural changes, some of which were implemented subsequently. The counties of Cornwall, Durham, Northumberland, Shropshire and Wiltshire all became single unitary authorities on 1 April 2009, while two were also then established in Cheshire. The Coalition Government announced that no further such changes were envisaged, and revoked other Orders already made for Norfolk and Suffolk. Subsequent to that, however, further unitary authorities have nevertheless been created – for example Bournemouth, Christchurch and Poole on 1 April 2019; Buckinghamshire on 1 April 2020; and North and West Northamptonshire on 1 April 2021. Section 8, however, remains relevant for any other potential boundary alterations between authorities, though the provisions of ss 17 and 18 about residuary bodies and staff commissions seem unlikely to be used in the foreseeable future. Unitary plans for unitary authorities in 2023 for Cumbria, North Yorkshire and Somerset have received ministerial approval.

When local government area changes are made, a wide variety of other matters need to be addressed. All sorts of things need to be similarly adapted to the new boundaries. They are effected partly by the principal statutory instrument making the boundary alterations themselves, and partly by the general Local Government Area Changes Regulations 1976, SI No 246, amended by SI 1978 No 247. There is a useful Ordnance Survey website www.election-maps.co.uk.

The Local Government Act 1972 had also created a Local Government Boundary Commission for Wales, and prescribed a boundary review procedure in ss 53-59. Though necessarily somewhat amended, these provisions continued following the Welsh reorganisation under the Local Government (Wales) Act 1994 (some amendments to ss 58-60 and s 68 were made by s 168 of the Local Government (Wales) Measure 2011). Under s 162 of the 2011 Measure, the Welsh Ministers were given power to make an amalgamation order to combine two or three local government areas. If one or more of the areas to be amalgamated was already operating a mayor and cabinet executive, a referendum had to be held under s 164 of the 2011 Measure on whether the new authority should also operate a mayor and cabinet executive system, while the Welsh Ministers could anyway – subject to prescribed conditions – direct that one be held where a mayor and cabinet executive was not already operating: s 165 (and see also M in chapter 4). These amalgamation provisions, contained in chapter 2 – that is, ss162-171 – of Part 9 of the Local Government (Wales) Measure 2011, were repealed by s 150 of the Local Government and Wales Act 2021.

The provisions in Wales are now governed by reviews carried out under the 2021 Act by the Local Democracy and Boundary Commission (see s 11 and sch 1). Part 7 of the 2021 Act, ss 121-150, provides in detail for both voluntary and compulsory mergers of authorities.

C. LOCAL GOVERNMENT ELECTORAL BOUNDARIES

In England, the Local Government Boundary Commission must under s 56 of the 2009 Act from time review the areas of principal councils, and determine whether electoral changes should be made. The review and implementation procedures are set out in ss 58-59, and the considerations to be taken into account are set out in sch 2 to the Act. Under s 57 a principal council with whole-council ("all out") elections not already divided into single member wards may request a review to consider the desirability of changing to them. Section 65 further deals with electoral changes necessitated by council boundary changes.

See also D below about related ward and electoral changes necessitated by a community governance review (parish council changes).

For Wales the approach had necessarily to be modified when unitary local government was introduced by the Local Government (Wales)

Act 1994. Sections 6 and 7 of the 1994 Act accordingly substituted s 64 of the Local Government Act 1972 and amended sch 11. Electoral arrangements for Welsh local authorities are now provided, however, following reviews by the Local Democracy and Boundary Commission under s 11 of, and sch 1 to, the Local Government and Elections (Wales) Act 2021.

D. PARISHES AND COMMUNITIES

Part II, ss 9-25, of the Local Government and Rating Act 1997 had provided a new code of powers for district and unitary local authorities in England to review their areas and to make recommendations to the Secretary of State for the creation, abolition or amendment of parishes. That review procedure in its turn has been entirely repealed and replaced by Part 4, ss 75-102, of the Local Government and Public Involvement in Health Act 2007.

Reviews had been matters for the Electoral Commission to oversee since the passing of the Political Parties, Elections and Referendums Act 2000, but since the operation of the Local Democracy, Economic Development and Construction Act 2009 the Commission no longer continues to have a role: the powers to make orders about electoral area boundaries under s 92(3) of the 2007 Act, and to issue guidance, were transferred to the Local Government Boundary Commission for England (see para 32 of sch 4 to the 2009 Act). The 2007 Act, however, put parish reviews on a wholly different footing.

The initiative, assuming they wish to take it, lies much more clearly with the relevant principal council for the geographical area concerned; it is much more onerous, and much more an active duty; and the procedures are couched in the context of a "community governance review." Greater London, where formerly there could be no parishes, is now included within these provisions' scope.

There had previously been some uncertainty as to whether a parish review could be conducted confined solely to potentially increasing the size of the council's membership. Historically, an order to this effect could be made under s 50(1) of the Local Government Act 1933, and empowering words were included in s 16(1) of the Local Government Act 1972. The Local Government and Rating Act

1997, however, had deleted these words, and so left doubt. There seems no doubt now however, from the references to electoral arrangements in s 90(2) of the 2007 Act relating to existing parishes, that the number of members is a competent consideration, though it also seems relatively unlikely that any review would be confined to such a specific issue alone.

The Local Government (Parishes and Parish Councils) (England) Regulations 2008, SI No 625 provide for the necessary implications where a reorganisation order is made following a community governance review. They were accompanied by the Local Government Finance (New Parishes) (England) Regulations 2008, SI No 626.

Significant additional powers about parishes were introduced by the Local Government and Public Involvement in Health Act 2007. Under s 75, inserting several new sections into the Local Government Act 1972, parishes may be grouped according to alternative styles, namely known (in what becomes s 12B(5) of the 1972 Act) a "group of communities," "a group of neighbourhoods," or "a group of villages." The group parish meeting and trustees will be known as the community meeting and community trustees, and similarly for neighbourhoods and villages. Ungrouped single parishes or meetings may also adopt the same styles under s 12A(2) of the 1972 Act, and there are ancillary provisions including such matters as de-grouping and making appropriate notifications. Section 76 of the 2007 Act enables parish councils to appoint (as opposed to co-opt) councillors via the additional s 16A of the 1972 Act. Note also that under s 92 of the 2007 Act a community governance review may make recommendations about desirable consequential changes in ward and county electoral division boundaries. For an example of such an Order see the Kettering (Related Changes) Order 2009, SI No 2786 (though made by the Electoral Commission, whose relevant powers have since been transferred to the Local Government Boundary Commission for England – see para 32 of sch 4 to the Local Democracy, Economic Development and Construction Act 2009).

The advent of neighbourhood development plans (see R in chapter

4), grafted onto the Town and Country Planning Act 1990 by s 116 of, and schs 9 and 10 to, the Localism Act 2011 will have considerable implications for parish councils. Section 61F(13) of the 1990 Act enables Regulations to make provision "as to the consequences of the creation of a new parish council, or a change in the area of a parish council, on any proposal made for a neighbourhood development order." See SIs 2012 No 637, 2015 No 20 and 2016 No 873.

In Wales the previous provisions of the Local Government 1972 (ss 27-29) were substituted and augmented by ss 8-12 of the Local Government (Wales) Act 1994. There had been no direct Welsh community council equivalent of the current provisions in England about conducting a parish review, nor a Welsh equivalent for communities of the potential alternative styles for parishes in England described in the previous paragraph. This was all changed by the Local Government (Wales) Measure 2011. Chapter 2 of Part 2 of the 2011 measure, comprising ss 100-115, provided a new and flexible regime for the organisation of communities and their councils.

Community meetings may apply to the relevant principal council for an order establishing a community council, or for an order dissolving its separate community council. There are also powers to group communities together with a common council, to add to, subtract from and dissolve those groupings. These steps, and the associated implications, are the subject of ss 27A-27L of the Local Government Act 1972, variously added by ss 101-112 of the 2011 Measure. In addition section 27M, added by s 113, gives the Welsh Ministers power to alter the voting thresholds in connection with the organisation of community councils.

CHAPTER 28
THE MODERNISATION PROCESS

"...it seems unlikely that the current fragmented arrangements for electoral administration in Great Britain would be considered as a serious option if designing a new set of structures from scratch."

This damning statement about the UK's present electoral was taken from page 1 of the Electoral Commission report *Electoral Administration in the United Kingdom* of August 2008. The report made several recommendations for change. This followed a period of considerable and varied piloting of different kinds of election and polling arrangements – for those interested, they were described at some length in chapter 25 of our seventh edition, *Running Elections 2013*.

It is a recurrent theme of this book that our electoral system is now more exposed than ever as a product of nineteenth-century Victorian England, and is becoming more and more unsuitable for twenty-first century society. The former significant levels of public trust in the system have been shaken by some high-profile cases of fraud, particularly in relation to postal voting (of which more later). There has been no coherent systematic approach to reform by central government but simply a series of reactive, piecemeal items of statute that could in no sense be considered as satisfactory. Continual tinkering with an already complex and archaic set of rules often makes the situation worse rather than better.

This has been further exaggerated as differing Government departments are left to pursue their own electoral activities, and to draft legislation to reflect their objectives. While there is some sharing of practice across government, and a group that endeavours to achieve co-ordination, until one single government department leads on elections and hence legislation etc, the problem will continue and grow. Practitioners need to be aware of this, and the associated issues and risks that this causes.

This is not, however, the only issue. In 2007 the legislative changes introduced to deal with so-called postal voting fraud were made in an untested and considerably under-resourced way. Tremendous problems occurred at those elections. In an unprecedented step the Association of Electoral Administrators produced its first ever post-election report stating that "these were the most difficult set of elections to administer within living memory." Their report also describes "the inappropriate approach by Government to funding and resourcing electoral services and how the determination to introduce new measures to combat fraud without proper and rigorous testing almost brought the service to its knees."

The Electoral Commission has taken a more leading role in respect of this topic over recent years. The 2007 combined elections in Scotland were a far from smooth process, with a high proportion of rejected ballot papers from the Scottish Parliamentary elections, problems with the electronic counting system used, and issues with the printing and delivery of postal voting packs. A report on what had happened was commissioned from a Canadian expert, Ron Gould (the Electoral Commission's remit, however, does not extend to Scottish local elections), and he made a number of interesting recommendations that many would argue are also relevant south of the border, namely:

• Electoral legislation needs to be rationalised and consolidated;

• A Chief Returning Officer for Scotland should be appointed to be responsible for overseeing Scottish Parliamentary and local elections (a similar post already exists for Northern Ireland);

• Combined elections are a disservice to local government and its candidates. Separate elections better enable voters to engage with the campaign in a meaningful way and make a knowledgeable decision;

• There should be timetable changes, as the provisions for postal voting do not allow sufficient time for printing the ballot papers following the close of nominations. The report recommends that the close of nominations should be twenty-three days before polling day rather than sixteen. The final day for postal vote applications should also be set earlier; and

- As polling now closes at 10pm, there should be no overnight counts.

Clearly, there are some radical ideas here, and the authors would readily concede that they may not have universal support within the electoral community (either north or south of Hadrian's Wall!). Following the Gould report, however, the Electoral Commission published a further report (December 2007) presenting views on the key challenges for the administration of elections and referendums across the UK as a whole. The Commission continued to express its concern in this report (and others) that the current structure for the delivery of electoral administration is stretched almost to breaking point.

In March 2008 a further issues paper was published for consultation and discussion involving the usual electoral stakeholders (including SOLACE). This paper attempted a more detailed analysis of the key challenges facing those responsible for electoral administration in the UK. All this led up to a further report in August 2008.

The Commission reflected that significant changes were needed at once, from returning officers and electoral registration officers, governments and legislative bodies and the Electoral Commission itself, to improve the delivery of electoral administration. These changes were required to clarify roles and responsibilities for the delivery of elections, improve coordination of returning officers and electoral registration officers and strengthen leadership and accountability for electoral administration professions.

The Electoral Commission did not believe, however, that there is currently a compelling case for removing responsibilities for the administration of elections and electoral registration from local authority control and re-configuring them under a single officer or body in Great Britain. They believed that it would be necessary, in the following five to ten years, to consider more fundamental changes to management arrangements for electoral registration functions, in the context of the future implementation of individual electoral registration in Great Britain. They made six recommendations for change for electoral administration in the UK, namely that:

1. Electoral Management Boards should be established in Great Britain, including all returning officers and electoral registration officers for each area;

2. The chairs of Electoral Management Boards should be given statutory powers to direct returning officers and electoral registration officers [a proposal that would have implications for the personal accountability of returning officers, and their insurance arrangements];

3. The Electoral Commission's role in driving and monitoring performance improvements for electoral administration in Scotland should be further developed;

4. The legal framework for electoral administration in the UK should be simplified and consolidated;

5. Steps should be taken to address structural causes of funding shortfalls for electoral administration in Great Britain; and

6. The potential for, and implications, of a co-ordinated electoral registration service across the UK should be considered.

The Electoral Commission wrote of the need for reforming action, saying in their Report on the administration of the 2010 general election:

"Our central message from this report is that the basic building blocks of electoral administration need long-term reform, support and maintenance: it is not enough simply to trust that the machinery of electoral administration will always work well and deliver elections to a consistently high standard; it is not enough simply to trust that those who want to undermine elections will resist the temptation to exploit the system; it is not enough simply to trust that people and systems will be able to adapt and cope with change without proper time to prepare."

Change, however, is in the wind, though certainly not imminent. Potentially the most significant changes to electoral law in our working lifetime may come from the Law Commission's review of electoral law. Following submission by the Electoral Commission, the Law Commission announced in 2011 that it would be including a project on electoral law in its eleventh programme of law reform. That project, which commenced in 2012, produced a highly detailed and universally supported interim report early in 2016.

In that, the Commission stated that the UK needs a new, modern and rational legal framework to govern the conduct of elections and referendums. They said:

"Electoral law in the UK is spread across 17 major statutes and some 30 sets of regulations. It has become increasingly complex and fragmented, and difficult to use. The turn of the century saw a steady increase in the numbers and types of election, and each of these election types comes with its own set of rules and systems. When these elections take place on the same day, yet more complexity is introduced by rules governing the "combination" of polls.

In today's interim report, the Law Commissions of England and Wales, Scotland and Northern Ireland outline the public response to their consultation on areas of electoral law that are in need of reform, and make recommendations to government for how that work might be done. The aim of the recommended reforms is to:

•rationalise the laws governing elections into a single, consistent legislative framework governing all elections and referendums,

•make electoral laws consistent across all types of election, and

•simplify and modernise out-of-date and complex laws, many of them Victorian in origin.

In particular, the Commissions are recommending that the process for challenging elections should be modernised, making it easier for parties to understand and use, and that judges be given the power, in appropriate cases, to limit the potential costs for challengers. The interim report also recommends that existing electoral offences be updated and made easier for the electorate, officials and prosecutors to understand, and that the maximum sentence for serious electoral offences be increased to 10 years.

Based on the interim report submitted by the three Law Commissions, governments will decide whether to ask the Commissions to proceed to the next stage of the project, which would involve submitting final recommendations for the reform of electoral law, along with draft legislation.

Nicholas Paines QC, Law Commissioner for public law, who is leading the project for the Law Commission of England and Wales, said:

"Elections are fundamental to democracy. They are the mechanism by which citizens exercise their democratic rights. The price we pay as a democracy when the electoral process loses credibility is high and potentially catastrophic.

Electoral law must be simplified, modernised and rationalised so that it can be more easily understood and used by administrators and candidates, and the public can have more certainty as to their rights. The law must be set out in such a way that policy development by Government, once properly scrutinised by Parliament, can be achieved by one legislative change, rather than a dozen spread out across several years. We are pleased to make these recommendations for reform and are hopeful that this opportunity to make electoral law more principled and efficient will be taken forward."

Lord Pentland, Chairman of the Scottish Law Commission, said:

"Inconsistencies and ambiguities risk undermining the credibility of our electoral process. It has become essential for electoral law throughout the UK to be streamlined and put into a modern, accessible and user-friendly format that is fit for the 21st century.

Throughout the project, we have stressed that our recommendations will be made taking into account the existing and emerging devolutionary framework, and we look forward to discussing this further with the Scottish Government. We have been delighted to participate in this important work and hope that the interim report will be received favourably."

The Hon Mr Justice Maguire, Chairman of the Northern Ireland Law Commission, said:

"The laws governing elections in Northern Ireland suffer equally from being spread out across different statutes and secondary legislation. In some cases older instruments are difficult for the public, or even legal professionals, to access. We are very pleased to recommend that the laws governing elections in Northern Ireland should be set out within a single and consistent legal framework and look forward to hearing the UK Government's response."

Subsequent to that, little has happened. The Law Commission have now announced that:

Due to the unprecedented demands on Parliamentary business arising out of leaving the European Union, Government made clear that there was no immediate prospect of introducing an electoral law bill to take forward our recommendations. We moved to explore with the Cabinet Office [now DLUHC] other ways to implement some of our reforms, in particular through secondary legislation. We have now agreed with Government that the project will move to producing a final report, which we aim to publish our final report in early 2020.

Electoral Integrity and Voter ID

In the Queen's Speech in October 2019, the Government announced its intention to introduce a requirement for voters to produce photographic ID at polling stations. People who do not have an approved form of photographic ID will be able to apply for a free local electoral identity document.

The Government states that requiring voters to show some form of ID will reduce the risk of voter fraud and improve the integrity of the electoral process. Showing ID will prevent people from pretending to be someone else at the polling station, an electoral offence known as *personation*. The proposals do not have implications for other forms of electoral fraud, such as offences relating to postal votes or campaign expenses. Critics have argued that the requirement will make it more difficult for people to vote and will disproportionately affect marginal groups.

The Electoral Commission analyses cases of electoral fraud. In 2017, one person was convicted for the crime of personation at the polling station. Eight police cautions were given in relation to other offences. In 2018, there were no convictions or cautions for personation. One person was convicted and two accepted a caution for electoral offences other than personation.

Several local authorities piloted different voter ID schemes at the local elections of 2018 and

2019, under provisions of the Representation of the People Act 2000. In 2018, about 340 people were turned away at the polling station for not having the right form of ID and did not return to vote. In 2019, there were 740. This was between 0.03% and 0.7% of all voters in each local authority. The Electoral Commission said afterwards that the pilots *"ran well but several important questions remain about how an identification requirement would work in practice."*

We now have the Election Bills 2022, referred to in detail in chapter 33. As we say in that chapter, however, the main matter of concern that urgently requires legislative time – namely the recommendations of the Law Commission regarding wholesale consolidation and reform – has not yet been taken forward.

During 2007, the Joseph Rowntree Reform Trust commissioned Stuart Wilks-Hegg of the University of Liverpool to undertake an independent, evidence-based review of UK electoral processes and procedures. The review's task was to establish the extent to which available evidence highlights potential threats to the integrity of UK elections. The report, *The Purity of Elections in the UK: Causes for Concern*, published in April 2008, concluded with a paragraph that certainly encapsulates the current position –

"The possibility cannot be dismissed that root and branch reform of British electoral law and administration is required, as opposed to

further consolidation of legislation and administration procedures originating in the nineteenth century. The nature of this task may be less onerous than it would seem. It has been widely noted in recent reviews of UK elections procedures that many viable solutions to the problems that have emerged in recent years are already in place in one part of the UK. Over the past decade, electoral reforms introduced in Northern Ireland have provided for more accurate electoral registers, strengthened the role of electoral administration, sharply reduced accusations of malpractice, and raised public confidence in the electoral process. The task of emulating these achievements in mainland Britain is the key challenge facing electoral policy today."

Can such reform driven by both a desire to modernise and a wish to drive corruption from the system be achieved? Sadly, it must be reported that, as we said ten years ago and as we now enter 2022, it seems highly unlikely to be forthcoming.

The new Elections Bill does not take us forward enough, nor comprehensively.

The authors (and other valued colleagues) have lobbied the Government via Ministers and civil servants for over thirty years, but with no real substantial success to report. Pleas at Parliamentary Select Committees and hearings are always given a polite and reasonably positive welcome, but without producing any actual results. Excuses such as lack of Parliamentary time (and drafting resources) are now of high mileage…but the cause will continue to be pursued.

CHAPTER 29
POLICE, FIRE AND CRIME COMMISSIONER ELECTIONS

The Police Reform and Social Responsibility Act 2011 established that elections for police and crime commissioners (PCC) for all existing police authority areas in England and Wales (except London) would take place on 15 November 2012 and in each subsequent fourth year thereafter on the ordinary day of local elections (though under s 50(4) that date may be varied by the Secretary of State by Order). As a result, much of England and Wales experienced the supplementary vote system for the first time on that date. The 2020 elections were postponed to 2021 because of the Covid pandemic, with the terms reduced accordingly to three years, so that the next elections are due on 2 May 2024.

The Policing and Crime Act 2017 introduced measures enabling PCCs to submit a proposal to the Home Secretary to take on governance of a Fire and Rescue Authority where a local case was made. Where this happens, the PCC is re-titled a Police, Fire and Crime Commissioner ('PFCC'). In this book we generally refer just to PCCs.

When the first PCC elections took place in November 2012, there was much criticism of them but practitioners faced an election at an unfamiliar time of year, using a system with which most were also unfamiliar, and which was combined with new responsibilities such as election addresses. The elections and counting officer provisions are summarised in O in both chapters 4 and 5. The Police and Crime Commissioner Elections (Local Returning Officers' and Police Area Returning Officers' Charges) Order 2021 is SI No 390, and the Police and Crime Commissioner Elections (Returning Officers' Accounts) Regulations 2012 are SI No 2088 (as most recently amended by SIs 2016 No 488 and 2021 No 179).

The regional nature of these elections meant that, with appropriate modifications, much of the regime and working practices for both European Parliamentary elections and the 2011 AV referendum were re-used for the forty-one police areas. Those regional practices have now evolved and become well established within individual areas. Consistency between the areas is both impractical and unrealistic. Geography, local circumstances and experience – as well as local operating practice – dictate how different regions operate. Nevertheless, while police area returning officers (PAROs) with legal responsibility for the elections had powers of direction under reg 4 of SI 2012 No 1918, very few directions were issued; the majority relied upon a combination of encouragement, good will and agreement to achieve a consistent approach across their police area.

The two most significant issue for the majority of both PAROs and local returning officers (LROs) in these elections is the supplementary vote (SV) process (particularly the adjudication of doubtful ballot papers), and the editing role for PAROs in relation to election addresses under para 7 of sch 8 to SI 2012 No 1917.

On the former, experience from mayoral elections, which are also conducted on the supplementary vote process, indicated that up to 20% of ballot papers can be regarded as "doubtful." Although some are not "doubtful" in the technical legal sense, they are invalid for a simple reason – for example, that a second preference vote cast for the same candidate as was given the first preference vote cannot be counted.

The number of doubtful ballot papers may accordingly be considerable, so that the process and logistics of their adjudication require very careful consideration. The conduct of mini-counts, for example, though preferred by many, can produce particular logistical issues. As a result the logistics of an SV count require much more careful planning and consideration than may initially seem obvious.

In addition, PAROs have to determine whether or not to verify and/or count locally or centrally. If they verify and count centrally, then they clearly have physical oversight in terms of consistency of approach on doubtful ballot papers (although practically, with a very large count, this can be questioned). The majority of PAROs at each of the PCC elections to date have decided to both verify and count locally, and therefore it has been important to ensure that each of the local counts followed the same criteria and standards.

In Hampshire, the PARO (one of the present authors) works with the LROs for each of the fourteen local counts on the process for the local count and the handling of doubtful ballot papers, basing that entirely on the Electoral Commission's guidance. Copies of the Commission's sample doubtful ballot papers are then posted at each local count. The aim is to ensure that those who adjudicate them follow the same approach, and also to demonstrate that consistency to candidates, agents and scrutineers, so that they could be assured that a ballot paper considered doubtful in one part of the police area would also be considered doubtful in another.

The other significant issue different for most PAROs for the police and crime commissioner elections concerns the production and validation of election addresses. This was the first time that returning officers had had overall editorial control – in relation to both party political and independent candidates – to adjudicate on the acceptability and validity of promotional text, with associated photographs and emblems. SOLACE took advice from Tim Straker QC on a framework within which PAROs could work. That advice remains available from SOLACE to all returning officers. There are, however, some useful points if a similar approach is adopted elsewhere (though other legislation may of course be differently worded) –

1. For the police and crime commissioner elections, election addresses are governed by sch 8 to the Police and Crime Commissioner Elections Order 2012, SI No 1917. The wording of that schedule is prescriptive, and needs to be applied literally.

2. In the absence of any legal prescription or requirements, common sense is required.

3. Under sch 8, the PARO has statutory powers to make any minor corrections considered necessary to ensure the address complies with the legal requirements. Such discretion should be exercised with circumspection, and PAROs are advised not to 'second guess' what someone else was seeking to say.

4. Paragraph 5(2) of sch 8 specifies that an election address shall contain only material about that elections, and shall not contain material about other candidates. In addition, advertising material (except promoting that candidate for this election) is prohibited.

5. There is a prohibition against any material referring to any other candidate at police and crime commissioner elections, but if words are included without a notional finger pointing directly to one or more other candidates, rather than making general reference to political policies (provided those cannot be directly linked to a specific candidate), then those words should be allowable: see para 42 of Tim Straker QC's Opinion.

6. Prohibitions against indecency, obscenity and offensiveness require particular thought. Counsel's advice was that it is the PARO's view that matters, although they should clearly bear in mind anyone else's view about obscenity, offensiveness or indecency.

The concluding paragraph from Counsel's Opinion summarised the position both eloquently and briefly –

"The relevant legislation provides a series of steps which need, in accordance with the election timetable, to be worked through. Many of the individual points mentioned ... will not often arise. However, when they do, a common sense approach in accordance with the advice is recommended."

It should also be noted that the National Police Chiefs Council (NPCC) produce additional guidance on interacting with candidates. Some interpret that guidance as applying additional prohibitions on the content of election addresses. It does not do this, but it provides very useful assistance to constabularies, so that they are consistent in terms of how they approach candidates who, for example, include photographs of serving police officers in uniform standing alongside police cars with badges, which the NPCC considers inappropriate. The enforcement of that, however, may not be for the PARO, and hence may be a difficult issue.

For PAROs, liaison with both the offices of the police and crime commissioner and chief constables is crucial – especially in the context of any unfamiliarity with the realities of holding elected office. The two are separate, although clearly linked; both will have an interest in the conduct of the next election (in police force terms, from an operational perspective not least), but unlike national and local government councils both are unused to operating in a political environment – and certainly not at the intensive level in which many returning officers operate on a day-to-day basis. They will require support and assistance, and should very much welcome a PARO who spends time with them working on issues such as publicity; liaison with candidates; what is acceptable and what not; etc.

Unfortunately in 2012, turnout was very low, leading the Electoral Commission to describe it as *"a concern for everyone who cares about democracy"*. Across all forty-one areas, turnout (including spoiled ballots) was 15.1%. The Government said that low turnout in a first-time election was to be expected; the Prime Minister said that it takes time to explain a new position, and it was predicted that voting numbers would be much higher next time. One polling station in Newport, Wales however, was reported to have had no voters at all, and many polling stations had individual turnouts of between 2% and 5%. Turnout subsequently has been higher, though as the poll was combined that is perhaps not surprising.

CHAPTER 30
THE 'DAY JOB'

Returning officers will be one of the most senior officers working in their local authority. They will, therefore, have regular contact with their councillors who may personally, or whose party may, be contesting a forthcoming election.

That can put the returning officer in a difficult position. As a result of that, it is appropriate to reflect upon the 'day job,' and how it will be exercised during the time that the same person is undertaking the role of the returning officer. 'Chinese walls' will help but, as always with elections, planning for the foreseeable problems – and dealing with those insofar as the returning officer can in advance – minimises not only the risk of their occurrence, but also gives a firm footing upon which to act. For example, many local authority chief executives/monitoring officers issue guidance for their councils covering the period between publishing the notice of election and polling day (the so-called 'purdah period' referred to in (iv) in chapter 8). That guidance varies between councils – reflecting local issues – and also varies between elections. For example, a European election was unlikely to have the same issues arising through the dissemination of material produced by the council as, say, a local election where perhaps the leader of the council is standing for re-election. Nevertheless, matters such as s 2 of the Local Government Act 1986 and the 2011 *Code of Recommended Practice on Publicity* will still be relevant. Whilst such issues are not necessarily relevant for the returning officer, the same officer may be required to rule or deal with such an issue wearing a different hat during the time they are returning officer – drawing them into a political level of debate and antagonism better avoided. Accordingly, having robust and clear arrangements in place in advance, and duly promulgating them so that the dividing line is clear and unequivocal before the issue arises, enables clarity on roles and responsibilities to be discharged and the criteria for what is (and what is not) acceptable to be publicly established. Hence decisions will not then be seen as made up on the spur of the moment, perhaps reached with a view to favouring (or dis-favouring) one party over another, and so on.

Such protocols or guidance can usefully include a number of particular topics; suggested areas that could be covered are –

(i) The principles underlying whatever guidance is given are the normal legal principles applicable to local authorities and their operation, as well as matters such as the *Code of Conduct* for Members, disciplinary rules and procedures for officers as well as documents such as any member/officer protocols in place.

(ii) The basic principle, particularly for officers, is not to undertake any activity which would call into question their political impartiality, or could give rise to the criticism that public resources are being used for party political purposes.

(iii)   A statement of the duties (and limitations on the powers) of a returning officer is sometimes helpful.

(iv)   In terms of decision-making, authorities can get into difficulty in relation to either making (or not making) controversial decisions prior to an election. Since the case of *R (On the Application of Kevin Paul Lewis) v Persimmon Homes Teesside Ltd* [2008] EWCA Civ 746; [2009] 1 WLR 83, the law has also been changed by s 25 of the Localism Act 2011 so that prior indications of views on particular matters at any time do not necessarily amount to pre-determination. Accordingly a council is not prevented from taking decisions it needs to take, provided that those decisions are taken correctly. The key aspect of the Persimmon decision was that a controversial planning matter fell to be determined during the pre-election period, and was featured in election literature. The council's decision was challenged on the basis that there had been pre-determination, but the Court of Appeal decided that there was no evidence of members having pre-determined the issue, but more a pre-disposition towards an outcome. The decision is helpful because the case confirmed (and this is a different point from that about pre-determination at non-election times) that local authorities are not precluded from the conduct of their normal business during election periods – but they must not, of course, disregard the potential for unfair electoral advantage or disadvantage by their actions. Any presumption of a freeze on decision-making, however, is flawed; business as usual is the starting point, but judgement needs to be exercised in each case. There will be situations where making a decision will be appropriate, or necessary, notwithstanding an imminent election.

Consultation issues can nevertheless sometimes mean that decisions are postponed or set aside. Certain consultations that may compete with the candidates for public attention, or may result in distortion because of their significant interest within the electoral process, will have to be revisited, and this can result in decisions being delayed. Matters or decisions may become issues in the election campaign, and this may distort the decision-making and create a risk that, rather than on its merits, the decision will be made on such overt, party political grounds that it becomes challengeable.

For this reason, provided that the law allows, chief officers should consider what steps should be made, for example, by extending a consultation period and/or putting out extra publicity for the consultation after the election in order to revive interest. Consultation processes can, in certain circumstances, subject to any legal constraints, be put on hold once the notice of election has been published – but a better approach might be to schedule such matters so that they do not take place during the election period.

Clearly, certain consultations, for example, those aimed solely at professional groups, will not have the same impact as a public and wide-ranging consultation on a controversial issue, so that each matter will have to be considered in the round.

(v) During an election, there may be more requests for information under Freedom of Information Act and/or Environmental Information Regulations. Requests should be treated even-handedly, and should be handled in accordance with the council's law, constitution and appropriate guidance. It should be 'business as usual.'

(vi) Publicity (specifically under s 2 of the Local Government Act 1986, which states that a local authority shall not publish any material which appears to be designed to affect public support for a political party) is, in one sense, fairly straightforward. It is also important to recognise, however, the significance of the 2011 *Code of Recommended Practice on Publicity* issued under s 4 of the 1986 Act. As a starting point it is worth bearing in mind that this requires the council to "have regard" to the Code. There is not, therefore, an obligation to follow it, although the authors of this book suggest that you should have an extremely good reason for departing from its provisions.

The Code contains guidelines specific to election periods, stating that

"Local authorities should pay particular regard to the legislation governing publicity during the period of heightened sensitivity before elections and referenda ... It may be necessary to suspend the hosting of material produced by third parties or to close public forums during this period to avoid breaching any legal restrictions."

This period referred to above, the period between publication of the notice of election and polling day itself is based on the statutory timetable in the relevant legislation, and is usually about six weeks. The Code goes on to say that

"During the period between the notice of an election and the election itself, local authorities should not publish any publicity on controversial issues or report views or proposals in such a way that identifies them with any individual members or groups of members. Publicity relating to individuals involved directly involved in the election should not be published by local authorities during this period unless expressly authorised by or under statute. It is permissible for local authorities to publish factual information which identifies the names, wards and parties of candidates' elections."

It concludes by advising that

"In general, local authorities should not issue any publicity that seeks to influence voters. However, this general principle is subject to any statutory provision which authorises expenditure being incurred on the publication of material designed to influence the public as to whether to support or oppose a question put at a

referendum. It is acceptable to publish material relating to the subject matter of a referendum, for example, to correct any factual inaccuracies which have appeared in publicity produced by third parties, so long as this is even-handed and objective and does not support or oppose any of the options which are the subject of the vote".

(vii) One local authority faced a specific question about correcting factual inaccuracies in media or other publicity. The issue was highly contentious in that the alleged inaccuracy appeared in material being circulated by the principal opposition party during a hotly contested local election. The legal advice was that only those inaccuracies that can be identified may be corrected. The council could not go on to explain, or otherwise summarise or interpret, save as was necessary to correct any factual inaccuracies. If the council were minded to consider issuing such a correction, it need clearly to identify what inaccuracies existed. Those should be cited in any correction letter, as well as the correction itself. There was a vast difference between factual inaccuracies and interpretation. One should not be confused with the other; the former was a lawful basis for issuing a correction, the latter not.

Even if factual inaccuracies could be identified, there was still a requirement demonstrating need to issue a correction in all the circumstances. Timing was critical and crucial. The more distant in time the inaccuracies, the less likely the need. Equally, if earlier statements had been superseded by subsequent media reports, that lessened the need. Furthermore, the council must be clear that there was a legal need to correct an inaccuracy, as compared to returning the matter to the political arena to be debated between parties as part and parcel of the normal round of pre-election debate and manoeuvring. Finally, matters raised within the ambit of this issue were likely in any event to relate to electoral issues that participants in the election could reasonably have expected to debate and discuss in a political arena, and as such the council would have no role in participating in that debate, and should take very great care to ensure that it remained strictly apolitical in its conduct.

(viii) Any guidance should address the issue of the use of resources, both by councillors and by officers. It is useful if such guidance is concerned with both aspects separately, so that members see, for example, that a member who breaches this rule may well be subject to action under the *Code of Conduct*, and that for officers, disciplinary action will be taken).

(ix) Given the number of premises that are visited by those campaigning during an election period, and the disparate way in which such premises can now be under the responsibility of one landowner but occupied by a multiplicity of public and/or private sector individuals, some guidance about access to council establishments (or joint establishments) can be beneficial – not least to make it clear who is responsible for what (in principle), and what might happen. For example, a prohibition against involving council establishments in overt electioneering is a fairly simple and standard requirement. In the case of joint establishments, however, it is appropriate to identify who is the relevant chief officer (not the returning officer) for that establishment. Where the properties are not controlled by or the responsibility of the local authority (for example NHS-related properties, schools etc) those bodies and/or individuals will be responsible for the decisions and, of course, will be expected normally to treat the candidates of all parties in an even-handed way. Particular care must be taken in relation to education establishments not to involve children in overt or indirect campaigning, electioneering or inappropriate media coverage. Sometimes an event will be authorised by a third party in premises that are also utilised by council staff and, in this case, local authority staff may be instructed by the relevant chief officer to ensure that they are not visibly or publicly involved, not photographed and not seen as participating in an event – all to avoid compromising their impartiality.

(x) It is often useful to include within the guidance the legal rules that entitle candidates or campaigners as of right to use, free of charge for election meetings, certain rooms which are the responsibility of a local authority – both to rehearse the requirements and to make it clear how such arrangements will be managed. "Free of charge" means free of hiring costs: incidental outgoings costs like heating still have be paid by the hirer or user.

The benefit of guidance such as the above has over the years assisted many senior officers and returning officers; although as already stated such guidance is broadly related to the operation of the council, and is therefore issued by whomsoever is the responsible council officer for the council's benefit, returning officers – either in their 'day job' or through their electoral role – can get drawn into such issues. Providing clarity on the rules and guidance, as well as on designated particular responsibilities, well in advance can therefore greatly assist.

CHAPTER 31
"IT'S NOT WHAT YOU DO, IT'S THE WAY THAT YOU DO IT"

This book, by its nature, has focussed on the law and many of the details about how returning officers discharge their duties in a range of electoral activities and referendums. On top of that, however, we must not lose sight of the characteristics that they must bring to bear on their roles and responsibilities.

Returning officers cannot unfortunately rely on everyone else to be polite and respectful, nor can they rely on others always adhering to the law. As senior, if not the most senior, officers in their councils, they will often find themselves intervening in what are highly contentious issues, and being expected to be judge, jury and (occasionally) executioner. The expectation often is that the returning officer will make an instant decision, supporting the view of whomsoever is standing in front of them (frequently to the detriment of others). Many of those decisions when made are made in haste but regretted at leisure. One of the safeguards available to a returning officer is that their role is tightly prescribed by a vast raft of legislation: primary legislation in the form of Acts of Parliament and secondary legislation in the form of Regulations. Election timetables are almost entirely prescribed and immovable, and hence the law will often state what you must (and must not) do, and by when. There is often no discretion. You may be able to bring more resources to deal with a crisis, but you cannot make more time. Even if something has gone wrong, compliance with the law at all times must be achieved. Do, however, remember that the law will assist. Section 46 of the Electoral Administration Act 2006, discussed in chapter 33, is potentially often helpful. Also, decisions made under the rules whereby clerical or minor errors in nomination papers or home address forms can be corrected by returning officers (eg rr 10 of SIs 2006 Nos 3304 and 3305 for local elections; and para 12 of Part 1 of sch 3 to the Police and Crime Commissioner Elections Order 2012, SI No 1917). Otherwise errors by the returning officer cannot be challenged in any other way other than by an election petition. First, though, always take time to think and reflect – and if necessary, take advice before responding. Bear in mind that the law is also your friend and a shield.

In terms of how the role is discharged, much has been said in the preceding chapters, but there are undoubtedly a few particular aspects that are worth bearing in mind. In the previous chapter, we focussed on potential conflicts, and methods of minimising them, between the 'day job' and the returning officer role.

In terms of how you deal with candidates and agents during the electoral process, courtesy, goodwill and pleasantness will always go far. With that you will need to encompass confidence in terms of authoritative advice – as well as assistance upon the rules, regulations and procedures.

Ultimately, however, political neutrality and all that the concept of neutrality means, is an absolute byword. Senior council officers are well versed in it.

That neutrality – being "politically restricted" as the Local Government and Housing Act 1989 terms it – can sometimes be described as stuffiness or "standoffishness," but a returning officer who is seen or believed, however incorrectly, to be partisan towards one party or candidate will struggle to convince the remainder of their neutrality. However closely you work or have worked with a particular party, or indeed, with the leader of a political party in your authority, and however many years they have been in control, once you are the returning officer, the approach has to be both professional and politically neutral.

Conducting briefings for candidates and agents at an early stage prior to the nominations process, supplying forms, being helpful (yet neutral) as well as being available during the count and in other ways will assist. Being clear where the line in the sand is, where there is discretion around acceptable behaviour or otherwise is, again, important. (We also touch on some aspects of this in (vi) in chapter 8.) Sometimes, even if you are not going to support a particular argument put by a candidate or agent, time spent listening and appreciating, even if you ultimately do not accept their point of view, will be appreciated. None of this will be new or strange to senior council officers in their 'day job', but in terms of the returning officer role, it is that bit different and can sometimes require a slightly different style of approach.

Compliance with the law is, of course, an absolute given. As already stated, it is your shield in so many ways. Yet how you go about applying that, interpreting it, and implementing it, particularly when electoral law by its very nature does have, unfortunately, many 'grey areas,' can be a challenge. Make sure that you do not get rushed into rapid decisions, even at the count. Take the time that you need to check the law. If necessary, discuss it with your electoral services manager and team, and/or pick up the telephone and talk to one or more returning officers that you know and respect. The regional elections leads are often contacted by colleagues for local and general elections and, of course, are happy to give their views. But do this out of sight of everyone else in the count!

A key *mantra* is that you must always look in command and control, even if underneath you are a seething mass of worries and concern. So create yourself a space, whether it is a side room or if you are using a large theatrical hall, even on the stage behind the curtain, where you and others, can look through law books and do all you want to do. On the floor of the count, however, you need to exude confidence and authority, while empathising and listening as appropriate!

CHAPTER 32
EXTERNAL RELATIONSHIPS

The Society of Local Authority Chief Executives and Senior Managers (SOLACE) has established an Elections and Democracy Policy Network, the third of SOLACE's policy networks as part of an ongoing programme to actively engage a growing number of SOLACE members in the Society's activities in key policy areas. The Network was established following a review of previous arrangements.

The principal purpose of the Network is strategically to influence electoral policy, legislation and practice to raise the profile of electoral services; to drive up standards; and to facilitate the exchange of knowledge and ideas. The Network clearly focuses both on electoral legislation and practice and also on the wider policy agenda around localism and democracy. The aim is that the Network will maintain the position of SOLACE as the principal professional body for electoral registration officers and returning officers.

As a result, electoral registration officers and returning officers should familiarise themselves both with the Network's output and current discussion topics. Meetings take place quarterly, minutes are circulated, and information is shared using various channels including an e-bulletin.

Returning officers should find the networking opportunities and the sharing of practice issues useful, and are recommended to consider participating. In addition, there are other bodies and groups that are worthy of note.

The Electoral Coordination & Advisory Board (ECAB) chaired jointly by the DLUHC and the Electoral Commission, aims to set consistently high standards of service across the UK to voters and to those standing for election or campaigning in the management of electoral registration, elections and referendums. There is a commitment to principles of maintaining trust, supporting participation and ensuring no undue influence – as well as recognising clear separation between the responsibilities of Government and Parliament for policy, legislation and election funding on the one hand, and the responsibilities of those independent of Government (such as returning officers, counting officers and electoral registration officers) who are responsible for the actual management of electoral work. The Board's aims are to advise Government, Parliament and the Commission on the right framework, resources and support for the administration of electoral registration, elections and referendums, as well as supporting the Commission in delivering high quality guidance and an effective framework for standards and monitoring. A further objective is to address wider strategic issues that affect the administration of electoral registration and elections and referendums, ranging across voter and campaigner behaviour and new technology, as well as the current and future capacity and capability of the various organisations and structures.

ECAB's membership is under review but has included the ten regional returning officers for the European Parliamentary regions of England and Wales, the convenor of the Electoral Management Board in Scotland, the Chief Electoral Officer for Northern Ireland, the Chief Executive and Director of Electoral Administration at the Electoral Commission, and representatives from the DLUHC, SOLACE, the AEA, the Greater London returning officer and the regional returning officer for Scotland (if any of the above is not already a Board member).

Importantly, a working group supports ECAB, consisting predominantly of administrators who provide particular valuable assistance in looking at the detail, both of guidance and draft legislation relating to elections. There is also a communications network who assist in evolving not only broader Electoral Commission communications relating to elections and registration issues, but also in devising local materials that are so useful to returning officers, particularly at national elections. In addition, an Integrity Round Table discusses integrity issues, both with administrators, political parties, and with representatives of the police and the Crown Prosecution Service.

Finally, it is important to note that what was the Electoral Policy and Co-ordination Group convened by the DLUHC has now been subsumed within ECAB. The role that that group took around overseeing and co-ordinating the development of electoral policy and legislation; considering the implications of proposed changes to legislation and funding arrangements; informing the development of electoral policy across Government generally; and working with appropriate other forums now falls within ECAB.

CHAPTER 33
THE ELECTIONS BILL 2022

The Elections Bill was introduced in the House of Commons on 5 July 2021. It proposes various changes to election law, and the Explanatory Notes confirm that these focus on the Government's priorities "that UK elections remain secure, fair, modern, inclusive and transparent".

Many within the election field feel that the Bill is a missed opportunity for an urgently needed wider reform of electoral law, which is accepted to be complex and fragmented. The Bill does not attempt to implement the Law Commission's recommendations for electoral reform, but instead introduces provisions to address issues which many practitioners do not regard as priorities. Returning officers, however, will ultimately be responsible for the implementation of whatever Parliament ultimately approves, so should be aware of both the policy proposals and also, as they develop, the intended delivery arrangements.

The Bill has gone through the first stages in the Commons and is expected to have Royal Assent by May 2022. It is therefore important to note that the Bill will have no impact on the conduct of the May 2022 elections.

Voter ID

The most controversial measure in the Bill is that voters must show photographic proof of identity before receiving a ballot paper in a polling station. The Government argues this will improve the integrity of elections and prevent someone's vote from being stolen – the electoral offence of *personation*. It proposes that a broad range of photo ID will be allowed, including a free voter card referred to above which will be available to those without any other form of ID.

Voters will be required to show an approved form of photographic identification before collecting their ballot paper to vote at a polling station for UK parliamentary elections in Great Britain, at local elections in England, and at PCC elections in England and Wales.

This is likely to extended to all other polls, such as parish and neighbourhood planning referendums, once the secondary legislation is made.

Prior to its introduction (likely to be in May 2023) it is planned that there will be comprehensive, targeted communications and guidance by the Electoral Commission. For those who have no scheduled polls until 2024, the first time that electors may be asked to produce photographic ID may be at the anticipated Parliamentary general election in 2024.

An elector who does not have any form of photo identification can apply for one, free of charge, from their local authority via the ERO. Current research suggest that around 2% of people may require identification issued by the ERO.

The deadline for applying for a free, local voter card will be set out in secondary legislation, but the current proposal is 5pm on the day before polling day.

There is potential for a digital solution so that electors can apply for a card online – similarly to online registration. This is currently being explored. Given the overlap with the poll itself and the fact that the electoral team usually undertakes both registration and election duties, EROs/ROs and their teams will need to be mindful of demand for voter ID being driven by electoral events, whatever is done to encourage early or timely applications ,he proposed deadline, is likely to bring further issues.

A broad range of documents will be accepted including passports, driving licences, various concessionary travel passes and photocard parking permits issued as part of the Blue Badge scheme. Any voter who does not have an approved form of identification will be able to apply for a free, local Voter Card from their local authority's electoral registration officer. It is likely that the Government will introduce a central online digital means of enabling voters to apply for a card online (akin to the registration system). There will be a paper based system also available for those who do not have the ability to access the online solution. In addition, absent voting applications (postal votes and proxy votes) will also be possible online through a further Government-led central IT system.

Opponents argue that personation is rare and that resources would be better directed at improving registration rates. They also point out that certain groups are less likely to have photo ID , so making it harder for some people to vote.

Franchise Changes for Overseas Voters and EU Citizens

The Bill will make two important changes to the eligibility to vote.

The first is for overseas voters – British citizens living overseas who are registered to vote in UK Parliamentary elections. Currently, overseas voters can only register to vote for up to 15 years after they have left the UK *and* provided that they were registered to vote before they left. The new rules will remove the time limit, introducing the so-called 'votes for life' Conservative manifesto pledge.

The registration period for overseas electors will be extended from one year to up to three years (currently an overseas elector needs to reapply every year), and electors will be able to re-apply or refresh their absent vote arrangements (as appropriate) at the same time as renewing their registration.

The Bill does not address the current issues with overseas voters, where the timetable allows very little time for ballot papers to be sent overseas, completed and returned by the close of poll. There have been issues and concerns with this. With more electors now able to vote under this changed regime, the problems that ROs often face are likely to be increased unless alternative approaches (such as e-voting, e-dispatch/receipt of ballot papers, different approaches to proxy votes for overseas voters etc) are considered.

The second important change is for EU citizens living in the UK. Now that the UK has left the EU, the Government is proposing to alter EU citizens' right to vote in local elections in England and Northern Ireland. This measure will amend the local voting and candidacy rights of EU citizens in local elections, as well as the PCC and combined authority polls.

EU citizens who have come to live in the UK since 31 December 2020 will only be able to vote in local elections if the UK has a reciprocal voting agreement with their home country. Currently Spain, Portugal, Poland and Luxembourg have agreed reciprocal voting treaties.

Once these measures are implemented, in addition to satisfying the usual eligibility requirements which apply to all electors (eg age, residence etc.), the following two categories of EU citizens will be able to participate:

• Citizens of an EU member state with which the UK has a voting rights agreement (currently Spain, Portugal, Luxembourg, Poland, plus others which may be added over time); or

• EU citizens who were resident in the UK at the end of the implementation period completion date (31 December 2020) and have retained lawful immigration status.

As a result, EROs will be required, when the revisions to the franchise are given effect, to remove from the register those EU citizens who are not eligible to be registered to vote.

Scotland and Wales have already changed their local voting to allow all legally resident foreigners to vote in local and devolved elections.

A Sanction for Intimidation

The Bill introduces a new electoral sanction for those guilty of intimidating a candidate or campaigner. This follows concerns about increasing levels of abuse, threats or intimidation.

The sanction will apply if someone is convicted of one of the offences of an intimidatory nature that are listed in the Bill. This applies only if the offence is committed because the victim was a candidate or campaigner. Someone convicted may be served a disqualification order which prevents them from standing for, being elected to, or holding certain elective offices for five years.

The Government says this would act as a deterrent, and that those convicted should not be permitted to participate in the democratic process they tried to undermine.

Digital Imprints on Campaign Material

An 'imprint' is information added to campaign material during an election or a referendum that tells potential voters about who produced the material.

Currently only printed campaign material requires an imprint, except in Scotland, where the rules have already been changed to include digital material too.

A key aspect of the Government's policy on this matter is to balance the need to avoid unreasonably restricting the free speech of individuals, and also to avoid imposing disproportionate measures which would discourage political campaigning. Under the new regime, all paid-for digital political material will require an imprint, regardless of by whom it is promoted. Further to this, certain campaigners, such as elected representatives and political parties, will also require a digital imprint on their organic material if it constitutes digital election material or referendum material.

The Bill will extend imprints to digital campaign material. This will help voters to know who is paying for what they see. It will also apply to some unpaid material if it is produced by a regulated party or campaigner. The imprint would be on the original material and so people sharing it online would not normally need to do anything.

The Electoral Commission's Strategic Priorities

The Bill would give the Government power to set the Electoral Commission's strategic priorities. It would also give the Speaker's Committee on the Electoral Commission the power to assess compliance by the Commission. Critics say this will risk the independence of the Commission.

The Bill will also prohibit the Commission from itself bringing prosecutions. The Commission had wanted to develop a prosecution role, but the Government's view is that this has never been agreed by Parliament.

Campaign Finance and Political Parties

The Bill will make changes to the registration requirements for political parties and third-party campaigners. These aim to tighten the rules that prevent foreign money being used in campaigning.

It will also amend legislation relating to 'notional expenditure' – that is goods and services received by candidates at a discount. This follows a 2018 court ruling that led to concerns that candidates and their agents could be liable for spending they were unaware of, or not involved in, but were seen to have benefitted from.

The Conservative Party called for urgent clarification of notional expenditure in the legislation. In 2019, it said it hoped "there is scope for cross-party agreement on this matter, and a short, technical amendment to legislation in this Parliament." The Labour Party said it "would support legislation that would serve to clarify Parliament's intention as to the extent the election agent is responsible for expenditure by third party campaigns to support their candidates" as part of a wider programme of reform.

Postal and Proxy Measures

These measures will strengthen the integrity of absent voting by addressing issues that have been highlighted as matters of concern at recent elections. The new measures will require those using a postal vote on a long-term basis to re-apply every three years. To negate 'postal vote harvesting' the Elections Bill bans political campaigners from handling postal votes. It also introduces a limit on the number of electors on behalf of whom a person may hand in postal votes to a returning officer or at a polling station. The Bill will provide that a person may be appointed to act as a proxy for a maximum of four electors, and among those four, no more than two may be electors who are not overseas electors or service voters. Finally, the measures add security to remote voting and protect those at risk of having their vote stolen by extending the secrecy of the ballot requirements in polling stations to absent voting.

Accessibility of Polls

To improve the electoral process for people with disabilities, the Bill places a new requirement on returning officers to consider a wider range of support for voters with disabilities in polling stations, supported through Electoral Commission guidance produced in partnership with the Government's expert Accessibility of Elections Working Group. The arrangements relating to the use of tactile voting devices will be consequentially amended following the successful challenge to the Government over this issue. The Bill also removes current restrictions on who can act as a 'companion' to support a voter with a disability to cast their vote at a polling station.

Other Matters

The Government is proposing to bring an amendment to the Elections Bill as currently drafted to change the voting system for both PCC and mayoral elections. Both will revert to first-past-he-post from the current supplemental voting (SV) system.

The Government is also proposing to abolish the Fixed-term Parliaments Act 2011, which would no longer to seek the approval of Parliament before calling a general election.

There has also been a suggestion that the timetable for Parliamentary elections be reduced from 25 working days to 17 working days. In our view, this was anyway impracticable prior to the introduction of the Bill; taken together with the other possible Bill changes, it would risk significant problems in the running of such important polls. Both SOLACE and the AEA oppose this proposal.

Finally, it is possible that a further amendment will allow electors to apply online for a postal vote in the same way that they can register online.

CHAPTER 34
WHEN IT ALL GOES HORRIBLY WRONG!

Elections are prone to things going wrong. Despite an increase in the use of IT (which in itself is not unknown to experience problems), elections are heavily reliant on people, and people do make mistakes. So things do and will go wrong. So what does the returning officer do when this happens? The first thing to do is not to rush in and do the first thing that comes to mind. Do some thinking; do some research; talk to colleagues; and if necessary consult legal experts.

The timetable for conducting an election is tight but you will have time, even if it is just a little time, to take advice before deciding what you are going to do. Do so, as experience has shown that an unconsidered initial response can create a bigger later problem than the original issue.

Do review the law. The Electoral Commission's guidance for those administering a poll is excellent and is of course based on the law, but there is no substitute for your looking at the relevant law itself. The law is your sword and shield it has been said, and that is true. The legal framework sets out what the returning officer must do, and to what timetable. It contains very little in the way of discretion.

The "conduct rules" are critical. These are the parts of the law that set out the specific rules under which specific elections are governed. For example, for Parliamentary elections, they are contained in the schedules to the RPA 1983. For local elections, in England and Wales, they are contained in the Local Elections (Principal Areas) (England and Wales) Rules 2006 (SI No 3304). The fragmentation and inconsistencies between the various 'Conduct Rules' will (one day) be addressed when the Government implements the Law Commission's recommendations. But for now, get the relevant "conduct rules" for whichever election or poll you are conducting, and study them in relation to the point at issue.

The legal framework is prescriptive. It sets out the steps you must take and the timetable within you must take them but if you follow that, you will be safe. So be clear that the issue that is concerning you is outside the legal framework – sometimes it is not.

Bear in mind that if an election is challenged over something the returning officer allegedly did wrongly, if that election was conducted substantially in accordance with the rules, and if the act or omission did not affect the result, then a challenge against the returning officer will probably fail (s 23 RPA 1983 – Parliamentary elections/s 48 RPA 1983 – local elections). Similar provisions exist for other polls.

It may sound odd to think of the worst case scenario, but to help you think through the issues, the options available to you and your potential courses of action, often there are serious consequences flowing from some options. If the "error" was not a substantial departure from the rules, and/or would have no impact on the result, that may clarify your decision as to what action you take, or do not take. One of the authors was faced with an error in the template of a ballot paper to be used in the European elections in 2009, namely a missing line along the foot of the ballot paper. Reprinting over 6 million ballot papers was one course open to him, but did the error warrant that? Was it substantial non-compliance? Would the omission of a line in question affect the result? No.

Section 46 of the Electoral Administration Act 2006 (which applies to local and parliamentary elections, similar provisions exist for other polls) is potentially very useful, and has been referred to a number of times. Section 46 states:

1. "A returning officer for an election to which this section applies may take such steps as he thinks appropriate to remedy any act or omission on his part, or on the part of a relevant person, which—
a. arises in connection with any function the returning officer or relevant person has in relation to the election, and
b. is not in accordance with the rules or any other requirements applicable to the election.

2. But a returning officer may not under subsection (1) re-count the votes given at an election after the result has been declared.

3. This section applies to—

a. a parliamentary election;

b. a local government election in England and Wales (within the meaning of the 1983 Act).

4. These are the relevant persons—

a. an electoral registration officer;

b. a presiding officer;

c. a person providing goods or services to the returning officer;

d. a deputy of any person mentioned in paragraph (a) to (c) or a person appointed to assist, or in the course of his employment assisting, such a person in connection with any function he has in relation to the election."

So what this means is that a returning officer for a Parliamentary or local government election may take such steps as they think are appropriate to remedy any act or omission on their part, or on the part of a relevant person, which arises in connection with any function that the retuning officer or that other person has in relation to the election, and is not in accordance with the rules or any other requirements applicable to the election. Relevant persons are the electoral registration officer, a presiding officer, a person providing goods or services to the returning officer (eg a printer of election documents), or a deputy of these persons, or a person appointed to assist, or in the course of their employment assisting such a person in connection with any function they have in relation to the election. Where a returning officer for a Parliamentary or local government election is guilty of an act or omission in breach of their official duty, but they remedy that act or omission in full by taking steps under s 46(1) above, they shall not be guilty of an offence under s 63 of the 1983 Act (breach of official duty) (s 63(4) of the 1983 Act, as inserted by s 46(6) of the 2006 Act). This provision does not affect any conviction which takes place, or any penalty which is imposed, before the date on which the act or omission is remedied in full (s 63(5) of the 1983, as amended).

The application of s 46 was material in 2021 when a number of returning officers experienced significant printing issues. There were concerns some might have only limited numbers of ballot papers, or even none at all. Despite an absence of specific powers, could a returning officer in that case postpone or cancel the poll, and plan for or announce a new date for another poll?

The answer to that question is an unequivocal no.

There is no scope in the rules for such a step, and *Baxter v Fear* [2015] EWHC 3136 clearly indicates that an absence of power on the part of a returning officer signifies an inability to act. Further, s 46 of the Electoral Administration Act 2006 does not permit such a step to be taken.

The only possibility for postponement is adjournment at a polling station until the next day in the case of riot at the polling station: see r 42 of the Principal Area Election Rules 2006, SI 2006 No 3304 and corresponding rules for other polls.

Any attempt to call off or postpone the poll (other than under r 42 or its equivalent) could be challenged, the appropriate remedy being to apply to the courts for an order of *prohibition* preventing the returning officer from purporting to exercise a power which a returning officer does not have. Furthermore, an order of *mandamus* could be sought requiring the election to proceed. Finally, in addition, the question of breach of official duty, which has a criminal sanction under the RPA1983, could arise.

Moreover, there would be the probability that the 'new' election would be invalid. Such a purported 'election' called or arranged in the way contemplated would not be an election properly and lawfully held.

It follows that returning officers have to carry on regardless, to do the best they can for the elections. "The show must go on". The role of a returning officers is to run the election as required by law. Amongst other things, the law specifies when they should take place. To illustrate, even if there were no ballot papers the election must still proceed; with no ballot papers and no votes, there would be a tie and the result determined by lot. A petition would surely inevitably follow, which would succeed and result in a new (and lawful) election.

Section 46 of the Electoral Administration Act 2006 did, however, provide assistance. This section enables a returning officer to take such steps as they think appropriate to remedy any act or omission on the part of the returning officer or any relevant person, which includes those providing goods or services (such as printing) to the returning officer. Taking a step includes *not* taking a step. put the matter positively, that is taking the step of allowing, for want of anything better, an imperfect document (in this case ballot paper). aim to consider the intended outcome, namely in this case the availability of ballot papers on which votes are marked.

Rule 47 of the 2006 Rules (and its equivalent in other rules) makes plain what is required for a ballot paper to be counted. That is still required. A returning officer should always endeavour to achieve the necessities so that valid ballot papers can be counted, but if let down by the printers may achieve that end result in what is otherwise an imperfect way. If this is kept in mind there will be a proper poll, which is likely to be unaffected (in terms of formal validity) by the errors or omissions.

Keep in mind the relevant legislation and s 46 in particular. Also keep in mind the object: namely in this case securing that there are ballot papers that can be marked and counted. A voter may well mark the paper invalidly, but in order to be counted there must be an official mark and the paper must not be void for uncertainty. (This would be the case if, for example, all the candidates' names were not on the paper before it came into the hands of the voter).

Do also note that s 46 only applies to errors made by certain individuals, and cannot be used to address errors made by candidates or agents. Also it does not enable votes to be recounted. But aside from that, its powers are broadly expressed. Do take advice before using it, but do consider its use.

And do take advice, talk to colleagues and seek their views. They may have experienced a similar issue, and as we all know, a problem shared is a problem halved.

Finally, consider taking expert legal advice if you need to.

CHAPTER 35
COVID-19 REQUIREMENTS AND EXPERIENCE

For the elections in 2021, we issued a *Supplement* to accompany our eighth edition of *Running Elections 2020* which addressed Covid-19 and related matters on which returning officers needed to focus. At the time of writing this ninth edition for the 2022 polls, Covid-19's Omnicom variant is with us, and although we are not in formal lockdown, there are restrictions in place which currently differ between England, Northern Ireland, Scotland and Wales.

As planning now gets under way for the polls in May 2022, we cannot know where we will be 'Covid-wise' then, but great uncertainties undoubtedly remain. With that in mind, SOLACE and the AEA are in essence advising that the approach in 2021 should be the approach adopted for 2022. In our words, plan for the worst, hope for the best. It is easier to relax restrictions late in the day than tighten them.

This chapter has two Parts. Part I suggests responses and adaptations to election stages and requirements that need to be re-considered, or differently planned, to allow for social distancing and other precautionary measures. Part II then records significant statutory changes since 1 March 2020 – principally of course occasioned by the Covid-19 situation. Both Parts refer to the foregoing principal text, of this edition, and have been updated to 1 February 2022.

PART I – Responses and Adaptations to Election Stages and Requirements which Need to be Re-considered, or Differently Planned

First, we set out various practical considerations and recommendations about the polls in 2022. Then, chapter by chapter related to this book, we consider a number of specific possible or necessary adaptations to election planning and polling day requirements which need to be re-considered, or differently prepared, to allow for social distancing and other precautionary measures necessitated by the Covid-19 situation.

Regard should of course also be had, as always, to advice and guidance from the Electoral Commission.

Introduction; and the Legal Regime

Much work has already been done on the practicalities of how elections should be run in May 2022. Preparations in some areas are well advanced. That is to be commended, but there is still a lot to be done, and there is of course great uncertainty around what the pandemic situation will be before and during the May election period. Returning officers can only do what they can do – which is to be as ready as they can be, and prepared for whatever may be thrown at them!

The starting point, as always, is the legislative regime. It is a well-known saying in relation to elections that the law is your sword and shield. This is because the legal regime sets out what you must do and when you must do it, but it contains less prescriptive detail than you may think. This time, this framework is even more important. In May 2022, the law is still your sword and shield. It will also justify, and be the basis for, some difficult conversations and decisions.

The starting point for reviewing the legal territory of elections is always the relevant primary legislation, which varies depending on the nature or the type of the election or poll concerned, given the fragmentation of the legal regime. For local elections it will be the Representation of the People Act 1983 (RPA) as amended. You must then study the relevant 'Conduct Rules', namely the details about what the returning officer must do, and within what timetable those steps must be taken. For local government elections, these are contained in the Local Elections (Principal Areas) (England and Wales) Rules 2006 SI No 3304 (as amended). The references to these statutory instruments (and their amendments) are given in the relevant sections of this book.

The Electoral Commission's guidance is always to be commended, but for 2021 it was rightly commended even more strongly. For

2022 it will be no doubt reviewed and revised, but much will remain in place. Specific guidance has been produced by the Commission with input from a range of practitioners, as well as from health advisers and the Government, and it is being continually expanded and amended as experience and expertise develop around how to run elections in 2022 in a Covid-19 environment. As well as exploring key considerations, anticipated guidance for 2022 will be made available on absent voting, nominations, polling stations, the count, and on attendance by candidates and agents at key events.

Accordingly, this reinforces the normal framework for elections with which you will be familiar, and which is fully addressed in full in our book – namely that the legal framework is prescriptive; it sets out the steps that you must take, and the timetable by which you must take them. If you follow these, as returning officer you will be safe from successful challenge.

This has not changed, and in considering how to run an election under Covid-19 it is important always to revert to that fundamental legal framework. Custom and practice have developed in many areas, but in looking back at them to see how an election can be run in a Covid-19 environment – subject to whatever social distancing or other obligations we are under to make sure that everybody involved in the process is safe – you should always go back to the legal framework. Often, it does not say what you think it might say: assumptions are understandably made because of custom and practice, but usually the legal framework gives you the answer.

Do always bear in mind – which may seem a strange point to raise at this early run-through of the steps that need to be taken to run a safe and legally valid election – that the legislation is clear: if the result is challenged because of any alleged act or omission by the returning officer, this will only succeed if the election was not conducted substantially in accordance with the rules, and the act or omission concerned affected the result. That can be found in s 48 of the RPA 1983 Act for local elections. In these difficult times, there is also something of the concept of 'herd immunity' about everyone moving together and acting similarly.

Before turning to some specific aspects of running the 2022 polls, it is worthy of note that on the Government's legislation website – legislation.gov.uk – there is a specific section dealing with coronavirus legislation. Certain aspects of this specific legislation are applicable to elections – see Part II of this chapter below. Further statutory amendments should be anticipated to facilitate the running of the elections. In addition, as set out in our earlier chapters, very significant other permanent changes unrelated to the pandemic are being made in Wales.

As already stated, the legal framework is the returning officer's sword and shield, within which you will find your roles and responsibilities delineated. It is also valid to remember, however, that as returning officer you have, in essence, four substantive responsibilities, namely –

- To see that everyone who is eligible has the opportunity to vote (and to do so reasonably conveniently);

- To ensure eligible candidates who wish to are able to stand;

- To ensure that the choice of the electorate is implemented; and

- To maintain the integrity of the democratic system.

These responsibilities can be useful in risk-assessing how you decide to deal with particular issues as they arise; returning officers need to understand their roles and duties, and what has to be done to ensure that there is a systemic and robust approach to delivery. You also must ensure that the system can be resourced, and – something which is particularly critical for 2022 – that you can make appropriate contingency plans.

Capacity and Resilience

As a starting point, we recommend that you consider building in extra capacity and resilience wherever you can. This is not simple, but where additional capacity and resilience can be incorporated into early planning, doing so now will provide additional flexibility, and (it is hoped) the ability to cope with the unforeseeable later in the process, when time and resources may be at a premium.

A key feature of these elections is likely to be that, for some of the events, you cannot finalise plans until very late in the day. As was the case in 2021, we believe the Government will be clear that the elections in May 2022 will take place. Assuming that the underlying pandemic situation is not so serious in April that the polls do have to be cancelled or postponed at the last minute, you could be running them in a pandemic situation – but with varying degrees of social isolation and other measures in place. You will need to be fleet of foot in changing circumstances, and may need to change things at the last minute. Building in that extra space for thought, capacity and time is really important.

Many of the issues that are likely to arise in preparing for these elections are going to be about the capacity and resources that the returning officer is able to deploy at any given time. As a result, it is necessary to have an early and determined focus on the capacity and resources available and required. What would happen if the returning officer – you – were unable to function? Or your core team? This assessment and gap analysis of all capacity must be ongoing, and the returning officer needs to be very clear about where the limits might be – and if there are capacity and resilience limitations, understand what those limitations are.

This assessment and its outcomes then feed into the planning process. Elections rely heavily on detailed project planning, but for this election it is will be important to be prepared to change that planning. Put simply, until the last minute there is likely to be less certainty in these polls than any others previously. That fact is new for most returning officers and their teams, and is something that everyone is going to have to deal with.

The Returning Officer Role versus the 'Day Job'

Returning officers need to have the confidence of all the participants in elections, but in 2022, in making those fleet-of-foot last-minute decisions which may be perceived by some to be prejudicial – in terms, for example, of their ability to attend key events – this confidence in you is even more important. Controversial and last-minute decisions or changes of plan may be unavoidable, of course, but must also be seen as being made not with a political agenda but for health and safety reasons in the best interests of everyone.

For that reason, it is even more important that the returning officer's independent role and politically neutral position is clearly presented by you and your team in all that you do – and also in the 'day job,' so that your independence and political neutrality can be acknowledged by all. The outcome will be that when as returning officer you must make those difficult decisions, candidates, agents and voters do not start from a position where they believe that you are in some way 'tainted,' prejudiced or politically biased.

Below are advice and comments relating more directly to individual chapters above in *Running Elections 2022*:

Chapter 5 – Returning Officers and Deputies

Consider whether the possibility of infection, or simply the requirement to self-isolate in quarantine following possible contact with the virus, may mean that the appointment of one or more additional deputies (whether for limited or all purposes) should be considered. The scope for home working is limited in relation to functions that must be completed to any extent in person (like the nomination and count processes). If you are the returning officer and your team physically meets together at any time, the risk that you all could be compromised is magnified.

Chapter 7 – Polling Stations

The siting and dynamics of all polling stations need to be re-considered. Double stations may be a particular problem, as will temporary polling huts and anywhere else with very limited space or accessways – these probably cannot be used, except as a very last resort. Do stations allow for staff to be distanced from each other? Can this be eased at all where two or more people otherwise in a private 'bubble' at home can work together? Do arrangements for kitchens and lavatories need different arrangements? If you do need to re-site any stations, or even alter any polling places, do you have the necessary powers and/or delegations to do this in time?

Can voters, who may well have to come in one at a time, queue safely outside? How will that be marshalled? What about hand sanitising, and wiping down of anything likely to be touched? Voters do not have to use a pencil – but will they be reminded that it is desirable to bring a suitable writing implement of their own? Will the person handing out the ballot papers wear gloves? Will presiding officers (who need full briefing about all this) have a box of spare pencils in case of need?

There have now been elections in 2021 as well as a number of by-elections carried out successfully under significant Covid-19 related limitations and obligations. The learning from those will be incorporated into the Electoral Commission's guidance – and it is highly recommended that you make yourself familiar with this. Ensure that you learn from this good practice elsewhere, and do not attempt to 'reinvent the wheel.'

Providing safe polling stations will be a critical part of the electoral process for all returning officers and their staffs. As indicated above, you will need to review the suitability of all your usual venues in the light of current circumstances and any additional requirements specific to these polls. This will include such issues as the size of the venue including social distancing space, as well as planning for the venue's actual operation. Many if not most utilised a one-in-one-out approach to polling stations, with a 'door marshall' (or equivalent title) at each polling station to help deliver the necessary health obligations, and also to manage the one-in-one-out system. Such an approach raises the likelihood of queues, but if the usual buildings have multiple entrances and exits to enable the implementation of a one-way system, existing buildings can clearly be used. You will need to consider cleaning protocols before you open the polling, again progressively during the day, and yet again if some issue arises in the polling station during the day. As the returning officer you (and your presiding officers) have a legal duty to allow designated individuals into venues for certain electoral processes – for example, candidates and agents must be allowed to oversee certain proceedings, and given certain opportunities particularly in relation to personation. Those requirements and opportunities must be maintained.

Of course, some venues in 2021 were not be suitable (or available). Similar issues may arise, and some alternative venues may themselves not be available in 2022. Many returning officers are already now booking venues for May 2022; some have gone a long way down this route, as well as organising staff. That is to be commended for obvious reasons. While public venues such as schools and libraries must be made available to the returning officer, private venues have a choice, and if they choose not to make themselves available for the 2022 elections then returning officers will have to look elsewhere for alternative venues for polling stations or the count.

Do bear in mind that the legal polling station review process for polling stations relates to Parliamentary general elections, and not to local elections or PCC elections. If you do have to change a venue (particularly one used for a long time and so familiar to local voters), you should, however, be entirely open and public in explaining what is going on and why. Take account of the legal constraints mentioned at the beginning of this section, and consider – as already mentioned above – whether you need to seek lawful authority to make changes should they become necessary shortly before polling is due.

If changes should become necessary, ensure that candidates and agents have been told repeatedly that you must continually review your venues, and may have to move polling station sites and locations. This is always potentially a contentious issue for candidates and agents, but in the current environment there are very likely to be more polling station issues than usual or presently anticipated. Returning officers should make sure that they communicate that loudly and clearly to candidates and agents as early as possible, and then obviously in the lead up to polling day itself. Do whatever is advisable in your area to ensure that the electorate know that they have to go to a different place to vote, where that place is, and why the change has been necessary.

When presiding officers are briefed, give thought to what will happen at polling stations at poll closing time, when there may be queues outside – not because people have arrived too late, but because they are simply waiting in a socially distanced line. This was provided for in s. 19 of the Electoral Registration and Administration Act 2013, which inserted r. 37(7) into the Parliamentary Elections Rules. Anyone outside in a queue "for the purpose of voting" must still be allowed to do so – see chapter 19 above.

Chapter 8 – Things to Do First for Elections: Suppliers

There needs to be regular and ongoing contact to ensure that suppliers are currently able to open for business, and can deliver what you need. Ongoing active management is important, as is an understanding of their contingency plans. You may not be facing the most acute Covid-19 limitations in your area, but your suppliers may be in theirs. In which case, are they able to function sufficiently well; are their staff able to work; and are they able to deliver to you on time? Suppliers may tell you that there are longer lead-in or delivery times, in which case you will need to consider how that impacts upon your plans, and whether you need to vary orders and expectations with them accordingly to make sure that their actual delivery performance will meet the statutory timetable. How do you minimise risk, capacity and resilience issues for them? Make sure that they understand your key dates, so that if they need to change their arrangements to meet those key dates because of pressures they are facing, they can review the situation and discuss solutions with you early on. The need for contact with, and active on-going management of, suppliers must be a high consideration on any risk register.

Major issues were experienced by some returning officers in 2021 in relation to printing – especially ballot paper printing. We have already referred to this in chapter 34. Be aware of this possibility, and take account of it in planning for how you will manage suppliers. It is not just your capacity and that of your team that may affect your ability to deliver a poll, but also that of your suppliers. Whatever or whoever the issue lies with, however, the responsibility – and accountability – remains vested with the returning officer.

Consider in addition the attitudes and outlooks of local political parties – and indeed any individuals whom you know intend to stand as independents. It is important that you know their points of view, and understand how your local political parties and other candidates intend to cope with the necessary arrangements; what their level of relevant engagement and experience is, and what their expectations are. How ready are they to contest an election in a Covid-19 world?

Chapter 9 – Insurance

There are inherently greater risks in running an election – and in organising the counting – in the present climate. As returning officer you must carry adequate insurance (without any excess at all, if possible), both for that role as such and also as the personal employer of election staff. Do not overlook the employer's liability requirements! Many insurers are excluding coronavirus-related risks from their policies on renewal, so it is important to check what exclusions apply following on from or since whatever arrangements you made on appointment, and have since annually and routinely renewed. There may, for instance, be conditions about the employing of people over a certain age, or with known disabilities or vulnerabilities. Do check all this now!

Chapter 10 – Appointing Election Staff

Common-sense provisions apply about the appointment of staff – and some 'regulars' may this year be unavailable because of shielding, underlying health conditions, or previous contacts that necessitate quarantine. That means making sure that spare appointees are identified – and that existing appointees are reminded to notify you as soon as they become aware of any risk to their availability on polling day. All staff will need to be briefed this year – not just presiding officers etc. That can be done online, so long as you are able to be satisfied that those involved have viewed it.

Staffing is probably best examined from two directions: first, considering the core election staff including the returning officer personally and deputies, the polling station staff, the count and other support staff (such as communications, IT, security etc.); secondly, approaching your requirements by thinking of the staff needed for each stage of the process (such as nominations, handling absent vote requests and inquiries from the public, polling day, the count etc.). Adequate and competent staffing is obviously critical to each stage of the process, but looking at your requirements from various angles will help to inform and support sound contingency planning.

Returning officers must (as in all staffing contexts) consider their needs for core staff, capacity and resilience – but particularly the importance of deputy returning officers. At least one deputy must be appointed at every election anyway, with authority to run every aspect of the process, and others may of course be appointed for certain roles only. Circumstances under Covid-19 are different. The likelihood of illness, or the need to self-isolate, is much greater. So contingency provisions are prudent as well as the normal precautionary cover. So, how many deputies will you appoint – perhaps more than normal? Will they be full or partial-authority deputies, and will they all be from within the core team or will deputies also be appointed from other areas, in case you and your core team also succumb to illness? Note what chapter 22 above says about payments, pension contributions (not applicable for deputies), and national insurance contributions.

Returning officers will also want to consider temporary staff generally, and how they may provide back-up capacity to all parts of the process – but in particular how they, or staff seconded from other areas of the authority, can provide contingency support to the core team. Do not forget to make appropriate and/or provisional insurance arrangements accordingly – and bear in mind what we say in relation to the section on chapter 9 (insurance) above about possible exclusions or special terms relating to older people and/or those with disabilities or vulnerabilities.

Vitally important, in general terms, is how people will not only be made to *be safe*, but also to *feel safe* when they are performing their various roles.

Chapter 11 – Working with Election Agents

Election agents too must be briefed about whatever ways you are having to modify the election preparations and practices that they are used to – and it will be sensible to remind them (although not your responsibility) about their own campaign conduct – using helpers, knocking on doors, appointing polling agents and tellers at polling stations, etc. It is understood that at the current time, the Government guidance on campaigning that was issued in 2021 is unlikely to be re-issued for 2022.

Chapter 12 – Handling the Nomination Process

The law on nominations has not been changed. It is understood that for 2022, there will be no reduction or change in the 'normal' legal requirements for nominations.

Just as you no doubt would normally encourage candidates and agents to make appointments before coming to submit nomination papers, the same is more than ever important when social distancing needs to be arranged. You cannot, however, refuse to consider a submission, and there may be some of which you have had no notice – but you can expect those concerned to act reasonably in order to protect yourself and your staff, as well as themselves. That in turn requires you of course to act reasonably too – which is just a matter of good customer service.

In dealing with nominations, the normal processes involve a number of interactions between the returning officer or their staff and the candidate or election agent. There may be a briefing of known potential participants. Draft nomination papers may be brought in, which may then be reviewed, and followed by a conversation to explain what needs to be changed, varied or altered. That process is an iterative one, and may have several cycles. When you look at the legislation relating to the nomination process, however, you find that the only physical human interaction that must occur as prescribed by law is the delivery of the nomination papers to the returning officer.

Submission of drafts can be done virtually; briefings can be done by Zoom or other online meetings; and the iterative processes can be undertaken by telephone Zoom meetings or by email. The only step that needs to be done on a face-to-face basis is when the final candidate nomination papers are handed to the returning officer (or appointed deputy) for formal receipt and decision about validity. The legislation is clear about this: it is one of the reasons why it is important that you reconsider usual practice, and do not start from what you normally do (or from what you understood to have been done in the past) – but that *you start from what the law says you must do.* It then becomes clear how the nomination process can be managed safely. This is fully reflected within the Electoral Commission's excellent guidance on this topic.

Chapter 15 – Absent Votes

The Electoral Commission have produced bespoke guidance for dealing with absent voting in a Covid-19 situation. 2021 showed that whilst voters made more use of postal votes, the level of usage was not as high as some expected. Nevertheless, returning officers need to be prepared to receive more postal votes and proxies, and consequentially to build capacity and resilience to administer them, as well as providing suitable back-up arrangements. Whatever plans you have for dealing with postal votes must still provide the legal rights of access that candidates, agents, observers and scrutineers all have to observe postal vote opening.

In 2021 the Government introduced what became known as 'Covid-Proxies'. Individuals who needed to self-isolate because of coronavirus were still able to vote because of an amendment to emergency proxy voting rules. The legislation allowed anyone who was self-isolating due to Covid-19 to access an emergency proxy vote, up to 5pm on election day.

Although this legislation was scheduled to have lapsed by May 2022, it is understood that the Government will be providing for these 'Covid proxies' to continue for the May 2022 polls.

Chapter 16 – Polling Agents and Tellers

You will know who has been appointed as a polling agent (though maybe not until very late in the process). They will need to be briefed about how you are planning to run the polling stations, and any special considerations which may be involved. You probably will not know in advance who will be the tellers at any location – it will be important to impress on agents the need to use responsible people who can be briefed about how polling stations are having to operate. Tellers have no special position or rights – and if there are queues outside, they may be tempted to approach voters too closely. In extreme cases presiding officers might have to call on Police assistance if moderate persuasion is insufficient. You could give presiding officers a leaflet to give to tellers who arrive at their polling station, saying what needs to be said.

Chapter 17 – Planning the Count

These various complementary requirements below will – as they always do normally – comprise much of the wider experience and public judgement of how well you ran the election.

Each of the principal aspects of a successful and smooth count operation will have to be re-thought with social distancing and contact hygiene in mind, and later briefings given accordingly:

The floor layout, when space is usually at a premium anyway without two-metre   distancing;

How to admit and seat your count staff (and whoever normally operates the count venue);

How to admit and marshall the candidates, agents and counting assistants;

How to enable ballot boxes etc. to be smoothly delivered and received with minimal delays;

How to operate your role as returning officer, make declarations, etc.

arrangements for the media;

The cloakroom and lavatory arrangements, with safe distancing etc.;

What will happen should the count need to be adjourned for any reason, and/or people need to take breaks, have refreshment etc.;

What will happen once the count is over, and when ballot papers and everything   else must be safely packed and removed to storage.

See also the section below on chapter 20 – Conducting the Count.

Chapter 18 – Handling the Media

It will be important to explain to the local media, as to the election agents, whatever adaptations you are having to make to run the elections safely – but still in accordance with the law. A particularly sensitive issue, for instance, may be that of queuing to enter polling stations – something in the past that has been a symbol of poor election management for which the returning officer is personally accountable. (See the chapter 7 section above.) Local media – and local radio stations – could be helpful here in helping to prepare voters for what the adapted voting process will be (and perhaps to remind them to bring their own pencil, etc.) It should help to mitigate any adversely critical coverage later if media outlets knew beforehand what was likely to occur, and played a part in shaping public expectations of it.

Communication is an important part of the returning officer's role normally; it was more critical in 2021, and will be again in 2022. The messaging has already started as the Electoral Commission's media campaign has been launched and is being adopted locally by many returning officers. The Commission's campaign is simple but concise, namely that –

It will be safe to vote in a polling station;

If you want to vote, but not in a polling station, the absent vote process provides an opportunity through either proxy voting or postal voting;

If you choose to vote by proxy or post, you will need to apply (if not already registered to do so), and we suggest that you apply early;

As polling day draws near, the messages will become more detailed and localised, to reflect individual circumstances and requirements – such as for example that polling stations will be safe but some venues may change; or that if you go to vote you will need to wear a mask, bring your own pen or pencil, and be prepared to queue, etc.

Also, it is worth starting to communicate how the count will take place, whether it is going to take place overnight or not, and whether it may take longer than usual. If any of this means that results may declared later and/or more slowly, you should say that too.

As already stated, relevant for any communications campaign is the duty under s 69 of the Electoral Administration Act 2006 to encourage electoral participation (to the extent that this applies to local elections). Similar provisions exist in other legislation for other polls, for example reg 12 of SI 2012 No 1917 for PCC elections, which contains the same duty.

Chapter 20 – Conducting the Count

See also the section above on chapter 17 – Planning the Count.

The scheduling of counts – bearing in mind that most places are facing combined elections and hence multiple counts – is the first issue to be considered, since once scheduling decisions have been made, venues and staff etc. can be booked.

There is no right or wrong to this, but an early decision can be very helpful to returning officers in taking the heat out of the situation by deciding that, for example, there will be no overnight counts (part of your building capacity and resilience into the process). How counts are to be scheduled, the order of counts, and the time at which counts will take will also be informed by the capacity and practicalities of the venues. As such it is an iterative process, but one that is useful to plan early. Because social distancing may well still be applicable in May 2022, it is possible – even likely – that there will be fewer counters in a count venue. If there are fewer counters, the counting process itself will take longer. That will mean different considerations apply about lengths of shifts, comfort breaks, rest periods and adequate refreshments.

There will also need to be responsible and pragmatic local discussions with candidates and agents about their attendances at the count. They will have to manage their expectations accordingly, and comply with whatever social distancing and other obligations are in place for that particular count. Achieving this will require as much tactful but explicit explanation as possible, shared as soon as possible. There are of course many statutory rights to attend, but (although obviously is important to be able to demonstrate publicly that counts have been fairly and validly conducted) counts can in principle take place with none of those who have such rights actually present. They are rights to attend – not requirements that the relevant people must do so.

Finally, you must consider how the media will operate at the count, as that is likely also to be different. How can they be managed and supervised safely to facilitate their access to candidates, agents, and the democratic process generally, but without prejudice to the safety of everybody else involved?

Chapter 33 – When It All Goes Horribly Wrong!

As always, and we keep saying, the legal framework is your sword and shield. It is never more critical than when you have to deal with the possibility of a failure or omission on your part, or in your name. If there is the possibility of a failing or a deficiency in the process for which you are responsible, do remind yourself that the power to correct clerical errors in s 46 of the Electoral Administration Act 2006 is a useful tool in your armoury. Do additionally bear in mind that provisions similar to s 46 exist for other kinds of polls. For example, for the PCC elections it is provided in reg 6 of the Police and Crime Commissioner (Functions of Returning Officers) Regulations 2012, SI No 1918.

You will recall that challenging the returning officer will only succeed if the election was not conducted substantially in accordance with the rules, and the error or omission affected the result. At present, it appears more likely that returning officers will have to make judgements where the need to take action to ensure the safety of all engaging in the electoral process is balanced against the delivery of that electoral process. We have not (yet) encountered a problem where we have been unable to assist colleagues with some advice that has not enabled both intentions to be served.

Often assumptions about what the legislation says is based on guidance which not only includes the formal legal requirements but also what is usual or best practice – or what is done customarily.

This has then been assumed to be the strict legal position. It is distinctly possible, however, in the authors' view that returning officers will have to make judgments in the 'grey areas' around the edges of the legislation – in which case not only should they seek advice first if possible, but they should remember their primary roles and responsibilities, as well as the only basis upon which a result can be challenged for an alleged failing or invalidity by themselves. No one should ever set out simply to comply substantially with the rules, though the law will not uphold a challenge if there has been substantial compliance with them. Furthermore, if there is an alleged breach of the rules, has that alleged breach, that act or omission, affected the result? That is, has it affected the declared outcome, as opposed to merely the numbers of votes cast, or whatever?

These matters should be borne in mind before a 'grey area' decision is made but, as always, we and indeed others would point out that, although the timetable is tight and must be followed, there is always some time to think, to consult or to take advice – and we commend that position, as always, to all colleagues who may be facing such an issue. Talk to a colleague; take legal advice!

Conclusion

We recommend creating time and space in your governance arrangements and planning to have time to think, react and be flexible. Plan for the worst, hope for the best!

Be prepared to change (and to be obliged to change at the last minute) how you are going to deliver this election. Let others be aware your plans may have to change, and ask them to accept this.

Keep your risk register in view, and update it regularly while you plan for contingencies in so far as you can. Consider using others with expertise in this area – the local resilience framework team and your emergency planning colleagues should be very helpful in this regard. Your plans need to be fluid, but of course must remain embedded within the legal framework. Get into the habit of making timed and dated, recorded or written records which can if necessary be reviewed and proved in evidence later – especially of key decisions. It may very well be that you will need to make some decisions that are in those legal 'grey areas' when it will be particularly important to record at the time what you did, and why and when you did it.

Take advice, and think. You will have a little time to think, even in a tight time frame.

Finally, ensure that you are connected into whatever networks or information flows there are for you, both locally and nationally. Information is key here, as is understanding what others are – and are not – doing.

Everyone has a part to play in helping you in delivering a successful election process despite all the difficulties. It cannot be done without procurement, property services, administrative, clerical, IT, office caretaking, and all the other vital work that must happen, when and as you need it. Remember to tell your support staff how much you recognise and appreciate their roles, even though their roles do not represent the same personal responsibility for them that election work does for you. Your success will be theirs too!

APPENDIX 1
FURTHER READING AND SOURCES OF INFORMATION

Surprisingly, for such an extensive area of local government work, there are comparatively few books written upon this subject. The two standard textbooks appear in encyclopaedia form and are widely consulted by all electoral practitioners; they also figure in all law libraries. *Parker* appears in three volumes and sets out to concentrate upon Parliamentary elections, although there are elements of cross-referencing to local elections. It is published by Butterworths; their address is referred to below. The other encyclopaedia is *Schofield*, which now appears in five volumes. Originally designed to deal with local elections, it now also contains material relevant to Parliamentary and other elections. It is published by Shaw and Sons, who also produce electoral stationery used by practitioners – eg nomination forms, the booklet *Guidance as to Doubtful Ballot Papers*, etc.

SOLACE and the AEA co-operated during 1998-99 to produce much training material for the European Parliamentary elections of June 1999. This was facilitated by a Home Office grant, and text books on legislation as well as training manuals were printed. There was also an evaluation report on the European election prepared by the University of Swansea. For the June 2004 elections the Electoral Commission took the lead in publishing a range of guidance and training materials, and also the subsequent evaluation. They continue to do this, also organising (often on a regional basis) a range of seminars and workshops.

The AEA, as the principal electoral administrators' organisation, provide examined courses leading to their Diploma or Certificate, and also as part of their range of professional activities run training seminars – as does SOLACE – for both newly appointed and experienced returning officers; written material is usually distributed also at these events.

Prior to each Parliamentary election the DLUHC's predecessors (going back in sequence the Cabinet Office, the MoJ, the DCA, the Lord Chancellor's Department and the Home Office, used to produce a guidance manual for acting returning officers – dealing with such matters as expenses, nomination of candidates, the count, etc. The Electoral Commission now publishes the equivalent general election guidance for those administering the poll, and also (usefully) guidance for candidates and agents.

The Electoral Commission also produces much further information and guidance, including circulars for returning officers and administrators. The addresses of the Commission's various offices are given below. The DLUHC too provides much more information and news about election-related issues than was formerly published. In March 2005 the Commission for Racial Equality published a 26-page briefing entitled *Elections and Good Race Relations*.

In 2006 the Committee on Standards in Public Life, then chaired by Sir Alistair Graham, investigated the work and role of the Electoral Commission in a very wide-ranging way. One of the original authors of this book (David Monks) gave evidence, and the Committee also visited his authority (Huntingdonshire) twice as well as with many other councils. The Committee's eleventh report *Review of the Electoral Commission* (Cm 7006) was published early in 2007. The National Audit Office has also investigated electoral registration and intended to report to the Speaker's Committee by the end of 2006. Again SOLACE submitted evidence and the National Audit Office visited Huntingdonshire to take evidence from David Monks. The Joseph Rowntree Trust report *Purity of Elections in the UK: Causes for Concern* was published in April 2008.

LEGISLATION AND COMMENTARIES

Legislation, including particularly new statutory instruments, can be accessed at http://www.legisation.gov.uk/new. Generally, http://www.legislation.gov.uk is the website to access legislation including that as currently amended, rather than as originally enacted.

Parker's Law and Conduct of Elections
Butterworths, Halsbury House, 35 Chancery Lane, London

WC2A 1EL
Schofield's Election Law
Shaw & Sons, Shaway House, 21 Bourne Park, Bourne Road,
Crayford, Kent DA1 4BZ

APPENDIX 2

LOCAL ELECTIONS TIMETABLE

THURSDAY 5 MAY 2022

Publication of Notice of Election	By Tuesday 29 March
Receipt of Nominations	By 4pm Wednesday 6 April
Publication of Statement of Persons Nominated	By 4pm Thursday 7 April
Withdrawal of Candidate	By 4pm Wednesday 6 April
Appointment of Election Agents	By 4pm Wednesday 6 April
Publication of Notice of Election Agents	Wednesday 6 April
Last Date for Registration	Tuesday 19 April
Receipt of Postal Vote Applications	By 5pm Wednesday 20 April
Publication of Notice of Poll	By Wednesday 27 April
Receipt of Proxy Vote Applications	By 5pm Wednesday 27 April
Appointment of Polling and Counting Agents	Thursday 28 April
First Day to Issue Replacement Lost Postal Ballot Papers	Friday 29 April
Receipt of Emergency Proxy Vote Applications	By 5pm Thursday 5 May
Last Day to Issue Replacement Spoilt or Lost Postal Ballot Papers	By 5pm Thursday 5 May
Polling Day	7am to 10pm Thursday 5 May
Declarations of Candidates' Expenses	By Thursday 9 June

APPENDIX 3

TABLE OF CASES

Aehmed v Afzal [2009] EKHC 1757

Ashby v White (1703) 2 Ld. Raym. 938 Holt C.J.

Begum v Tower Hamlets (Lawtel Document No AC94004651)

Considine v Didrichsen [2004] (Lawtel Document No AC0107399)

Knight v Nicholls [2004] EWCA Civ68

Medhurst v Lough and Gasquet (1901) 17 TLR210

Morgan v Simpson [1975] Q.B. 151

Pilling v Reynolds [2008] All E.R. (D) 54; [2008] EWHC 316

R (On the Application of Kevin Paul Lewis) v Persimmon Homes Teeside Ltd (also v Redcar and Cleveland Borough Council [2008] EWCA Civ 746; [2009] 1 WLR 83

R v Balanboff, Ex Parte De Beer (2002) (Lawtel Document No.C9500809)

R (Vote Leave Ltd) v Electoral Commission [2019] The Times 27 December

Robinson v Secretary of State for Northern Ireland [2002] The Time 26 July

Scarth v Amin and Reeves [2008] EWHC 2886; [2009] PTSR

Watkins v Woolas [2010] EWHC 2702

APPENDIX 4

TABLE OF STATUTES

APPENDIX 5
TABLE OF STATUTORY INSTRUMENTS
ORDERS AND RULES

INDEX

PUBLISH YOUR BOOK

Why APS Books?

Because we love new books and hate that good writers get such low percentage royalties for their efforts or even feel they have to pay to be published…

– You write
– We do a final edit
– We provide cover art
– We publish print on demand paperbacks and eBooks
– We don't charge for our input
– We do traditionally printed books too
– We both market your book
– You get 50% royalties

Does that sound fair? We're a publishing co-operative which aims to produce excellent books not exploit authors.

We have already publishing around 250 books by over 60 authors and photographers as well as limited editions for private circulation by authors who aren't seeking open availability of their work yet. We're also happy to organise book printing for 10 or more copies at affordable prices and are moving into hardcover printing and audio books too.

andrew.sparke@icloud.com
www.andrewsparke.com

Printed in Poland
by Amazon Fulfillment
Poland Sp. z o.o., Wrocław
25 February 2022

ea09af7c-e899-42c9-a54c-f389d3fa89dfR01